"I enjoy reading Phil Moore's books. He writes about Jesus and the Christian life with perception, wisdom and wit."

– Nicky Gumbel – Vicar, HTB London

"In taking us straight to the heart of the text, Phil Moore has served us magnificently. We so need to get into the Scriptures and let the Scriptures get into us. The fact that Phil writes so relevantly and with such submission to biblical revelation means that we are genuinely helped to be shaped by the Bible's teaching."

– Terry Virgo

"Fresh. Solid. Simple. Really good stuff."

– R. T. Kendall

"Most commentaries are dull. These are alive. Most commentaries are for scholars. These are for **you**!"

– Canon Michael Green

"These notes are amazingly good. Phil's insights are striking, original, and fresh, going straight to the heart of the text and the reader! Substantial yet succinct, they bristle with amazing insights and life applications, compelling us to read more. Bible reading will become enriched and informed with such a scintillating guide. Teachers and preachers will find nuggets of pure gold here!"

– Greg Haslam, Westminster Chapel, London, UK

"A strong combination of faithful scholarship, clear explanation and deep insight make these an invaluable tool. I can't recommend them highly enough."

– Gavin Calver, Director of Mission, Evangelical Alliance

"The Bible is living and dangerous. The ones who teach it best are those who bear that in mind – and let the author do the talking. Phil has written these studies with a sharp mind and a combination of creative

– Joel Virgo, Leader o

T0339269

"Phil Moore's new commentaries are outstanding: biblical and passionate, clear and well-illustrated, simple and profound. God's Word comes to life as you read them, and the wonder of God shines through every page."

– Andrew Wilson, Author of Incomparable and If God, Then What?

"Want to understand the Bible better? Don't have the time or energy to read complicated commentaries? The book you have in your hand could be the answer. Allow Phil Moore to explain and then apply God's message to your life. Think of this book as the Bible's message distilled for everyone."

– Adrian Warnock, Christian blogger

"Phil Moore presents Scripture in a dynamic, accessible and relevant way. The bite-size chunks – set in context and grounded in contemporary life – really make the make the Word become flesh and dwell among us."

– Dr David Landrum, Evangelical Alliance

"Through a relevant, very readable, up-to-date storying approach, Phil Moore sets the big picture, relates God's Word to today and gives us fresh insights to increase our vision, deepen our worship, know our identity and fire our imagination. Highly recommended!"

– Geoff Knott, former CEO of Wycliffe Bible Translators UK

"What an exciting project Phil has embarked upon! These accessible and insightful books will ignite the hearts of believers, inspire the minds of preachers and help shape a new generation of men and women who are seeking to learn from God's Word."

– David Stroud, Leader of Christ Church London and author of Planting Churches, Changing Communities

For more information about the *Straight to the Heart* series, please go to **www.philmoorebooks.com**.

You can also receive daily messages from Phil Moore on Twitter by following **@PhilMooreLondon**.

STRAIGHT TO
THE HEART OF

Job

60 BITE-SIZED INSIGHTS

Phil Moore

MONARCH
BOOKS

Published by
Lion Hudson Limited
Wilkinson House, Jordan Hill Business Park
Banbury Road, Oxford OX2 8DR, England
www.lionhudson.com

ISBN 978 0 85721 976 3
e-ISBN 978 0 85721 977 0

First edition 2020

A catalogue record for this book is available from the British Library

Printed and bound in the UK, April 2020, LH26

This book is dedicated to my father, who suffered from a crippling illness for over a quarter of a century with the patience of Job and without cursing the Lord.

CONTENTS

ACT TWO: SOME NEW ANSWERS

ACT THREE: GOD'S OWN ANSWERS

EPILOGUE: JOB'S COMFORT

About the *Straight to the Heart* Series

On his eightieth birthday, Sir Winston Churchill dismissed the compliment that he was the "lion" who had defeated Nazi Germany in World War Two. He told the Houses of Parliament that *"It was a nation and race dwelling all around the globe that had the lion's heart. I had the luck to be called upon to give the roar."*

I hope that God speaks to you very powerfully through the "roar" of the books in the *Straight to the Heart* series. I hope they help you to understand the books of the Bible and the message which the Holy Spirit inspired their authors to write. I hope that they help you to hear God's voice challenging you, and that they provide you with a springboard for further journeys into each book of Scripture for yourself.

But when you hear my "roar", I want you to know that it comes from the heart of a much bigger "lion" than me. I have been shaped by a whole host of great Christian thinkers and preachers from around the world, and I want to give due credit to at least some of them here: Terry Virgo, Dave Holden, Guy Miller, John Hosier, Adrian Holloway, Greg Haslam, Lex Loizides, Malcolm Kayes and all those who lead the Newfrontiers family of churches; friends and encouragers, such as Stef Liston, Joel Virgo, Stuart Gibbs, Scott Taylor, Nick Derbridge, Phil Whittall, and Kevin and Sarah Aires; Jon Oliver and Jessica Gladwell at Monarch Books; the pastors and congregation that serve alongside me at Everyday Church in London; my great friend

Andrew Wilson – without all of your friendship, encouragement and example, this series would never have happened.

I would like to thank my parents, my brother Jonathan, and my in-laws, Clive and Sue Jackson. Dad – your example birthed in my heart the passion which brought this series into being. I didn't listen to all you said when I was a child, but I couldn't ignore the way you got up at five o'clock every morning to pray, read the Bible and worship, because of your radical love for God and for his Word. I'd like to thank my children – Isaac, Noah, Esther and Ethan – for keeping me sane when publishing deadlines were looming. But most of all, I'm grateful to my incredible wife, Ruth – my friend, encourager, corrector and helper.

You all have the lion's heart, and you have all developed the lion's heart in me. I count it an enormous privilege to be the one who was chosen to sound the lion's roar.

So welcome to the *Straight to the Heart* series. My prayer is that you will let this roar grip your own heart too – for the glory of the great Lion of the Tribe of Judah, the Lord Jesus Christ!

Introduction:
Why Does God Allow Suffering?

"Shall we accept good from God, and not trouble?"
(Job 2:10)

The British actor Stephen Fry isn't shy about explaining why he doesn't believe in God. He says that all the suffering in the world makes faith impossible. When asked in a TV interview what he would say if he were wrong, and if he found himself standing before God, he didn't hesitate:

I'll say: bone cancer in children – what's that about? How dare you? How dare you create a world where there is such misery that's not our fault? It's utterly, utterly evil. Why should I respect a capricious, mean-minded, stupid God who creates a world which is so full of injustice and pain? That's what I'd say.

When the astonished interviewer asked him how he hoped to get into heaven with such words, he insisted:

I wouldn't want to. I wouldn't want to get in on his terms. They're wrong... The God who created this universe, if it was created by God, is quite clearly a maniac, utter maniac, totally selfish... It's perfectly apparent that he is monstrous, utterly monstrous, and deserves no respect

*whatsoever. The moment you banish him, your life
becomes simpler, purer, cleaner and more worth living.*[1]

Stephen Fry is by no means alone in his views. Any Christian
who tries to share their faith with their friends quickly finds
that this is by far the most common objection thrown back in
their faces. Nor is this anything new. People have been grappling
with this question since the earliest of times. The Ancient Greek
philosopher Epicurus stated the same problem, well over 2,000
years ago, in its simplest terms:

> *Either God wishes to take away evil, but he is unable; or
> God is able to take away evil, but he is unwilling; or God
> is neither willing nor able to take away evil; or God is
> both willing and able to take away evil. Well then, if he
> is willing and unable, then he is feeble, which is not in
> accordance with the character of God. If he is able and
> unwilling, then he is malevolent, which is equally at
> variance with God. If he is neither willing nor able, then
> he is both malevolent and feeble. If he is both willing and
> able, which alone is suitable to God, then where does evil
> come from and why doesn't he rid the world of evil?*[2]

Twenty-three centuries have passed since Epicurus summed
up our great dilemma in those few short sentences, but each
succeeding generation has continued to grapple with it. For
those who believe in God, the existence of suffering poses a
major problem to their faith. How can a God who is both loving
and powerful allow such things to happen on his watch and
in his world? At the same time, our reaction to the existence
of suffering makes it very hard to be an atheist too. After all, if
there is no God, and if we all evolved by chance out of a fierce

---

[1] Stephen Fry interview with Gay Byrne on Ireland's RTÉ One TV show *The
Meaning of Life*, 29th January 2015.

[2] Epicurus died in 270 BC so most of his writings are too ancient to have survived.
We know that he wrote these words because he is quoted by Lactantius in
about 315 AD in his treatise *On the Anger of God* (13.20–21).

survival of the fittest, then why do we care so much about the suffering in the world? Why do we sense so acutely what's right and wrong that we nod at the words of Stephen Fry? Why do we care so much about justice and kindness and compassion and all the other virtues that the Bible says God possesses and has placed within the human heart to help us find him? The suffering that we witness in the world makes both faith in God *and* lack of faith in God seem a bit too easy. And so, the Scottish philosopher, David Hume, observes, the search for an answer goes on:

> *Epicurus's old questions are yet unanswered. Is he willing to prevent evil, but not able? Then he is not omnipotent. Is he able, but not willing? Then he is malevolent. Is he both able and willing? Then whence cometh evil? Is he neither able nor willing? Then why call him God?*[3]

A whole book of the Bible is devoted to answering this question of why God allows such suffering in the world. Halfway through the Old Testament, sandwiched between the history books and the prophets, are the five books that together form the "Wisdom Literature" of the Bible. They are Job, Psalms, Proverbs, Ecclesiastes and Song of Songs – the first and oldest of which is devoted to this first and oldest question. At forty-two chapters long, the book of Job isn't short, but that's because God knows that our biggest question requires more than a cursory answer. If we are willing to take the time to read it slowly and carefully, then God promises to give us real answers.

The book of Job is *anonymous*. As we will see when we meet him in a moment, Job experienced his sufferings any time from around 1850 BC, and they were recorded later by a nameless Hebrew author. Through that ancient record, God invites you to step back to a time long before Epicurus and to grapple with humanity's oldest question.

The book of Job is *honest*. Some of the things that we are about to hear Job and his friends say about God are meant to

---

[3] David Hume wrote this in 1779 in his *Dialogues Concerning Natural Religion*.

make our toes curl. They are every bit as shocking as what Stephen Fry said to his astonished TV interviewer. God is therefore inviting you to be real with him about your questions as you read, so that he can give you real answers.

The book of Job is *poetry*. It begins with two chapters of prose but from then on, other than a few verses at the start of chapter 32 and at the end of chapter 42, the book of Job takes the form of a very long poem. That's because poetry moves our hearts in a way that prose cannot. It deals not just with facts, but with how those facts make us feel. It deals not just with our heads, but with our hearts. God is therefore inviting you to engage with him throughout the book of Job on more than an intellectual level. He wants you to be honest about your emotions and about the anger that you feel towards him because of all the suffering in the world. Alfred, Lord Tennyson apparently called the book of Job, "the greatest poem of ancient or modern times". My prayer is that, as we journey through this

Chapters 1–2	Prologue: Job's Suffering
Chapters 3–27	Act One: The Same Old Answers
Chapters 28–37	Act Two: Some New Answers
Chapters 38–41	Act Three: God's Own Answers
Chapter 42	Epilogue: Job's Comfort

ancient book together, you will sense that too.

The book of Job follows a basic structure:

It's a simple structure, and I'm eager to make a start. So find the book of Job, right in the middle of your Bible, and let's begin reading it together. It is one of the oldest books ever written and it deals with one of oldest questions ever asked: *Why does God allow suffering?*

Let's find out what God has to say in reply to Epicurus, to David Hume, to Stephen Fry, and to you and to me.

Prologue – Job 1–2:

Job's Suffering

The Perfect Man
(Job 1:1–5)

In the land of Uz there lived a man whose name was
Job. This man was blameless and upright; he feared
God and shunned evil.

(Job 1:1)

Job is the perfect man to help us grasp why God allows so much suffering in the world. These opening five verses underline that several times.

Job is perfect because his life is like a blank sheet of paper to us. We are told that he is married, but we are never told his wife's name. We are told he has ten children, but they remain unnamed too. We are never told the name of his parents or of his wider ancestry. You don't have to have read much of the Old Testament, with its love of genealogies, to spot that this is quite unusual. The writer of the book of Job deliberately withholds this detail from us in order to hold Job up for us as a clean mirror in which we can see our own reflection. He is everyman and everywoman.

Job is also perfect because he lived in the dark recesses of history. The writer doesn't formally date Job's life for us, but he peppers his book with clues that Job lived in the same period of history as the Hebrew patriarchs Abraham, Isaac and Jacob.[1] Like the patriarchs, Job's wealth is measured by how many sheep and camels and cattle and donkeys are found in his herds. Like the patriarchs, he lives to a far greater age than was possible for later generations. Like the patriarchs, he acts as priest on

---

[1] Ezekiel 14:14 and 20, and James 5:11, should leave us in no doubt that Job was an actual historical person.

behalf of his own family.[2] The fact that it never occurs to him in his anguished search for God to set out for the land of Israel indicates that he lived at a time before there were any Hebrew Scriptures or any Tabernacle of Moses for him to turn to in his hour of need. Job is very isolated spiritually. He's the perfect man to reflect our own sense of utter loneliness whenever the sparks of suffering start to fly.

Job is perfect because he isn't the author of his own story. We've all read the memoirs of people who feel that they have been hard done by. Their accounts of their own suffering are a lot harder to swallow than the objective account of historians sometime later. That's why it helps us that the book of Job is history, not autobiography. We can tell that he and his friends actually spoke the words that are attributed to them, because the Hebrew text of their conversations uses lots of archaic vocabulary and grammar that is found nowhere else in the Bible.[3] The writer of the book of Job turns their speeches into poetry (we aren't really expected to believe that they spoke poems to one another!), but he also gives us a massive clue that he hasn't tampered with the substance of their speeches, because whereas he uses the name *Yahweh* thirty-one times to refer to God while acting as narrator, Job's friends never once refer to God as *Yahweh* in all their speeches and Job only calls him *Yahweh* once in all of his replies.[4] The book of Job is therefore the best of both worlds – both an accurate account of what Job said and an objective view of why he said it. It is no sob story, written and exaggerated by the sufferer.[5] It was produced

---

[2] Compare Job 1:3 and 42:12 with Genesis 12:16, 24:35, 30:43 and 32:5. Compare Job 42:16–17 with Genesis 25:7, 35:28 and 47:28. Compare Job 1:5 with Genesis 12:7, 26:25 and 35:1–4. Don't be confused by the mention of iron tools in Job 19:24 and 20:24. Tools were forged from meteoric iron 1,000 years before the Iron Age began.

[3] Some of the Hebrew words used in the book of Job are so archaic that the Jewish translators of the Greek Septuagint in the third century BC show signs of struggling to grasp what every word exactly means.

[4] Job refers to the Lord as *Yahweh* in 12:9.

[5] Job longs in 19:23–24 for somebody to write a record of his story. His anguished prayer was answered!

when God inspired a poet to take the oral history of Job and to turn it into a formal written record for every generation of humanity.[6]

Job is perfect because he isn't a Hebrew, like the narrator of his story. We aren't given much detail about Job's life, but the very first thing emphasized is that he lived in the land of Uz. This might mean that he was an Aramean living to the north of Israel, in modern-day Syria, since Uz was the name of one of the Aramean founding fathers.[7] Alternatively, it might mean that he was an Edomite living to the southeast of Israel, in modern-day Jordan, since the Bible speaks elsewhere about *"Edom, you who live in the land of Uz"*.[8] We discover later that one of Job's friends was a descendant of Esau, so it seems more likely he was an Edomite than an Aramean, but his exact nationality is beside the point.[9] The writer of Job is less interested in locating Job's homeland for us than he is in emphasizing that it wasn't the land of Israel. Job wasn't a Hebrew. He was a Gentile, an outsider to the family of Abraham. He lived in a pagan land and he might have been forgiven for worshipping the pagan idols of his friends.[10]

But he didn't. That's the point the writer wants to make.

---

[6] We do not know exactly when the book of Job was written, but it may have been as early as 1800 BC, making it the oldest book in the Bible. Those who date it later tend to argue that God only revealed his name as *Yahweh* when he met with Moses at the Burning Bush (Exodus 3). However, God is called *Yahweh* much earlier than that (see Genesis 26:22, 26:28–29 and 49:18). The mother of Moses is called *Jochebed*, meaning *Yahweh is Glorious* (Exodus 6:20), so there is no problem with an early dating of Job.

[7] Genesis 10:23 and 22:21. The *War Scroll*, one of the Dead Sea Scrolls, also mentions an Aramean land of Uz.

[8] Genesis 36:28 and Lamentations 4:21. Job lived among the people of the *East*, not of the North.

[9] Eliphaz was descended from Esau's grandson Teman (2:11 and Genesis 36:15). This probably makes Job a contemporary of Joseph's grandchildren, living any time from 1850 BC onwards.

[10] The name that Job's parents gave him suggests that they were believers in the Lord who predicted that their son would find it hard to follow the true God in a pagan land. Job means *Hated* or *Persecuted*.

Job wasn't just the perfect man to mirror our own sufferings. He was the perfect man, end of story. The writer tells us five things about this foreigner, living in a land of foreign idols. First, he was *blameless*. Second, he was *upright*. Third, he *feared God*. Fourth, he *shunned evil*, turning away from anything that he knew displeased the Lord. Fifth, he got up *early in the morning to sacrifice a burnt offering* to the Lord. There are hints that Job was unsuccessful in passing his faith on to his children. The Hebrew word *mishteh* in verses 4 and 5 refers literally to *drinking feasts*, and Job suspects his children of cursing God in their hearts as they party.[11] But this doesn't detract from his own remarkable devotion to the Lord.[12] In case we haven't fully grasped that Job was even godlier than the Hebrew patriarchs, the writer ends these five verses by emphasizing that *"this was Job's usual custom"*. He wasn't an up-and-down believer, sometimes devoted to God and sometimes backsliding into sin. He was a day-in-day-out worshipper of the Lord.

That's why Job is the perfect man to help us understand why God allows suffering. The truth is, we don't take too much issue with the Lord inflicting suffering on those who practise evil. When bad things happen to bad people at the end of books and movies, we rather enjoy it as a fitting resolution to the story. What we can't abide is when good things happen to bad people, and when bad things happen to good people. We dislike it in our books and movies, and we certainly can't bear to see it in the real world. The writer feeds this expectation that good things ought to happen to good people by assuring us that Job is married, has lots of children, is staggeringly wealthy and is more honoured than anybody else in the East. He is what we expect to see in a well-run world.

---

[11] The Hebrew word for *cursing* in Job 1:5, 1:11, 2:5 and 2:9 is *bārak*, which normally means *to bless*. The writer fears God too much to use anything other than a euphemism for cursing him, just like 1 Kings 21:10 and 13.

[12] The Old Testament focuses on God's plan to make the Hebrews his holy nation, but it also says he called many non-Hebrews to follow him too. Alongside Job as early Gentile believers stand Melchizedek the Jebusite (Genesis 14:18–20) and Jethro the Midianite (Exodus 3:1).

Now for the sucker punch. It is to this man, this perfect man, this paragon of virtue that suffering suddenly came. The book of Job isn't going to give us any cheap and easy answers to the question: *Why does God allow suffering?* It sets the scene by telling us that all of the suffering we will read about in the book of Job happened to the perfect man.

Real (Job 1:6–12)

One day the angels came to present themselves before the Lord, and Satan also came with them.

(Job 1:6)

In the surreal science-fiction movie, *Her*, Joaquin Phoenix's character falls in love with the virtual assistant on his computer.[1] While most people simply issue commands to Siri or Alexa or Google Assistant, he conducts such long conversations with the voice of Scarlett Johansson that he starts believing she is the woman of his dreams. It is only when she briefly goes offline for a system upgrade that it finally dawns on him that he isn't in a real relationship at all. His girlfriend is a robot that has been pre-programmed to serve him up whatever answer he wants to hear. It's a pretty weird movie, but it helps us to understand the message of the book of Job.

The writer of Job never used the virtual assistant on a computer. He never had to grapple with the ethics of artificial intelligence. But he is more alert than we are to the kind of God that we are wishing for whenever we point our finger heavenwards and complain that God allows so much suffering in the world. He begins to answer our question *Why does God allow suffering?* by pulling back the curtain on heaven so that we can see how committed God is to cultivating a relationship with us that is real.

In verse 6, the writer uses the name *Yahweh* for the first time. He wants to make it clear to us that, while some lesser god might be happy with a race of automatons, the real God is committed to allowing his creatures to choose. This is the

---

[1] *Her* was written, directed and produced by Spike Jonze (Warner Bros Pictures, 2013).

God of the Bible, the God that most people have in mind when they say they don't believe in him. That's part of the paradox of atheism, defining God to deny God, accepting what the Bible says about God's love and power in order to accuse him of not having enough of either. It's the paradox that the philosopher Sidney Morgenbesser tried to expose in his famous question: "Why is God making me suffer so much? Just because I don't believe in him?"[2]

The real God, the writer shows us in these verses, is no tyrant. He is immensely powerful – that much is obvious from the way a mighty host of angels throng about his throne and seem to know instinctively that they need his permission to act in the world – and yet what we see here is more than power. It is power voluntarily curtailed. Here is a God who has decided not to rule by *might*. He is determined only to do what is *right*.

The Hebrew phrase in verse 6 that is translated into English as *angels* means literally *the sons of God*.[3] It reminds us that the Lord did not create the angels to be a troupe of celestial scullery boys. He entrusted them with real executive power. Here they stand before him like a king's trusted council, as if God has decided to make himself accountable to them for the way in which he uses his divine power. He wants them to testify to the righteousness of his rule, and we know from the rest of the Bible that this is more than mere show. God didn't want a friendship with his angels that was similar to Joaquin Phoenix's character's relationship with a virtual assistant, so he gave them genuine freedom to choose whether to love and worship him, or whether to rebel and oppose him. He even allowed one of his most powerful angels to lead a third of his angels in revolt against his rule.[4] The big surprise in these verses is that this angel is still permitted to stroll into God's throne room to

---

[2] Quoted in Sidney Morgenbesser's obituary written by Douglas Martin in *The New York Times*, 4th August 2004.

[3] The same phrase is used again to refer to angels in 38:7, as well as in Psalms 29:1 and 89:6.

[4] Isaiah 14:12–17, Ezekiel 28:11–19, Luke 10:18, and Revelation 9:1 and 12:1–12.

witness how he uses his power. That's how committed the Lord is to real accountability for how he rules the world.

Five times in these seven verses, the writer refers to this fallen angel literally in Hebrew as *"the satan"*.[5] We are not wrong to translate this as a proper name, *Satan*, but the definite article is there for a definite reason. Satan is the Hebrew word for *Accuser*, just as Devil comes from the Greek word for *Liar*, so the writer wants us to grasp that God allowed him to survive his fall from heaven so that he could continue to play a role in God's council. The Devil is the great *Fault Finder*, and he confesses as much when he admits he has been *"roaming throughout the earth, going to and fro on it"* (1:7). He has been combing over God's creation to find any grounds upon which he can lodge an accusation that God is not ruling righteously.[6] The apostle Paul hints at this when he tells us in Ephesians 3:10–11 that God's *"intent was that now, through the church, the manifold wisdom of God should be made known to the rulers and authorities in the heavenly realms, according to his eternal purpose that he accomplished in Christ Jesus our Lord".*[7] God has not brushed our sins under the carpet, but satisfied the demands of justice against our sin through the blood of his own Son.

The Devil has clearly found no grounds here upon which to accuse the Lord of wrongdoing, but he acts unimpressed with the world that he sees. It doesn't look as if God was the winner of their celestial struggle. The nations are awash with sin, hoodwinked into worshipping demons dressed up as idols instead of worshipping the Lord. Even Jacob's family look a lot more like the Canaanites and Egyptians than they do the God

---

[5] He is called *"the satan"* again in Zechariah 3:1–2, but then called *Satan* as a proper name in 1 Chronicles 21:1 (and possibly Psalm 109:6). The New Testament picks up on this, referring to him as *Satan* thirty-five times.

[6] The Lord knows where Satan has been in 1:7, just as he knew where Adam was in Genesis 3:9. He is simply inviting the Devil to declare the very worst of what he has seen.

[7] The death of Jesus paid the price tag for our sin so that God saves by *right*, not just by *might*. See Genesis 2:17, Mark 10:45, Galatians 3:13, Romans 6:23, 1 Timothy 2:5–6, Hebrews 9:15, 1 Peter 1:18–19, and Revelation 5:9 and 14:4.

they claim to worship. God's plan to let people choose to worship him clearly isn't working. Maybe he ought to have created a race of virtual assistants, after all! Instead of throwing Satan out of his courtroom, God appears to welcome this scrutiny. The accountability that we witness here is real.

The Lord tells the Devil to take a good look at Job. Now *that's* the kind of worshipper that only comes about when choice is real.[8] The Lord confirms what the writer told us in verse 1 – Job is blameless and upright, fearing God and shunning evil – but then he goes even further by declaring that *"my servant Job"* is godlier than Jacob and his children.[9] His life is proof of the wisdom of God's salvation plan. What a load of rubbish, retorts the Devil. There's nothing real about Job's worship. He is merely using the Lord as the means to an end. His true god is his wealth and his faith in God is a prosperity gospel. If he were to lose his riches, he would lose his piety too. Job isn't a real worshipper at all.

And so the scene is set. The Lord allows Satan to test whether his commitment to let his creatures choose to worship him has been a blunder. He grants Satan permission to test Job and to reveal to God's celestial council if the worship that he offers to the Lord is real.

---

[8] The Lord asks Satan literally in Hebrew, *"Have you set your heart on my servant Job?"* Now here is a man who can prove to my heavenly council that you are wrong to question the wisdom of my plan of salvation.

[9] This is an illustrious title which the Lord endows elsewhere on Abraham (Genesis 26:24), on Moses (Numbers 12:7–8), on Caleb (Numbers 14:24), on David (1 Kings 14:8) and supremely on Jesus (Isaiah 42:1).

No Excuses (Job 1:12)

The Lord said to Satan, "Very well, then, everything
he has is in your power, but on the man himself do
not lay a finger."

(Job 1:12)

The book of Job is one of many ancient writings that philosophers refer to as a *theodicy*. The Greek words *theos* and *dike* mean *God* and *justice*, so a theodicy is an attempt to put God on trial for all the suffering in the world and to vindicate his righteousness. A theodicy is an attempt to answer the dilemma which Epicurus summed up for us. If God is truly good, he would want to make his creatures happy. If he is truly powerful, he would be able to do so. But since his creatures are not happy, it seems that God lacks either goodness or power or both. How can such a God expect us to put our faith in him?

The book of Job is one of many ancient theodicies, but it differs fundamentally from all the others. For a start, it is much longer. The book of Job never tries to offer us glib answers or easy shortcuts through our pain and confusion. It never tries to fob us off with clichés or with the cheery quotations that clog up many of our Facebook feeds. It insists that we must go on a slow journey through the land of suffering if we want to emerge on the other side with answers real enough to sustain our trust in God under fire.

An even bigger difference is that the book of Job never tries to make excuses for God. It doesn't try to dodge our questions or to blame somebody else for what happens in the world. The theodicy, *Dispute Between a Man and His Soul* (Egypt, about 1850 BC), ends without giving the man any real explanation for his suffering. His soul simply promises to try a little harder to make him happy. The *Dialogue Between a Man and His God* (Babylon, about 1650 BC) sounds in places like the book of Job (*"A young man was weeping to his god like a friend, constantly praying... I do not know what sin I have committed!"*) but it too offers little in the way of real explanation. The man's idol never explains why he is suffering. Once he feels better, it simply warns him, *"Now you must never forget your god until the end of time!"*

The same is true of the *Poem of the Righteous Sufferer* (Babylon, about 1300 BC), where a man loses his possessions and his health, while remaining convinced he has done nothing to offend his god. When he recovers, he attributes his healing to his idol but remains none the wiser for his pains. He never advances beyond the confusion he expresses early on in the poem: *"I wish I knew what was pleasing to a god! What seems good to oneself could be an offence to a god. What in one's heart seems detestable could be good to one's god. Who then can grasp the reasoning of the gods?!"* The sufferer in the *Babylonian Theodicy* (Babylon, about 1000 BC) fares even worse. We are not even told that his god delivers him. His complaint that, *"Those who neglect the god go the way of prosperity, while those who pray to the goddess are impoverished and dispossessed"* evokes some sympathy from his friend, but it is met with stony silence from heaven.

The book of Job is fundamentally different from those pagan theodicies because it never seeks to dodge our questions and/or make excuses for the Lord. Although there are clearly forces at work in Job's life that exonerate God, the writer never uses them to downplay God's role in the drama. He makes it very clear that the Lord is in control.

The writer could pass the blame onto Satan. After all, a literal reading of verse 12 makes it clear that the hand behind Job's suffering isn't God's. It is Satan's. *"Look, everything he has is in **your hand**, but on him you shall not stretch out **your hand**."* Yet the writer never tries to use this to disguise the Lord's own role in Job's sufferings. He deliberately ignites our sense of outrage by recording God's conversation with Satan in the most unflattering of terms. When the Lord asks literally in verse 8, *"Have you set your heart on my servant Job?"*, the writer makes the two of them sound a bit like the callous company directors who wreck Dan Ackroyd's character's life for the sake of a wager in the movie *Trading Places*.[1] Satan is at work here, but the writer is honest with us that the Lord could stop him in a moment.

The writer could also pass the blame onto Job. After all, he is part of a human race which has given Satan legitimate authority to inflict suffering on the earth.[2] Had there been no Fall, there would be no suffering. Whenever we point the finger at God, we are therefore pointing three fingers back at ourselves. We see this in 1 Kings 22:19–23, which echoes these verses in Job, where the Israelites reject God's truth and decide to embrace lies, so the Lord grants permission to one of the deceiving spirits at his council to go out and lead them astray. The Israelites reap what they have sown. They get what their deeds deserve.[3] But the writer of the book of Job doesn't use the reality of human sin to make excuses for the Lord. He reasserts in verse 8 that Job is entirely innocent. In his life at least, the Great Accuser and Fault Finder, can find no legitimate grounds for accusation.

Instead of blaming the Devil or humanity as a whole, the writer tells us that the Lord is sovereign over all of the suffering that befalls Job. This courtroom scene portrays no clash of equals. The Devil's very presence betrays that he knows, deep down, that he can only act on God's say-so. The way he sulks about Job's worship betrays that he lacks God's omnipotence. The way he conducts a constant reconnaissance mission throughout the earth betrays that he lacks God's omniscience and omnipresence too.[4]

---

[1] *Trading Places* (Cinema Group Ventures and Paramount Pictures, 1983).

[2] Luke 4:5–7, John 12:31 and Ephesians 2:2 all warn that Satan holds legitimate authority over us which is only overturned in Jesus. This is what Jesus means when he says the Devil *"has no hold over me"* (John 14:30) and what Paul means when he warns us, *"do not give the devil a foothold"* (Ephesians 4:27).

[3] Galatians 6:7–8, 2 Thessalonians 2:10–12, Judges 9:23, and 1 Samuel 16:14 and 18:10. Don't be surprised that demons stand in God's council here. He wants the righteousness of his rule to be scrutinized (Ephesians 3:10–11, and Psalms 82:1–2 and 89:5–7).

[4] For this reason, it is unlikely that the Devil is attacking you. If even the apostle Paul merely experienced *"a messenger from Satan"* in 2 Corinthians 12:7 (my

Even when he receives permission from the Lord to torment Job, it comes with very strict parameters. He is like a dog on a leash. Martin Luther is said to have described him as "God's Satan". He is a defeated foe, who knows he will never be permitted to tempt one of God's children beyond what they can bear.[5] He is like Gollum in *The Lord of the Rings*. When Frodo complains to Gandalf:

> *"What a pity that Bilbo did not stab that vile creature, when he had a chance!", the old wizard gently replies: "Pity? It was pity that stayed his hand... For even the very wise cannot see all ends... My heart tells me that he has some part to play yet, for good or ill, before the end; and when that comes, the pity of Bilbo may rule the fate of many.*[6]

In the same way that an act of Gollum's wickedness enables Frodo to succeed in his mission at the end, the Lord only gives the Devil enough rope with which to hang himself.

So don't miss the way that the writer refuses to dodge our question: *Why does God allow suffering?* He makes no excuses for the Lord. He doesn't hide behind the Devil's wickedness or the fact that we have given him legitimate grounds to work his mischief in our world. He simply asserts that God is wise enough to use Satan's evil actions to perform his greater good.[7] He simply assures us that, at the end of time, when we see things far more clearly than the brief glimpse we are given in these verses, we will worship the Lord for his wisdom and confess that what Romans 8:28 says is true: *"We know that **in all things** God works for the good of those who love him."*

---

translation), our own struggles are likely to be with Satan's junior demons too.

[5] 1 Corinthians 10:13, Matthew 8:29–31, Mark 5:6–13, Luke 8:28–33 and 22:31, and Revelation 12:12.

[6] This conversation takes place in J.R.R. Tolkien's *The Fellowship of the Ring* (1954).

[7] Elsewhere the Bible also apportions responsibility for Satan's actions both to Satan himself (1 Chronicles 21:1 and 2 Corinthians 12:7) and to God for permitting him to act (2 Samuel 24:1 and 2 Corinthians 12:8–10).

The Naked Worshipper
(Job 1:13–22)

*"Naked I came from my mother's womb, and naked
I shall depart. The Lord gave and the Lord has taken
away; may the name of the Lord be praised."*

(Job 1:21)

When my children were younger, one of their favourite party games was Pass the Parcel. Whenever the music stopped, they or one of their friends were allowed to strip away a layer of wrapping paper to find a sweet inside. When the final layer of wrapping paper was removed, a whole bag of sweets was revealed at the heart of the parcel.

Job got up early one morning with no suspicion that God had given Satan permission to test what lay at the heart of his own worship. He was not privy to the insight that we are given into the discussions of God's heavenly council. It must have felt to him like any another day. His sons and daughters were busy throwing yet another of their drinking parties when the Devil began his game of Pass the Parcel, starting to strip away the prosperous packaging of Job's life to reveal the naked worshipper on the inside.

In verses 13–15, a messenger arrives to inform Job that he has lost much of his property. The Sabeans were a nomadic tribe from the land of Sheba, in modern-day Yemen and Oman.[1] They were best known as traders, but when times got hard, they weren't above committing a little bit of violent crime. Job's

---

[1] The Hebrew word *shebā'* in 1:15 is the name of one of Abraham's grandsons through his concubine Keturah (Genesis 25:1–3). It is the same word that is used for the *Queen of Sheba* in 1 Kings 10 and 2 Chronicles 9.

servant reports that Sabean raiders have stolen all of the 1,000 oxen and 500 donkeys that we were told about in verse 3. They have also killed a third of Job's servants while battling to do so. This scene is the ancient equivalent of a modern investor suddenly discovering that he has been the victim of a Ponzi scheme. It comes as a devastating blow to a godly man who might well have expected the Lord to protect him from such disasters in a well-ordered world.

With the removal of the first layer of wrapping paper comes the first taste of something sweet. Job doesn't shout expletives. He doesn't point an angry finger towards heaven. As far as we can tell, he says nothing at all.[2] He is like my friend from church, who loves to give generously to the advance of God's Kingdom, but who discovered last month that he had been swindled out of thousands through a scam email. I've often seen my friend worship the Lord by giving generously, but I don't believe I've ever seen him worship more sweetly than right now, as he bears his loss without accusing God of having failed him. Job's sweet reaction to the ripping away of the first layer of wrapping paper makes us hope that Satan's accusations against him might yet prove false. Perhaps we will find that Job isn't simply using God. Perhaps he is a naked worshipper after all.

In verses 16–17, two more messengers arrive to strip away two further layers of wrapping paper. Job's 3,000 camels have been stolen by a second band of nomadic raiders (this time they're Chaldeans, from Babylonia) and another third of his servants have been killed in the raid. His 7,000 sheep and the remainder of his servants have also been struck and killed by lightning. This is even harder for Job to bear, since losses to raiders can be blamed on wicked people but natural disasters cannot. The writer highlights this by referring to the lightning as *"the fire of God"* (verse 16). Job might have coped with the

---

[2] The writer commends Job's self-control in 1:22 by telling us that Job avoided sinning by not saying any (literally) *"foolish thing"* to the Lord.

thought that his neighbours were against him, but the thought that God might also be against him comes as a far heavier blow.[3]

The Devil strips away these layers of wrapping paper so rapidly that one messenger has barely finished talking before the next one arrives with more bad news.[4] But Job doesn't use what little breath he draws between disasters to curse God. He chooses to keep on trusting, even now, and his faith goes up to heaven as sweet worship to the Lord.

In verses 18–19, the removal of a fourth layer of wrapping paper tears an even bigger hole in Job's heart. A messenger arrives while the first three are still catching their breath, bringing news that a windstorm has struck the house where Job's children were holding their drinking party. His seven sons and three daughters have all been killed.[5] Oxen and donkeys and camels and sheep can be replaced, but beloved children cannot. Job is beside himself with grief. He shaves his hair and tears his clothes, removing yet another layer of wrapping paper so that the true nature of his worship can be revealed for all to see. How will Job respond to such an avalanche of disasters? Will he still trust in God? Underneath the prosperous packaging of his life, is Job a naked worshipper?[6]

In verses 20–22, with this final layer of wrapping paper finally removed, we find that Satan was wrong to accuse Job of only worshipping God for what he could get out of him. Job

---

[3] God isn't against Job, as we can see from the fact that no fifth blow strikes down either Job or his wife. Satan acts only within the strict parameters God set for him. Nonetheless, it can often *feel* like God is against us.

[4] Satan is utterly cruel. He allows one servant to survive from each of the four disasters to become a messenger of evil news to Job. He also times their arrival perfectly to pummel Job with blow after blow.

[5] Don't be like one of Job's false friends, in 8:4, by blaming the deaths of Job's children on their drunkenness and sinful hearts towards God. They aren't innocent like their father, but one of the big themes of the book of Job is that jumping to simple cause-and-effect assumptions about God's judgment is never wise.

[6] The writer doesn't try to make excuses for God here. He will emphasize later that the Lord, and not Satan, is in charge of the windstorm and the lightning (36:30, 36:32, 37:3, 37:9, 37:11, 37:15, 38:24 and 38:35).

hasn't fallen for a prosperity gospel. The writer's summary of his worship song is glorious.[7] *"Naked I came from my mother's womb, and naked I shall depart. The Lord gave and the Lord has taken away; may the name of the Lord be praised."*[8] Suffering reveals Job to be a naked worshipper of the Lord.

We are not told how God's heavenly council reacted to Job's stripped-down worship. We have to imagine the reaction of the angels and the demons to this utter vindication of God's plan to allow his creatures to choose whether they want to worship him or reject him. No automaton could ever offer this kind of praise to God. It can only come as the glad expression of a heart that chooses to trust God in the midst of howling pain. It is the kind of worship that costs a willing person everything. It is the kind of worship that God is still looking for.[9]

It is the kind of worship that stirred Matt and Beth Redman to put Job's prayer to modern music in the days after the 9/11 attacks on the Twin Towers in New York City. They recall that:

> *The truth was, in most places we visited (or led worship in), there was a distinct lack of songs appropriate for this time. As songwriters and lead worshippers, we had a few expressions of hope at our disposal; but when it came to expressions of pain and lament, we had very little vocabulary to give voice to our heart cries... The truth is, the Church of God needs her songs of lament just as much as she needs her songs of victory.*[10]

---

[7] The writer clearly summarizes Job's much longer prayer into a single verse, since Job refers to God as *Yahweh* only once in all his speeches and yet he calls him *Yahweh* three times in this single verse alone!

[8] Job says literally that he will return naked *to his mother's womb* – in other words, that he will return empty-handed to the same place of dust and darkness from which he came (Genesis 3:19 and Ecclesiastes 12:7).

[9] 2 Samuel 24:21–24, 1 Chronicles 21:20–24 and John 4:23–24.

[10] Matt and Beth Redman tell this story in their book *Blessed Be Your Name* (2005).

And so they wrote a song, which I encourage you to sing with me now as an expression of your own desire to worship God, not for what you can get out of him, but for who he is even when he gives you nothing. It is the stripped-down worship song of Job.

> *Blessed be Your Name in the land that is plentiful,*
> *Where Your streams of abundance flow, blessed be Your Name.*
> *Blessed be Your Name when I'm found in the desert place,*
> *Though I walk through the wilderness, blessed be Your Name.*
> *Every blessing You pour out I'll turn back to praise.*
> *When the darkness closes in, Lord, still I will say:*
> *Blessed be the Name of the Lord, blessed be Your glorious Name.*
> *Blessed be Your Name when the sun's shining down on me,*
> *When the world's all "as it should be", blessed be Your Name.*
> *Blessed be Your Name on the road marked with suffering,*
> *Though there's pain in the offering, blessed be Your Name.*
> *You give and take away. You give and take away.*
> *My heart will choose to say: Lord, blessed be Your Name.*[11]

Can you sing that song with Job? When God allows pain in your life, do you still worship him? It's a bit like Pass the Parcel. Your response to suffering reveals whether you are worshipping God for God himself, or for what you can get out of God.

---

[11] *Blessed Be Your Name* (ThankYou Music, 2002).

Close to Home
(Job 2:1–10)

> *"Skin for skin!" Satan replied. "A man will give all he has for his own life. But now stretch out your hand and strike his flesh and bones, and he will surely curse you to your face."*
>
> (Job 2:4–5)

There once lived a man who was upright and blameless. He feared God and kept himself entirely from sin. He was more righteous than anybody else who ever lived, so we might have expected his life to be completely free from suffering. But note what happened to him immediately after God commended him publicly at his baptism in the River Jordan. Straightaway, Jesus was led by the Holy Spirit into the desert so that the Devil could test the reality of his decision to worship and obey God as his Father.[1]

There are many parallels between the lives of Job and Jesus in the book of Job, and it starts to become obvious for the first time in these verses. The Great Accuser returns to God's council, looking even more sorry than before.[2] His reconnaissance of earth has yet again failed to turn up any basis for a charge that the Lord is misruling his creation. Far from proving that the Lord has been unwise to allow his creatures to choose whether or not to love and worship him, Satan's attacks on Job have served to vindicate God's wisdom. It turns out that Job isn't using the Lord. He genuinely appears to love him.

---

[1] Matthew 3:13–4:11, Mark 1:9–13, Luke 3:21–4:13 and 2 Peter 1:17.

[2] The Devil is called *"the satan"* – that is, *the Accuser* – seven times in Job 1 and seven times in Job 2.

The Devil is fuming, so the Lord lets him have a second try. Don't miss the parallel between the words he spoke over Jesus at the River Jordan – *"This is my Son, whom I love; with him I am well pleased"* – and the words that he speaks over Job in these verses.[3] God commends Job with the same words that he used in chapter 1, but then he carries on with extra words which rejoice over Job's stripped-down worship. When the Lord points out to Satan that *"He still maintains his integrity, though you have incited me against him to ruin him without any reason,"*[4] we are meant to spot that this Hebrew word *hinnām* is the same word used throughout the Psalms to prophesy that the Messiah's enemies would hate him without reason too.[5] The Lord is therefore inviting Satan to try out on Job what he will one day try out much harder on God's Son. Having vindicated his wisdom once, God asks the Devil if he would like to run the risk of proving it a second time around.

Satan is quick to sin but he is a slow learner. He deceives himself into believing that he can win a second bout against the Lord, if only he can secure permission to strike closer to home. He convinces himself that the first bout was rigged. Job knew that God can replace lost possessions and he had also long suspected that his children were sinners. The Devil demands that this time Job's own body must become the battleground. *"Skin for skin!"* Satan demands. *"A man will give all he has for his own life. But now stretch out your hand and strike his flesh and bones, and he will surely curse you to your face."*

Many readers are offended by these verses. They accuse the Lord of acting unfairly by allowing the Devil to (or even goading the Devil into) launching a fresh attack against the

---

[3] Matthew 3:17, Mark 1:11 and Luke 3:22.

[4] The Hebrew word *sūth* in 2:3 is the same word used in 1 Chronicles 21:1 to describe Satan *inciting* King David to sin. The Lord isn't saying that the Devil did the same to him. He is saying: "Come on, Devil. I've let you try your worst on me and you've failed. Are you ready to give up yet or do you want to have another go?!"

[5] Jesus tells us in John 15:25 that Psalms 35:19, 69:4 and 109:3 are all prophecies about him.

undeserving Job. That's ironic, since Job himself refuses to accuse God of any wrongdoing in verse 10. It also overlooks the strict parameters that the Lord places here on what the Devil can and can't do. Satan wants him to stretch out his hand to strike Job's body, but the Lord insists, literally in the Hebrew text, *"He is in your hand."*[6] The Lord allows Satan to afflict Job with sickness, but not to lay a hand on the man's life. He doesn't have a licence to kill.

There is also an even bigger reason why we mustn't be offended by these verses. They contain one of the earliest predictions in the Bible that the Son of God, the only truly Righteous One, would one day surrender his physical body to a squad of Roman executioners. The Lord who stops short of putting Job's life on the line in these verses wouldn't stop short when it came to his own. The hands that the Lord refuses to stretch out against Job, he stretched out willingly at Calvary in order to save the world in his righteousness – not just by *might*, but by doing what is *right*. When you see the ministry of Jesus as the subplot to these verses, it is mind-blowing. It ought to make us want to lift up our own hands to God in grateful worship.

Satan goes off with permission to follow up the four bitter blows of chapter 1 with a fifth blow that is closer to home. He afflicts Job with sores on his skin, from the soles of his feet to the top of his head – sores that itch so fiercely that his only relief is to scrape his flesh raw with a piece of broken pottery.[7] Bereft of his possessions and bereaved of his children, Job now sinks even lower to cut a hideous and repulsive figure. We discover later that this sickness made his skin turn black and peel so that his friends no longer recognized him. It was also accompanied by terrible fever, by nightmares, by weight loss, by reeking

---

[6] *Hand* is singular in the Hebrew text of both 2:5 and 2:6, as the Lord deliberately reverses Satan's request. This echoes 1:11–12, where Satan also asks the Lord to stretch out *his hand* against Job and the Lord replies literally in Hebrew, *"Look, everything he has is in **your hand**, but on him you shall not stretch out **your hand**."*

[7] *Shehīn* is the same Hebrew word that is used in Exodus 9:8–12 to describe the sixth plague of *boils* or *ulcers*.

breath and by unrelenting pain.[8] Job collapses in the dust a broken man.

Job's wife has survived her husband's ordeals, but she can think of no kind words to comfort him. Some readers speculate that Satan spared her life to make her nagging form a sixth attack on Job, because discouragement is far harder to bear when it comes from a loved one, close to home. But many a carer can testify that it is harder to watch a loved one suffer than to bear the same suffering ourselves. We ought to see Job's wife as a victim, like her husband, who voices our own thoughts whenever we conclude that a God who allows people to suffer is not a God worth worshipping at all. *"Are you still maintaining your integrity?"* she asks her husband. *"Curse God and die!"*

Job ignores his wife's advice. As his suffering begins to strip away his very flesh, it reveals a heart of naked worship underneath the protective packaging of God's blessing. His faith is not in a prosperity gospel. He isn't merely using God to become healthy and wealthy. He loves the Lord for the Lord's own sake, and he chooses to carry on worshipping, even when he seems to get nothing back but trouble in return. Satan asked, *"Does Job fear God for nothing?"* (1:9). Job issues a resounding rebuke when he replies to his wife: *"You are talking like a foolish woman. Shall we accept good from God, and not trouble?"*

Now *this*, the writer tells us, is the kind of worship God is looking for. Not the forced worship of a virtual assistant, nor the cynical worship of a person out to get something from God, but worship that is freely given out of love for God himself, even when that love appears to bring nothing but trouble close to home.

---

[8] Job 2:12, 7:14, 17:7, 19:17–20, 30:17 and 30:28–30.

Job's Three Friends
(Job 2:11–13)

When Job's three friends, Eliphaz the Temanite,
Bildad the Shuhite and Zophar the Naamathite,
heard… they set out… to go and sympathise with him
and comfort him.

(Job 2:11)

If Job's three friends had a theme tune, then it would definitely be the Ronan Keating song, *(You Say It Best) When You Say Nothing At All*.[1] When they hear the news that Job has lost his herds, that his children have been killed and that he has contracted a hideous skin condition, they drop everything and set out from their homes to pay a visit to their suffering friend. The writer says that their intention is to *"sympathise with him and comfort him".* But we quickly discover that they do it best when they say nothing at all.

Eliphaz appears to be the oldest of the three friends, since he speaks first in each of their dialogues, which was a mark of deference towards one's seniors in the ancient world.[2] Eliphaz means *My God is Fine Gold*, but his ancestry is more significant than the meaning of his name. He comes from the family of Esau's grandson, Teman.[3] In other words, he is one of the famous

---

[1] The song went on to become Hugh Grant's theme tune instead in the classic 1990's movie, *Notting Hill* (Polygram Filmed Entertainment, 1999).

[2] The writer says in 32:4 that this is why Elihu has to wait to speak right until the end.

[3] Genesis 36:10–11, 1 Chronicles 1:35–36, Amos 1:11–12, Obadiah 8–9, Jeremiah 49:7 and 49:20. When seventy Jewish scholars produced the Greek Septuagint translation of the Old Testament in about 250 BC, they added a few extra sentences at the end of the book of Job which claim that Eliphaz was king

wise men of the land of Edom, but he helps Job a lot more in his seven days of silence than he does by unleashing four chapters of his wisdom on his friend.

Bildad appears to have been the second-oldest of the three friends, since he always speaks after Eliphaz. He is descended from Shuah, Abraham's son by his concubine Keturah, that he sent east into Arabia with his brother Midian.[4] Some people think his name means *Loved by [the Babylonian God] Bel*, while others think it means *Argumentative*. All we know for sure is that living in a pagan land has given Bildad some pretty strange views about God, and that he is definitely argumentative by nature. He comes across as a good friend to Job while he sits with him for seven days in silence, but when he starts to dispense three chapters of his wisdom to his friend, I find myself humming Ronan Keating. Bildad definitely says it best when he says nothing at all.

Zophar appears to be the youngest of the three friends. His hometown of Naamah was ruled either by the Amalekites or the Edomites, although the Israelites would later conquer it under Joshua.[5] His name means *Sparrow* and is the masculine form of Zipporah, the name of the Midianite wife of Moses, so he helps the three friends to represent a smorgasbord of all the greatest wisdom that the pagan East had to offer Job. Zophar only dispenses two chapters of wisdom, since Job tells his friends to stop their chatter before it comes back round to Zophar's third turn. Like his two friends, Zophar helps Job far more by sitting with him in silence than he does by delivering speeches.

Eliphaz, Bildad and Zophar are not bad friends. The writer tells us that *"they set out from their homes"* to come and offer comfort to Job. In other words, despite the fact that they were significant grandees in their home countries, they dropped

of the Temanites, but those extra sentences are probably fanciful since they also claim that Job was the grandson of Esau, that his wife was an Arab and that he himself was the king of Edom. It is better for us to stick to what we know about Eliphaz.

[4] Genesis 25:1–6.

[5] Joshua 15:41.

everything and made significant journeys to be there for Job in his hour of need. When they see their friend's shaved head and catch first sight of the gaping sores on his skin, disfiguring him almost beyond recognition, they are so devastated for him that they start to weep with all the loud lamenting of a Middle Eastern funeral. They identify with Job in his suffering by tearing their own clothes and getting down in the dust next to him. They demonstrate a remarkable commitment to their friend by sitting with him for seven days and seven nights without speaking a word, assuring him that they are as appalled as he is by all that has befallen him. They really do say it best to Job when they say nothing at all because, for now at least, they look like they are three great friends.

The truth, however, is that Job's three friends are nowhere near as sympathetic as they seem. We discover in Genesis 50:10 that seven days of loud weeping and mourning were what the wise men of the East observed whenever a close friend or family member died. We learn in 1 Samuel 31:13 that seven days of fasting and sprinkling dust on your head was what the people who lived east of the River Jordan did to mark the tragic demise of a friend. While Job's three friends simply sit with him, they provide him with a small shred of comfort, but the moment they open their mouths they betray what they are really thinking. They actually consider him as good as dead! They haven't come to bless him, but to bury him! They offer him no greater comfort than his wife does. They end up making him feel far lonelier in their company than he did before they arrived. He will eventually dismiss them as *"miserable comforters"*, speaking *"windy words"* of *"falsehood"* and *"nonsense"*.[6] With friends like these, Job has no need of enemies.

One of my favourite paintings at the National Gallery in London, near my home, is a self-portrait by the seventeenth-century artist Salvator Rosa. The painter looks out from the painting with a look of surly disdain and holds a Latin inscription in his hand: *"Aut tace aut loquere meliora silentio."*

---

[6] Job 13:4–5, 16:1–3 and 21:34.

Job's three friends might have heeded the artist's advice. The Latin text means: *"Either be silent, or say something that is better than silence!"*

We have reached the end of the writer's first two chapters of narration. The speeches are about to begin. We are about to discover that Job's three friends say it best when they say nothing at all.

Act One – Job 3–27:

The Same Old Answers

In the Dark (Job 3:1–26)

*"Why is life given to a man whose way is hidden,
whom God has hedged in?"*

(Job 3:23)

I don't know if you have ever been to one of those surprising talent shows where somebody opens their mouth and you simply can't believe that *that* sound can be coming out of *them*. That's how I feel about the first of Job's speeches, and not necessarily in a good way. Job seemed so full of faith in chapters 1 and 2 that it really catches us off guard in chapter 3 to see how much a week spent sitting grieving in the dust with his three friends appears to have altered his point of view. The first of Job's speeches is a lament in the dark about the anguish and utter misery that he feels.

I've heard some people argue that Job was not really a historical person and that the sudden mood swing in this chapter reflects the fact that the book which bears his name is an anthology of poems from many different mourners. There is a rather fatal flaw to this idea, however. The writers of the Bible are unequivocal that Job was a real person. The Lord himself lists Job alongside Noah and Daniel as one of the most righteous men in history.[1] That explanation also displays a total lack of understanding about the grieving process. Isn't this precisely how we feel in the midst of bereavement and tragedy? We have good days and we have bad days. After seven days of sitting in the dust with Eliphaz, Bildad and Zophar, you'd probably be having a pretty bad day too.

In verses 1–12, Job ends his seven days of silence by opening his mouth and starting cursing. It isn't the Lord he

---

[1] Ezekiel 14:14 and 14:20, and James 5:11.

curses, but he directs some very bitter language at the day when he was born. He calls for his birthday to be struck out of the calendar.[2] He calls for those who curse days to curse his birthday too.[3] He wishes that he had been stillborn, for then at least he would be lying dead in the grave, instead of suffering with the living.

If we re-read the first half of Job's poem slowly, we discover that he actually goes far further than lamenting his own birthday. His true lament is that the Lord ever created the world! On the first day, God created light, so let day be turned to darkness. On the second day, God divided the sea from the sky, so let gloom and utter darkness once more cloud the distinction between the two. On the fourth day, God created the sun, moon and stars to mark the seasons, so let the calendars be graffitied, let the morning stars burn out and let people wait in vain for the first sunrays of dawn. On the third and sixth days, God replaced the chaos of the primordial oceans with the dry land and its beautiful creatures, so let ancient Leviathan reassert its rule.[4] Job's frequent talk about darkness in the first stanza of this poem reflects how much he feels in the dark about God's actions all around him. His property is gone, his children are gone and his health is gone, so he starts to fear that God has gone and left him too. Job's initial reaction to disaster was to worship the Lord, but as the days roll on without deliverance he begins to conclude that the Lord must have abandoned him.

In verses 13–26, we learn a few important things about ancient Hebrew poetry. It doesn't rhyme, for starters, finding

---

[2] This may seem strange to our ears, but it wasn't strange for poetry in Job's day. David curses Mount Gilboa with no longer receiving rain because Saul was killed there (2 Samuel 1:21) and Jeremiah not only curses the day he was born but also the man who informed his father that he had a son (Jeremiah 20:14–18)!

[3] What on earth does Job mean by *those who curse days*?! Well, in the same way that our culture sees *Friday 13th* as an unlucky day in the calendar, ancient Eastern religions earmarked many other days as evil.

[4] We will see later, in Job 41, that *Leviathan* was an ancient name for the Devil and his demons, the "monster" that sought to keep the world in chaos before the Lord spoke, *"Let there be light!"* at the start of Genesis.

its beauty instead in its rhythm and its symmetry. This second stanza of Job's lament begins and ends therefore with a pair of bookends that seek relief from all his suffering. The stanza begins with a wish to find rest in death (verse 13) and it ends with a lament that there is no rest for the living (verse 26). The verses in between describe a man who feels anguished and suicidal.[5] *"What I feared has come upon me; what I dreaded has happened to me"* (verse 25). Job's worst fears have been realized. He has lost all that he holds dear. All he has left is a nagging wife and three false friends.[6]

So what are we to make of this? How can the man who trusted God so totally in chapters 1 and 2 have plummeted so quickly into such terrible despair? If you are asking such questions, then praise God. It means that you have not yet experienced first-hand real grief and tragedy. Anyone who has can testify that the human heart acts like a yo-yo, one day feeling full of faith and the next day unable to get out of bed for a debilitating sense of bleak despair. The writer of Job records this honest lament to help us trust that God is able to sustain our hearts on both the good days and the bad. Last year, I buried the child of a lady at the church I lead in London. When I saw her one Sunday recently, she confessed that she was having one of her bad days but she assured me through her tears that she knew one thing for sure: *What is true in the light is still true in the dark.*

That's what the writer wants to teach us through these verses. Job is truly in the dark. He knows nothing of the exchanges at God's heavenly council, that shed such light on these events for us, in chapters 1 and 2. The writer reminds us of those conversations by using the Hebrew verb *sûk* or *sākak* to record Job's complaint in verse 23 – *"Why is life given to a man whose way is hidden, whom God **has hedged** in?"* – since this is the same phrase that Satan used in his own complaint to the Lord in

---

[5] Job doesn't merely wish he had been stillborn in the Hebrew text of 3:16. He wishes he had been aborted. He uses shocking language to plumb the depths of human suffering and sorrow.

[6] Bankrupted, Job comforts himself in 3:13–19 that at least the rich and the poor are both equal in death.

1:10, *"Have you not **put a hedge** around him and his household and everything he has?"* From the bottom of his whirlpool of depression, Job imagines that the Lord has surrounded him with barbed wire and with misery. From the perspective of the angels in heaven, however, the Lord has surrounded Job with his love and protection.[7] Even in his sickness and pain, the Lord has forbidden Satan from laying a finger on the man's life. Job will not find his final respite in death, but in glorious resurrection when God vindicates him!

One day Jesus would hang from a cruel cross in deep darkness. He would cry out, *"My God, my God, why have you forsaken me?"*[8] He would walk in Job's footsteps to deliver him and you and me. He would plumb the depths of human sorrow so that, even when our days feel darkest, he is able to lead us out into the light of day. If you feel hedged in by tragedy, then God calls you to look up to the Righteous One who died and rose again. He reassures us that, even on dark days, he is hedging us in with his protection.

---

[7] Feelings are a terrible barometer for reality. We must only place our trust in God's unchanging Word.

[8] Matthew 27:45–46, Mark 15:33–34 and Luke 23:44–45.

The Best Answers in the World (Job 4:1–11)

Then Eliphaz the Temanite replied...

(Job 4:1)

I know that it's a bit of an unusual pastime, but I love reading newspapers from six weeks ago or, even better, from six months ago. I enjoy reading their confident predictions about election results and parliamentary votes and stock prices and sports matches – so many of which have been proven to be utterly false by the time I read them. They teach me not to be swayed too much by people's oh-so confident assertions today.

The speeches of Eliphaz, Bildad and Zophar are like very old newspapers. Although it's hard to imagine it now, there once was a time when their answers to the problem of suffering were regarded as the best answers in the world. One day, no doubt, people will look back on the writings of Richard Dawkins and Sam Harris and the other great thinkers of our generation and find it equally hard to believe that anybody ever swallowed half of what they say. It is easy for us, with the benefit of many centuries of hindsight, to look back on the speeches of Job's three friends and to see that their bold claims are riddled with flaws but, at the time, it wasn't easy. They represent the greatest thinking of the wise men of the East. They give Job the very best answers that the pagan world can offer him. They are meant to make us cry out for better answers from the Lord.

Act One of the book of Job (chapters 3–27) consists of three cycles of speeches:

Introduction:	Job's lament (3)
The first cycle of speeches:	Eliphaz (4–5) Job's reply to Eliphaz (6–7) Bildad (8) Job's reply to Bildad (9–10) Zophar (11) Job's reply to Zophar (12–14)
The second cycle of speeches:	Eliphaz (15) Job's reply to Eliphaz (16–17) Bildad (18) Job's reply to Bildad (19) Zophar (20) Job's reply to Zophar (21)
The third cycle of speeches:	Eliphaz (22) Job's reply to Eliphaz (23–24) Bildad (25) Job's reply to Bildad (26–27)

Eliphaz is the oldest of Job's three friends, so he tends to speak as the voice of *experience*.[1] Bildad is no spring chicken himself, so he tends to speak as the voice of ancient *tradition*. Zophar likes to think of himself as a bit more open-minded, basing his own arguments on *logical reasoning*. Although these three friends take three different approaches, what strikes us most during their three cycles of speeches is how little they actually have to say. They each keep on trotting out the same old answers, offering very little in the way of real comfort to Job. Their empty and repetitive speeches are meant to make us long for the Lord to silence them with better speeches of his own. As they summarize the best answers that our world has to offer to the question, *Why does God allow suffering?*, we are meant to start longing for answers from beyond our own world.

---

[1] The Lord addresses Eliphaz as the leader of the three friends in 42:7, another sign of his seniority.

At the start of chapter 4, Eliphaz presents his own answer. He is remarkably insensitive in verses 2–6, offering Job a lecture on religion instead of sympathizing with him in his pain. Eliphaz points out that Job has been quick to give advice to others in the past, so now it is his turn to shut up and listen. He has no right to feel impatient or discouraged or dismayed now that he finds himself on the receiving end of trouble. There is an easy way out for him. If he learns a simple formula, life will tip back in his favour and God will have to start helping him again.

Eliphaz reveals his formula with a flourish in verses 7–11. *"Consider now… As I have observed."* Eliphaz claims to have tested out his formula through many years of experience: *"those who plough evil and those who sow trouble reap it."* In other words, God never afflicts anybody who consistently does what is right, and God never prospers anyone who consistently does evil. We can summarize his formula like this:

> People who do evil + A loving, powerful God = People who are cursed
> People who do good + A loving, powerful God = People who are blessed

Before we rush to criticize Eliphaz for being too simplistic, let's face up to the fact that his formula still lies at the heart of Western spirituality today. He is a preacher of *karma*. What goes around comes around. Do good to others and good things will happen to you; do bad to others and don't be surprised when it catches up with you. Since most of us see ourselves as good people, this is the formula that makes us rage against God for not sheltering our own lives from suffering. It is also the formula that makes us angry that God seems to let evil people get away with their evil deeds scot-free. It is the formula that dominates the plot lines of our literature and movies. It's what makes Captain von Trapp and Maria celebrate their love for each other in *The Sound of Music* by singing that nothing can come from nothing, so in their childhood or youth they must have done something good.[2]

---

[2] Julie Andrews stars as Maria in *The Sound of Music* (Twentieth-Century Fox, 1965).

There's just one problem with the formula that is preached by Eliphaz and Julie Andrews. The experiences of Job are meant to show us that it simply isn't true! Yes, if we act foolishly then we are more likely to suffer.[3] If we drive our cars at double the speed limit, we are more likely to crash them. If we gossip behind people's backs, we are more likely to lose our friends. But the book of Job insists that bad things *do* happen to good people and that good things *do* happen to bad people. Cancer *does* seem to strike indiscriminately. Good people *do* seem to be in the wrong place at the wrong time. Evil people *do* appear to prosper. The wise men of the East were purported to have the best answers in the world, but all that Eliphaz shows us here is that the world has no real answers when it comes to the biggest question of them all: *Why does God allow suffering?*

---

[3] The apostle Paul agrees with Eliphaz in Galatians 6:7–9. But he also points out in 1 Timothy 5:24–25 that, while some people feel the full force of God's judgment in this life, other people feel it only when they die.

The Limits of Experience
(Job 4:12–5:27)

"We have examined this, and it is true. So hear it and apply it to yourself."

(Job 5:27)

I once got lost driving home late at night from one side of London to the other. I had been driving for over an hour when I found myself back at the same junction for the third or fourth time. That's how Eliphaz makes me feel as he finishes the first of his speeches. He won't engage with the real problem. He just keeps going round in circles.[1]

Eliphaz can tell that Job is unimpressed with his simplistic formula for why God allows suffering. Job is probably too emotionally exhausted to conceal his anger at being given a lecture instead of sympathy and prayer. But Eliphaz isn't in any mood to stop and hear out Job's objections. He ploughs on, asserting over and over again that his formula simply has to be true. He is an old man, so he claims to speak from experience about what *"I myself have seen..."* and about what he would do, *"If I were you..."* When Eliphaz finally stops talking, he ends arrogantly: *"We have examined this, and it is true. So hear it and apply it to yourself."* But all his speech does is reveal to us the limits of experience.[2]

In 4:12–21, Eliphaz shows us that *experience alone is a poor foundation for understanding.* When Job refuses to accept

---

[1] For example, 5:6 repeats 4:8. Trouble doesn't come to us by chance. We only ever reap what we have sown.

[2] Many of Eliphaz's insights are true. In 9:10, Job repeats the insight that Eliphaz shares with him in 5:9. The problem is that his insights are pot-bound by his over-reliance on experience alone.

his simplistic formula, Eliphaz tells him that he didn't make it up on his own. It was given to him one night by a spirit in a spooky dream. He started shaking (so it must have been God). His hair stood on end (proof that it must have been an angel). He heard the spirit talk to him about the fall of Satan's demons from heaven (which is in the Bible, so the rest of the dream *must* also be true).[3] The spirit confirmed that, if even angels sinned and fell from heaven, then Job cannot be as holy as he claims to be. His suffering therefore stands as proof that he has disobeyed the Lord.

Now don't get me wrong here. I believe in God-given visions and dreams. Scripture tells us to expect them, and many of my friends and I have experienced them.[4] My problem isn't with supernatural revelations, but with what foolish people often tend to do with them. One person argues that *their* dream resolves the matter. Another person is certain that *their* prophecy ought to carry the day. Still another claims to "feel no peace" about either revelation, so they press forward with whatever feels right to them. It's all so subjective. God doesn't give us supernatural revelations to spare us the need to think or so that we can use them to back up whatever we wish to be true. Visions and prophecies are meant to be a confirmation of, not a substitute for, what God says to us in his Word.[5]

In 5:1–7, Eliphaz shows us that *experience alone can never give us the full picture.* For all his confident bluster, he confesses to Job that he doesn't really know how to pray or who to pray to. He has seen enough of life on earth to speak smart words of wisdom which would not look out of place in the book of Proverbs, but he clearly has no idea about what is happening in

---

[3] The reason why so many people still fall for this sort of nonsense is that some of what is spoken is actually true. What Eliphaz says happened in 4:18 is corroborated by 2 Peter 2:4, Jude 6 and Revelation 12:3–12.

[4] Acts 2:17, 9:10, 10:3, 16:9–10, 18:9 and 26:19.

[5] That's why the New Testament commands us to *weigh* prophecy and *obey* the Bible (Matthew 24:23–25, Acts 17:11, 1 Corinthians 14:29, 1 Thessalonians 5:19–22, 1 Timothy 4:1, 2 Peter 2:1, 1 John 4:1 and Revelation 2:2).

the courtroom of heaven.[6] He has no place in his thinking for the Devil or for the idea that God might have a bigger agenda for our lives than making us healthy and wealthy in the short-term. His thinking is entirely earthbound.

In 5:8–16, Eliphaz shows us that *experience alone can't teach us how to help each other.* When he tells Job what he would do if he were in Job's position, he merely demonstrates how little he grasps what it is like to be Job. He insists that God will always deliver those who grieve, but that's precisely the problem. Job has been grieving in the dust for days, and God *hasn't* yet delivered him. Eliphaz insists that God always thwarts plans of the crafty and saves the innocent from their sword, but that's the problem too. God *didn't* thwart the plans of the Sabean and Chaldean raiders when they stole Job's herds, and he *didn't* spare Job's servants from their sword. No amount of experience and no amount of years can ever truly teach us what it is like to walk in another person's shoes. What has been relevant to our own life may prove irrelevant to theirs.[7]

In 5:17–26, Eliphaz shows us that *experience alone will never teach us God's way of salvation.* He isn't just insensitive when he urges Job to thank the Lord for disciplining him, or when he claims that Job would still have his property and his children would still be alive if only he had lived a better life. Eliphaz is also pretty ignorant about God's purposes.[8] He has no understanding of the death-and-resurrection pathway that God has laid out before Job, that he would one day lay out before his

---

[6] What Eliphaz says in 5:7 is one of the most memorable proverbs in the book of Job: *"Man is born to trouble as surely as sparks fly upwards."* He also speaks great wisdom in 5:2 – resentment looks back and longs for a different past, while envy looks forward and longs for a different future, but both are equally fatal to our happiness. Eliphaz speaks a lot of general truth, but he is sorely misguided in his short-sighted conclusions.

[7] What Eliphaz says in 5:13 is generally true. It is echoed by Psalm 9:15–16 and directly quoted by the apostle Paul in 1 Corinthians 3:19. Yet misapplied general truth is as deceptive as an outright lie.

[8] Eliphaz represents the wisdom of all the wise men of the East. Note how much his formula in 5:19 (*"from six... in seven"*) reflects other sayings of the wise in Proverbs 6:16, Ecclesiastes 11:2 and Amos 1:3.

Son Jesus, and that he still lays out before you and me today.[9] It never crosses Eliphaz's mind that God might have a higher purpose in taking people through the dark valley of suffering to teach them to worship him for his own sake, not for the sake of what we can get out of him. Eliphaz never stops to consider whether God might be more interested in real relationships than he is in our following a formula. Eliphaz's attitude towards the Gospel is: *If I don't understand it then it can't be true.* What is really scary about his speech is just how many people echo him today.[10]

In 5:27, Eliphaz ends his speech in a way that makes it clear that he cares far less about comforting Job than he does about proving his own formula. His life experience hasn't made his heart tender. It has made his heart stubborn and has deafened his ears to the genuine suffering of his friend. Instead of extending love to Job, he subjects him to a lecture. As he wanders round in circles, insisting that his formula simply has to be true, he demonstrates the limits of experience. Eliphaz's first speech is meant to convince us that we need more than human wisdom. We need a far better answer from the Lord.

---

[9] There is no room for the cross in Eliphaz's formula. Jesus didn't constantly suffer, but he often did, and so will anyone who follows him. See Matthew 16:21–24, Mark 8:31–34, Luke 14:26–27, Acts 14:22 and 1 Peter 4:12.

[10] It lies at the heart of the prosperity gospel. The promise in 5:26 that *"You will come to the grave in full vigour"* is patently absurd. If God promises to keep our bodies healthy until we die, then who would ever die at all?!

The Glory of Kings
(Job 4:12–5:27)

"Call if you will, but who will answer you? To which of the holy ones will you turn?"

(Job 5:1)

Every year I organize an Easter egg hunt for my children and their friends. They have a lot of fun, and they always think that it was worth the effort when they find their chocolate in the end. If you find yourself surprised at the length and rambling nature of the speeches in the book of Job, then try to view them as God's invitation to enjoy a little treasure hunt. One of the Bible's other books of Wisdom Literature tells us: *"It is the glory of God to conceal a matter; to search out a matter is the glory of kings."*[1]

Recently I got into a conversation with a Christian friend. I told her that I had just started writing a commentary on the book of Job, and I asked if she had ever read it. *I've read the first couple of chapters and then the chapters at the end*, she reassured me. *Is that what you mean?* Well, no, not really. God has laid out for us this lengthy treasure hunt for a reason. I could tell you about my trip to India. I could even lend you my guidebook. But it would be no substitute for you actually going there. In the same way, God resists giving us a set of bullet point answers to our questions about the suffering in the world. He wants to take us on a journey of discovery alongside Job and his friends. He offers us no shortcuts or easy answers, because he wants us to see the same things that they saw.

These speeches chart how Job and his friends come to

---

[1] Proverbs 25:2. The five books of Wisdom Literature are Job, Psalms, Proverbs, Ecclesiastes and Song of Songs.

understand *God himself*. It becomes evident in these early chapters that they initially knew very little about him, and that God turned Job's sufferings around for good by making them a vehicle to reveal his character to them. In 5:8, Eliphaz refers to God as *Ēl*, a Hebrew word that could just as easily describe any of the pagan idols of the ancient world. In time, El would become the proper name for the chief god of the Canaanites, who was married to the goddess Asherah and often pictured as a bull.[2] Eliphaz reflects the same lack of understanding that would later lead the Israelites to build a golden calf to worship the Lord.

Job and Eliphaz also refer to God five times in Job 3–5 as *Elōahh*.[3] This conveys a slightly better understanding of what the Lord is truly like, but only compared to referring to him as El. The word sounds very similar to one that the Babylonians used to describe their gods.[4] What's more, it is a singular noun. It describes a one-dimensional deity. It carries with it no hint that the Lord is three-in-one.

The Lord uses Job's suffering to change all this. As many a Christian who has experienced great pain and trauma will tell you today, it is often in the darkest places that we see God's light shine the most clearly. God arrests our attention in the valley of suffering far more easily than in fields of ease and plenty. In 4:17, Eliphaz confesses that the God he mentions is our *Maker*. In 5:17, he refers to God for the first time as *Shaddai* – the *Almighty*.[5] Perhaps most exciting of all, in 5:8, he refers to the

---

[2] The name *Ēl* is used to refer to *God* a total of fifty-seven times in the book of Job. That's well over a quarter of all the times that the name is used to refer to the Lord in the entire Old Testament.

[3] They call him *Elōahh* in 3:4, 3:23, 4:9, 4:17 and 5:17. The name is used forty-one times in total in the book of Job, and it is only used fifteen times in the rest of the Old Testament put together. On five of those fifteen occasions, it is used to describe a pagan false god rather than the Lord (2 Chronicles 32:15 and Daniel 11:37–39).

[4] The Babylonian word *Elāhh* is used ninety-five times in the parts of Daniel and Ezra that are written in Aramaic.

[5] This will go on to become quite a feature of the book of Job. The name *Shaddai* is used for God thirty-one times in Job, and only seventeen times in

Lord for the first time as *Elōhīm*. This is the normal name for God in the Old Testament and it is a name brimming with meaning. It isn't a Hebrew singular noun (referring to *one* god). It isn't a Hebrew dual noun (referring to *two* gods). It is a Hebrew plural noun which always takes a singular verb (referring to God as *three-in-one*). As Job and his friends grope around together in the darkness of his suffering, they actually stumble upon the Trinity.[6]

These speeches also chart how Job and his friends come to understand *God's plan*. We do not know whether Eliphaz's dream really came from God, but we do know from 4:15 and 18 that it convinced him of the reality of angels. He does not know in 5:1 to which of the *"holy ones"* Job ought to turn, but he at least begins to grasp that there is a spirit world beyond the world we see. This matters deeply to Job. At the heart of his lament in chapter 3 was a sense that he could cope with his sufferings if only he believed that there was more to life than what he sees. His despair wasn't so much over suffering as over suffering without meaning. Don't miss, then, the important progression in these first three chapters of speeches. Job talks at first as if death leads to nothingness and as if the same eternal fate lies in store for both the rich and poor, both the good and the wicked. But if there is a spirit world beyond the one we see, then perhaps Job might dare to hope for meaning in the midst of suffering.[7]

These speeches therefore chart how Job and his friends come to understand *God's Saviour*. We are still in the early stages of the speeches, but already this emerges as one of the book's greatest themes. Eliphaz confesses in 5:1 that he doesn't know which spirit might act as a Mediator between Job and

---

the rest of the Old Testament put together.

[6] This triune meaning comes out in Genesis 1:26, where *Elōhīm* says, *"Let us make man in our image."* The writer of Job uses this name eleven times in Job 1–2. Job and his friends only use it five times in their speeches.

[7] We will go on to see that this is one of the biggest themes of the book of Job, as his suffering gives him profound insight into the realities of heaven and hell, of God's final judgment, and of life beyond the grave.

God, but he speculates that there must be someone. Eliphaz might misapply much of his wisdom, but there's a reason why the apostle Paul quotes his words in 1 Corinthians 3:19. Quite a bit of what he says is true! Eliphaz urges Job in 5:8, *"if I were you, I would appeal to God; I would lay my cause before him."* He doesn't know any Mediator who can vindicate Job as righteous in the Lord's courtroom, but he and Job are starting to believe that there might be one out there.[8]

So don't fast-forward through these chapters, like my friend who assumed that only the first and last few chapters of the book of Job are worth reading. There is great gold to be found in here, if we are willing to get down in the dust to pan for it alongside Job and his friends. Job's suffering will prove to be the grit in the oyster's shell that eventually brings him to the Pearl of Great Price.[9] These chapters chart his treasure hunt through lengthy days of torment to discover the Good News about the suffering Son of God.

[8] We will go on to see that this is another massive theme of the book of Job. Through his suffering, Job will find out more about Jesus than any of the patriarchs or their peers.

[9] Jesus assures us in Matthew 13:44–46 that nor will anybody else who gains the Pearl of Great Price by losing everything in this life feel aggrieved in heaven. They will view their sufferings as deeply meaningful.

When the Sparks Start to Fly (Job 6:1–30)

"I would still have this consolation – my joy in unrelenting pain – that I had not denied the words of the Holy One."

(Job 6:10)

The *Hindenburg* was the largest aircraft ever made, both then and now. At 245 metres long and 41 metres tall, it was three times longer and twice as tall as a modern Boeing 747. But big is not the same as strong. On 6th May 1937, it only took a few sparks to bring the giant hydrogen balloon crashing down to the ground in a ball of fire. On the outside it looked impressive, but on the inside it was fatally flawed.

The book of Job was written to prevent our own faith in God from experiencing a *Hindenburg* disaster. Faith that looks impressive, singing loudly on a Sunday, can crash and burn in a moment if it is unprepared for the sparks of suffering that will inevitably come our way. That's why Jesus warned his followers to get ready for *"when trouble or persecution comes"*.[1] Note it's *when* it comes, not *if* it comes. Jesus warned that it is only when the sparks start to fly that the angels and the demons at God's heavenly council witness whether our faith is shallow and short-lived, or deep enough to go the distance under fire. The book of Job seeks to ready us for life's ups-and-downs in order to prevent our faith in God from going up in flames when the sparks start to fly.

In verses 1–13, Job replies to Eliphaz. He rejects his friend's simplistic formula and returns to his lament of chapter

---

[1] Jesus says this in his famous Parable of the Sower, in Matthew 13:20–21.

3.[2] He still feels so miserable that he wants to die, plagued by more anguished thoughts than there are grains of sand on the seashore. Notice the important progression as he picks up his lament a second time. This time around, he is convinced that the author of his suffering is the Lord. *"The arrows of the Almighty are in me... God's terrors are marshalled against me."* In chapter 3, Job lamented that God felt like a lousy friend. In chapter 6, he laments that God feels like his enemy.

Not everyone who claims to love the Lord can cope with such a feeling. In May 2014, a Pentecostal pastor caused a major stir by posting a blog entitled "Dear Yahweh, You're Fired: An Open Termination Letter for God". In the wake of finding out that his two nieces had been murdered, he declared that he could no longer carry on with his faith in God:

> *Our working relationship is not what it used to be... Some years ago I noticed that certain duties which are part of your job description were being neglected or mismanaged. I've called you several times, leaving you messages asking you to address the issues, but you have repeatedly refused to answer my calls... Well, enough is enough. Something has to be done about the situation... There's no point in continuing this working relationship. You do nothing useful... I am therefore terminating your position effective immediately and cancelling all contractual obligations between us... If you're thinking of using me as a reference in the future, don't bother. I wouldn't give you a good one. In fact, I'll be sure to tell everyone who asks not to waste their time, love, energy and resources on you... Good riddance. You're fired.[3]*

It wasn't a spoof blog. He went on to leave his church and become a computer salesman.

---

[2] Job essentially says to Eliphaz in 6:5: If your formula was right, I wouldn't be in any of this agony!

[3] Dennis Augustine on www.sonofsamuel.blogspot.com (14th May 2014).

Job feels equally tormented, but when the sparks start to fly his faith in God proves to be a lot deeper. He steps back from the brink of suicide, declaring that God alone has the authority to kill him. Unless he does so, Job is determined to keep on worshipping him. *"Then I would still have this consolation – my joy in unrelenting pain – that I had not denied the words of the Holy One"* (verse 10). Rather than accusing the Lord of mistreating him, Job insists through bitter tears that the Lord is holy – distinct from pagan idols, in a league all of his own. Job may not be able to understand him, but he can at least still choose to trust him.[4]

The writer wants Job's faith in God to do more than merely impress us. He wants his example to prevent a *Hindenburg* disaster when the sparks start to fly in our own lives. To do that, he lets us in on Job's big secret. He uses the Hebrew word *kāhad* in verse 10. Most translators take it to mean that Job refused to *deny* any of God's words, but it can also be translated as a refusal to *hide, conceal, cross out, cover up* or *cut out* any of them. The writer's point is that Job resolved early on in his walk with the Lord that he would not ignore a single verse of the Scriptures that God had given him.[5] In the words of the apostle Paul, he decided up front that he would submit to *"the whole will of God"* and believe that *"all Scripture is God-breathed and is useful for teaching, rebuking, correcting and training in righteousness"*.[6] Job refused to cherry-pick his Bible verses.

If we are honest, isn't this why our own faith begins to crash and burn so easily whenever the sparks start to fly in our own lives? We love many of the words of Jesus, but we conveniently cover over many of the Bible verses in which he warns us that following in his footsteps means walking the Calvary road by his

---

[4] In this chapter, Job calls the Lord three times *Elōahh* (*God*), twice *Shaddai* (the *Almighty*) and once *Qādōsh* (the *Holy One*).

[5] Job was possibly the first book of the Bible to be written, but before then the ancient believers studied prophecies from men such as Abel, Enoch and Noah (Luke 11:50–51, 2 Peter 2:5 and Jude 14–15).

[6] Acts 20:27 and 2 Timothy 3:16.

side.[7] Some of those verses warn us that we will be persecuted for our faith in him, just as Job suffered for being blameless – not, as Eliphaz suggested, for his sin.[8] Other verses warn that we will suffer simply as a result of living in a fallen world to which our Saviour has not yet returned. Either way, Jesus says that such times of suffering do not scupper faith. They reveal how much or little faith is actually there. He warns us in his Parable of the Sower, in Matthew 13:20–21, that *"The seed falling on rocky ground refers to someone who hears the word and at once receives it with joy. But since they have no root, they last only a short time. When trouble or persecution comes because of the word, they quickly fall away."* When the sparks begin to fly, it is too late. The time to deepen our faith in those Scriptures is now.

In verses 14–30, we see the fruit of Job's commitment to God's Word. He laments that, in his hour of need, his friends have proved to be as useless as a desert stream that dries up in summer, at the very moment when a thirsty traveller needs its waters most. He hasn't asked them for money, yet the only generosity he has received from them is in the amount of words they cram into their heartless speeches![9] Like Jesus in the Garden of Gethsemane, Job has three friends with him but he still feels utterly alone. The only thing that keeps him from a spiritual *Hindenburg* disaster is the Word of God that he has stored up within him. This, and only this, keeps him still trusting in God and keeps assuring him that Eliphaz's simplistic formula simply can't be true. "Take it back!" he says literally to Eliphaz in verse 29. "My righteousness still stands!"[10]

---

[7] Matthew 5:11–12, 8:18–22, 10:16–39, 16:24–25, 19:21, 23:34 and 24:9–14. That's just Matthew's gospel!

[8] The book of Job isn't simply about suffering. It is about suffering *because we are believers*. See 2 Timothy 3:12.

[9] The Hebrew word *ḥēsēd* in 6:14 is a word that is normally used in the Old Testament to describe the *covenant loving kindness* of God. Job's point is that their love has failed him, but he still has the love of God.

[10] My translation.

Get Real (Job 7:1-21)

"I despise my life; I would not live for ever. Let me alone; my days have no meaning."

(Job 7:16)

C.S. Lewis argues that:

> *What seem our worst prayers may really be, in God's eyes, our best. Those, I mean, which are least supported by devotional feeling and contend with the greatest disinclination. For these, perhaps, being nearly all will, come from a deeper level than feeling. In feeling there is so much that is really not ours – so much that comes from weather and health or from the last book read. One thing seems certain. It is no good angling for the rich moments. God sometimes seems to speak to us most intimately when He catches us, as it were, off our guard.*[1]

If C.S. Lewis is right, then Job's prayer in chapter 7 is brilliant. Having finished his reply to Eliphaz in chapter 6, he now turns to the Lord and gives him both barrels over how he really feels. Many readers are shocked by his forceful language and the contrast with his simple faith back in 1:21 and 2:10. But that's how grief works. Our feelings go up and down like a yo-yo. Job doesn't hide these fluctuations from the Lord. He gets real with God in this chapter, and he wants to teach us to get real with God in our prayers too.

In verses 1-5, Job gets real with God about *his situation*. If he ever hoped that the Lord would reward him for his righteous living, he has long since given up any hope that his payday

---

[1] He writes this in his *Letters to Malcolm: Chiefly on Prayer* (1964).

will come.[2] He spends his days longing for nightfall so that his so-called friends will finally go to bed and grant him a few short hours of respite. He then spends his nights tossing and turning, enjoying no respite at all. All he can see stretching out before him are endless months more of longing for dark in the daytime and for dawn in the dark.[3] His skin is a mass of sores and scabs. Some of his wounds are festering so badly that an army of maggots have decided to make his red-raw body their permanent home.

It all sounds pretty hideous, but the writer doesn't censure Job for his language. It would be even more hideous if Job tried to hide how he is really feeling and if he spouted religious platitudes instead of this impassioned prayer. The monk Thomas Merton is said to have told his novices, *"If you want to ascend to God, you have to descend into your own reality. God is too real to be found anywhere else but in reality."* If Thomas Merton is right, then Job is definitely doing well here. Job is shockingly real with God.

In verses 6–10, Job gets real with God about *his prospects*. He faces up to the fact that he has very little hope of seeing any happiness in whatever life is left to him before the grave. The Hebrew word he uses in verse 9 is *she'ōl*, which can either mean the *grave* (where everybody goes) or *hell* (as opposed to heaven). It is therefore one of the most negative words for death in the Hebrew language. Job hasn't lost his faith in God, but he has lost all pretence in his prayers.

In verses 11–16, Job gets real with God about *his feelings*. He refuses to keep silent about the anguish of his spirit and the bitterness of his soul.[4] He doesn't try to hide the fact that he

---

[2] Job is right. The Lord generally promises to reward us for what we have done (Psalm 62:12 and Matthew 16:27). But Job is also wrong. Our hope ought to be in the pay packet of Jesus, not our own (Romans 6:23).

[3] Job is not saying in 7:3 that months have passed since Job 1–2. He is lamenting his bleak future.

[4] The Hebrew words Job uses in 7:11 are *rūach* and *nephesh*. He is tormented body, soul and spirit.

feels that the Lord is treating him as he would a mortal enemy.[5] What kind of God would rob his worshippers of the few brief moments of sleep that their constant pain affords them by troubling them with nightmares which immediately wake them up again?[6] Job pulls no punches when he tells the Lord that he would rather be strangled in his bed than have to face another night sleeping in it. You won't find the honesty of his prayer request on many people's tongues: *"Let me alone; my days have no meaning"* (verse 16).

In verses 17–21, Job gets real with God about *how it feels to be one of his worshippers.* Job lived many centuries before King David wrote his worship songs, but don't miss his ironic inversion of Psalm 8:4. David marvels that the Lord should pay attention to mere humans in order to bless them; Job marvels that the Lord should pay attention to mere humans to cause them pain. Why does it bother God whether people love or disobey him? What does he gain through their love and worship anyway? Why not simply overlook their sins and let them all be happy?[7] Why does he keep on using Job's peeling body for his target practice?[8] Aaron would pray later, in Numbers 6:22–26, for the Lord to turn his face towards people and bless them, but Job prays for the Lord to turn his face away from people and to simply let them get on with their lives. If this doesn't sound much like how you pray, that's the point.

The writer wants us to get real. He is teaching us to pray here, but he is also doing more than advocating honesty. He is showing us where to find the answer to our question: *Why does God allow suffering?* It isn't found in denying the reality of

---

[5] We noted in 3:8 that Leviathan, or the great sea monster, is an ancient picture of the Devil. See Job 41.

[6] Job is addressing the Lord here, so he isn't talking about Eliphaz's scary vision in 4:12–21. Job has had many scary visions of his own.

[7] Job uses pretty strong language in 7:19, begging God literally to *"Leave me alone long enough to swallow my spit!"* This is a man at the end of his tether with God.

[8] Job's claim in 7:20 that God is using him for target practice links back to his claim in 6:4 that God has riddled him with arrows.

pain. That's Buddhism. Nor is it found in masking the reality of pain with religious words. That's Western Christianity. Nor is it found in watering down our expectations of the Lord. That's fatalism, masquerading as faith.

After the liberation of Auschwitz, one Jewish holocaust survivor reflected that:

> *It never occurred to me to question God's doings or lack of doings while I was an inmate of Auschwitz... It never occurred to me to associate the calamity we were experiencing with God, to blame Him, or to believe in Him less or cease believing in Him at all because He didn't come to our aid.*[9]

Job doesn't see this as faith. He dismisses it as fatalism. The answer to our question isn't found in pretending that God is less than he is. It's found in getting real with God.

It is only because Job gives voice to his real feelings that he suddenly stumbles upon a huge part of the answer. By asking the Lord to sweep sin under the carpet and to let bygones be bygones, he places his finger right at the heart of the issue.

God will never use his *might* to fix our world if it means riding roughshod over what is *right*. He will never rob his creatures of their freedom to choose whether or not to love him, or of their right to reap the consequences of the choice they have made. Job is still in the dark, but these verses ought to shed the light of the Gospel into our own hearts. God is so committed to his plan to save a sinful world in righteousness that he would one day come in person to suffer in the dust with Job to break the power of the grave that Job mentions here. He would rise again to lead his people out of a world of suffering and into his eternal glory.

That's what happens whenever we get real with God. We start to grasp his real answers.

---

[9] Quoted by Harold Kushner in his book *When Bad Things Happen to Good People* (1981).

Tradition (Job 8:1–22)

"Ask the former generations and find out what their ancestors learned..."

(Job 8:8)

When I think of Job's second friend Bildad, I find it hard to get the opening number from *Fiddler on the Roof* out of my head. The musical begins with the Jewish farmer Tevye, played by Topol in the movie, trying to insulate himself from a fast-changing world by clinging onto a way of life that has been handed down to his community for centuries by the rabbis. He sings and speaks into the camera: *"Traditions, traditions. Without our traditions, our lives would be as shaky as – as – as a fiddler on the roof."*[1]

That's Bildad the Shuhite in a nutshell. Unlike Eliphaz, who is forever boasting of his many years of life experience, Bildad is forever harping back to traditions forged in days long gone by. He does it here, in verses 8–10, in the first of his three speeches. *"Ask the former generations and find out what their ancestors learned, for we were born only yesterday and know nothing... Will they not instruct you and tell you?"* Bildad is full of old answers.

Sadly, we discover in verses 2–7 that Bildad isn't full of sensitivity. His scathing tone actually makes Eliphaz look as though he has a caring bedside manner! Bildad accuses Job of being a blustery old windbag, whose sinful children must have had it coming to them anyway.[2] He should pull himself together and go back to praying proper prayers. Bildad offers him a simple formula to get him back up on his feet. If Job recognizes

---

[1] *Fiddler on the Roof* (United Artists, 1971).

[2] Bildad compares Job's words to *"a blustering wind"* (verse 2) only a few days after Job's ten children were killed in a windstorm. His insensitivity is quite staggering.

the way in which God runs the world, then he will soon have fresh cattle and children aplenty.[3]

> A God who is just + A person who is suffering = Clear proof of sin
> A God who is just + A person who isn't suffering = Clear proof of virtue

In verses 8–22, Bildad tries to prove his formula by looking back to the wise men of previous generations. He claims that answering big questions such as *Why does God allow suffering?* is too difficult for us because we live such short lives, but if we stand on the shoulders of the giants of the past then we can give ourselves a longer view. Those giants tell us two things for certain: plants without water always wither and die under the hot sun, and people without virtue always wither and die under God's judgment.

The strength of Bildad's formula is that it is generally true that God punishes sinful people by afflicting them with suffering. The Old Testament is full of examples of this, and the New Testament has several examples too.[4] But the weakness of Bildad's formula is that the Bible also insists that God doesn't always punish sinful people in this way, and that he lets godly people go through long periods of suffering for a very different reason. Eliphaz says "experience" and Bildad says "tradition", but if you take a closer look then you will notice that their two formulae are essentially the same. Bildad simply trots out the same old answer that Eliphaz gave earlier. He just rephrases it a different way.

I like tradition. I live in one of the most traditional nations in the world and I went to one of its most traditional universities to study History – in other words, tradition. I'm about as sympathetic towards tradition as anybody that I know, but even I can tell that Bildad is merely trying to hide behind tradition here.

---

[3] The Hebrew word *tsedeq* in 8:6 means more than merely being *prosperous*. It means *just* or *right* or *righteous*. Bildad's formula reflects traditional views about the workings of God's justice.

[4] For example, in Acts 12:21–23, Romans 1:27 and 1 Corinthians 11:28–31.

Bildad appeals to tradition in order to avoid having to do any serious thinking of his own. If he can quote what the thinkers of yesterday said about the problem of suffering, then he hopes not to have to think too much about it today. Of course his ancestors were right to say that *"God does not reject one who is blameless or strengthen the hands of evildoers"* (verse 20). But that isn't an answer to our question; it's merely a restatement of the problem. Job is blameless yet it looks as though the Lord has rejected him. The Sabean and Chaldean raiders are evildoers yet it looks as though the Lord has strengthened their hands. Quoting the rhetorical question of our ancestors – *"Does God pervert justice?"* – doesn't absolve us of the need to think for ourselves. Their question merely stirs up more confusion that bad things *do* happen to good people, that good things *do* happen to bad people, and that God *doesn't* appear to be doing very much about it.

Bildad appeals to tradition in order to protect his shallow answers from scrutiny. He doesn't really know for sure that Job's children were drunken and sinful. The writer hints that they may have been, but he never says so explicitly. Even if they were, Bildad cannot prove that their tragic deaths were linked in any way to their lifestyle. After all, what about all the other drunk and sinful people who were not killed in the same windstorm? Bildad claims that our lives are too short for us to come to robust conclusions about why God allows suffering, but he never comes clean that the lives of our ancestors were equally short too! The Early Church leader Cyprian was right to warn us against people like Bildad: *"Tradition without truth is just error in its old age."*[5]

Bildad appeals to tradition in order to try to make the world feel a little tidier. He is like Tevye in the musical, hanging onto his traditions as a comfort blanket, because he knows deep down that what has happened to Job ought not to happen in a well-ordered world. He isn't honouring the dead here by

---

[5] He wrote this in the third century in a letter addressed to Pompeius (*Letter 74*).

seeking to recruit them to his team. He simply wants to use their words to silence the awkward questions of the living.[6] Whenever tradition is weaponized like this, it becomes the refuge of the rogue. It is what almost prevented the Bible from being translated into English, what almost kept church services in Latin and what almost kept the Gospel locked away during the Reformation. The truth is, the wisdom of the ages isn't wise enough. We need something better than the same old answers. We need to receive a proper answer from the Lord.

That's what the Lord gives us in the ninth chapter of John's gospel. The disciples spot a beggar by the side of the road who was born blind. They therefore bring out Bildad's formula and ask Jesus, *"Rabbi, who sinned, this man or his parents, that he was born blind?"* (John 9:2). Jesus lifts their gaze to see that something bigger is happening in the man's life, as was happening in the life of Job.[7] *"Neither this man nor his parents sinned, but this happened so that the works of God might be displayed in him"* (John 9:3).

Jesus calls us to lift our own gaze to see beyond the pot-bound thinking of traditional, formulaic answers. He says that God often allows good people to suffer temporary losses to grant them something of far greater value than mere happiness in the end.

---

[6] Jesus accuses the Pharisees of doing this too, building tombs to honour the dead prophets while murdering the live ones (Matthew 23:29–32)! We do the same if we pay lip service to the radical preachers of long ago.

[7] We are told explicitly in 1:1, 1:8 and 2:3 that Job did not deserve his sufferings. The Lord would restore his fortunes, as Bildad promises in 8:7, but only after achieving what he purposed through Job's suffering.

Lift Your Eyes (Job 9:1–35)

"His wisdom is profound, his power is vast."

(Job 9:4)

My youngest son and I love making elaborate mazes for his pet hamster. We take the books down from the bookshelves and we create a giant labyrinth on the floor, the hamster at one end and a bowl of food at the other. At first, the hamster runs around in circles at ground level, unable to access all areas. But then the hamster looks up and spots a way that we have made for it to climb up over many of the walls to explore the rest of the maze. Don't worry, no animals were harmed in the writing of this chapter. The hamster always gets its food in the end, and my son and I have a lot of fun together.

The first few chapters of speeches in the book of Job have made us feel a bit like my son's hamster. Eliphaz and Bildad have taken us round and round in circles without ever really answering our question.[1] Neither the formula of "experience" nor the formula of "tradition" has made much headway in explaining: *Why does God allow suffering?* They have merely restated the problem that Epicurus summarized for us earlier:

> *Either God wishes to take away evil, but he is unable; or God is able to take away evil, but he is unwilling; or God is neither willing nor able to take away evil; or God is both willing and able to take away evil. Well then, if he is willing and unable, then he is feeble, which is not in accordance with the character of God. If he is able and*

---

[1] Many of their insights are true. In 9:10, Job repeats the words of Eliphaz in 5:9. However, they don't lift their eyes to see what Job sees of God. Their insights are incomplete, so they continue round in circles.

unwilling, then he is malevolent, which is equally at variance with God. If he is neither willing nor able, then he is both malevolent and feeble. If he is both willing and able, which alone is suitable to God, then where does evil come from and why doesn't he rid the world of evil?[2]

That all changes when Job replies to Bildad in chapter 9. This marks the moment when, like my son's hamster, he lifts up his eyes and begins to discover a way out of the maze. When Eliphaz and Bildad mention God in their speeches, they merely use him to help balance the equations in their rigid formulae. But Job lifts his eyes up to God in this chapter and recognizes that the Sovereign Lord of the universe must have a bigger will and purpose of his own. This leads him to a breakthrough that has eluded his friends.

In verses 1–13, Job declares God's greatness. He announces that he knows one thing at least in answer to the question of why God allows so much suffering: it isn't because God lacks the power needed to put an end to it. Wisdom and strength lie at the epicentre of the Lord's character.[3] He is all-wise and all-powerful, which means that the question posed by Epicurus and by David Hume rests on a mistaken premise. It says:

1) we can't think of any justifiable reason why God would allow suffering;
2) therefore God can't have any justifiable reason;
3) therefore God can't be both powerful and loving.

But Job declares that such a view will always keep us at ground level, running round in circles like a hamster. God isn't just profoundly powerful and profoundly loving. He is also profoundly wise, which means that he may well have justifiable reasons for allowing suffering that are beyond human understanding. God has not shared them with us because his thoughts would blow

---

[2] Quoted by Lactantius in his treatise *On the Anger of God* (13.20–21).

[3] In the Hebrew text of 9:4, Job literally declares that *"He is wise in heart and mighty in strength."*

our tiny minds. It would be like trying to teach quantum physics to my son's hamster.

Job reminds us that the Lord is the God of volcanoes, the God of earthquakes and the God of solar eclipses. He is the God who created the stars and constellations.[4] He is the God who performs miracles. He is the God who defeated the Devil at the dawn of time, and the God who doesn't need to be told how well he's running the universe by the likes of you and me.[5] We have to concede that we don't fully know the answer to the question: *Why does God allow suffering?*, but we can rest assured that it is because God's wisdom tells him that he can achieve a world that is better by permitting evil than he can by preventing it. We may not be able to see such a reason. But God can, and he is right.[6]

In verses 14–20, Job points out another major flaw in both of the formulae that Eliphaz and Bildad have tried to peddle him. Nobody is truly righteous in the eyes of the Lord.[7] There are no "people who do good" and no "people of virtue", so both of their formulae are meaningless. How dare they lecture God on the ins-and-outs of his justice? Anyone who puts their hope in divine justice will regret it; the only hope we have of standing before God lies in his *mercy*. As Job lifts his eyes to see the holiness of the Lord, he sees a gaping flaw in our complaint that God allows bad things to happen to good people.

Job has made massive progress so far in this chapter. First,

---

[4] The Lord is so powerful that Job lists three constellations by name and then refers to the others literally in Hebrew as *"the bedrooms of the south"* (verse 9). The Lord is so great that vast galaxies are like mere bedrooms to him!

[5] The name *Rahab* in 9:13 is spelt differently in Hebrew to that of the woman in Joshua 2. It means *Proud* or *Insolent* or *Arrogant*, and it is another name for *Leviathan*. We saw in 3:8, and we will see again in 41:1 that both names speak of the Devil and his demons, viewed by the ancients as a monster that sought to keep the world in chaos before the Lord spoke, *"Let there be light!"* (Genesis 1:3). See also 7:12, 26:12, Psalm 89:9–10 and Isaiah 51:9.

[6] The Hebrew word for *resisting* God in 9:4 is *qāshāh* – the same word used for God *hardening* the hearts of his enemies so as to destroy them in Exodus 7:3 and Deuteronomy 2:30. This ought to sober us into silence.

[7] Job 14:4, 15:14–16 and 25:4–6, Psalm 14:1–3, Ecclesiastes 7:20, Mark 10:18, Romans 3:9–24 and 1 John 1:8–10.

he has lifted his eyes to see God's power. That clears up one thing at least: the suffering in our world is not caused by God's inability to prevent it. Second, he has lifted up his eyes to see God's wisdom. God always knows what he is doing, even when we do not. If God is big enough for us to blame for the suffering in our world, then he is also big enough for us to trust in the midst of it. Third, Job has lifted his eyes to see God's holiness. That's pretty sobering. Instead of complaining that God allows bad things to happen to good people, Job has recognized that none of us are good people at all. This leads on to the fourth insight that is still missing from the picture that Job has painted for us here. We don't just need a God who does good things to good people and bad things to bad people. We need a God who is merciful enough to make a way for *good* things to happen to *bad* people.

That's the theme which Job explores in verses 21–35. He confesses that the early signs do not look good. God is all-powerful, yet he allows the rulers of the earth to deny justice to their subjects, treating alike the blameless and the wicked. Worse than that, God appears to be doing so himself, holding Job guilty of some grave sin, when Job is convinced that he is as innocent as anyone.[8] Job longs to talk with God face to face so that he can add this fourth insight to the Gospel picture that he is painting for us here. We will look at the answer that God gives him in the next chapter.

---

[8] Job comes dangerously close in these verses to accusing the Lord of injustice and wrongdoing. God brings him to the end of his tether to reveal his Gospel to him, but not beyond his tether (1 Corinthians 10:13).

Courtroom Drama
(Job 9:32–35)

"If only there were someone to mediate between us,
someone to bring us together..."

(Job 9:33)

Many of the oldest texts that have survived from the ancient world are concerned with courtroom law. There is the Sumerian *Code of Ur-Nammu*. There are the Mesopotamian *Laws of Eshnunna*. There is the Babylonian *Code of Hammurabi*. And then there is the book of Job. If we want to understand Job's fourth insight into our questions about suffering, then we need to note how much this chapter of Job uses the language of a courtroom drama.

Bildad's speech encouraged Job to contemplate the workings of God's justice. He asked him, *"Does God pervert justice? ... Surely God does not reject one who is blameless"* (8:3, 20). In 9:1–13, Job therefore responds by asking Bildad, *"How can mere mortals prove their innocence before God?"* (9:2). The Hebrew word he uses here is *tsādaq*, which means *righteous* or *just* or *innocent*, and it cuts right to the heart of what is happening in the book of Job. The Lord is using Job's suffering to vindicate the wisdom of his rule before the angels and the demons that stand examining his actions in the courtroom of heaven, but this doesn't make Job a mere pawn in the drama. He begins to sense that the Lord has a marvellous plan to vindicate his suffering servant too.

Job confesses that any vindication will not come on the basis of his own actions. What Eliphaz said to him in 4:18–19 is indeed horribly true. He might be blameless in comparison to his neighbours on earth, but if he stood in the courtroom of heaven before the Lord then he knows he *"could not answer him one time out of a thousand"* (9:3).

In verses 14–20 of chapter 9, Job describes his sorry legal state even more bluntly. He calls the Lord his *Judge* and confesses freely that, although he could persuade any court on earth that he is innocent, he stands no chance of doing so before God and his holy angels.[1] He needs God's mercy, not his justice. The Lord is too strong to be resisted in battle and too just to be resisted in his courtroom. He rules both by *might* and by *right*.

In verses 21–31, the very thought of standing in God's courtroom begins to drag Job down into despair. He is certain that he is blameless in comparison to his sinful neighbours, but he is equally certain that he already stands condemned in comparison to God. He would only need to open his mouth in the courtroom of heaven for the Judge and jury to recognize that he might be the best of men, but he is still a man at best.[2] Job therefore laments that whether a person is good or bad on earth makes little difference. We are all guilty before God. We don't need a self-help plan. We need a Saviour.[3]

Job looks around for solutions and he quickly pulls up short. Bleach and laundry soap can wash the dirt from his clothes, but there isn't enough detergent in the world to wash the dirt from his soul.[4] Heaven's courtroom will instantly declare him guilty and throw him down into the slimy pit of hell.[5] Job's suffering has brought him a long way from declaring in chapter 3 that

---

[1] Job also uses the word *tsādaq* to describe his innocence in 9:15 and 20.

[2] Job uses the Hebrew word *tām* to describe himself as *blameless* in 9:20–22. This is the same word used in 1:1, 1:8 and 2:3, but it is *not* the word used in this chapter for legal innocence. This is important. Job is not flitting between two views of himself. He is contrasting his status on earth with his status in heaven.

[3] The Hebrew word for *innocent* in 9:23 and 28 is *nāqī*, rather than *tsādaq*, but it means something similar.

[4] Job lived a very long time ago, so he talks literally about doing his laundry with *snow water* and *lye*. His views on spiritual self-help are echoed by Isaiah 1:16–18, Jeremiah 2:22 and Malachi 3:2. See Romans 10:3.

[5] The Hebrew word *shahath* in 9:31 means a *pit* or *ditch* or *grave*. It is used to refer to *hell* in Psalms 16:10, 49:9, 55:23 and 103:4, in Jonah 2:6, and in Job 33:18, 22, 24, 28 and 30.

there is probably no life beyond the grave, to grasping now that there is heaven and hell. The only problem is that he knows he is on the wrong side.

In verses 32–35, Job therefore cries out for the Lord to provide him with the kind of defence lawyer that a guilty man like him requires. He does not know a technical term for what he needs from God (*yēsh-bēynēynū* simply means a *go-between*). All that he knows is that he needs some kind of advocate to stand beside him in the heavenly courtroom and to do whatever it takes to clear his name. He knows that he needs somebody to remove the rod of God's judgment from him and to grant him peace with God, instead of the terror and the fear that he feels right now.

Pregnant pause. Job looks up to heaven. Will the Lord answer his prayer? Will God provide him with a Defence Lawyer, a Mediator, a Saviour, in the courtroom of heaven? Job waits in silence and then sadly concludes: *"but as it now stands with me, I cannot"* (verse 35).

This sad conclusion is what tips Job back into despair in chapter 10, but the Lord has indeed heard his prayer. He sometimes simply chooses to leave a gap between convicting us of our sin and convincing us that we have been forgiven. We will worship him for saving us throughout all eternity, so he often takes his time to write the life story that will fuel our eternal song.[6] So as we finish this ninth chapter, let's take a moment to reflect on the Gospel that God has preached to us so far through Job's sufferings.

Jesus is the true and better Job, the truly Righteous One, who became a man and who lived the only human life that has ever been declared blameless and upright, not just on earth, but in the courtroom of heaven.[7] Jesus is the one who truly feared God and shunned evil. God could ask Satan, *"Have you considered*

[6] Later, Job receives the reassurance that he craves in 16:19–21 and 19:25–27.
[7] Can we detect a prophecy about his incarnation here when Job talks about the Lord walking on water? Compare 9:8 with Matthew 14:25–33 and John 6:19–21.

my servant Job?", but he could declare to the whole world, *"This is my Son, whom I love; with him I am well pleased."*[8]

Jesus was led by God's Spirit into the desert in order to be tested at the hands of the same Devil whose hands attacked Job. Jesus was hated without reason yet maintained his integrity in the face of it all.[9] Jesus had three friends with him during his agony in the Garden of Gethsemane, and those three friends let him down like the three friends of Job. Why do bad things happen to good people? That has only ever truly happened once, and Jesus surrendered his body willingly to suffering. He endured the slimy pit of hell for us, then rose back to life again on the third day.[10]

Jesus would be vindicated by the Lord at the end of all his sufferings, before ascending back home to heaven. He would stand in heaven's courtroom and declare once and for all that there is now a Mediator, a Go-Between, an Intercessor for the world.[11]

What a promise. What a Saviour. What a breathtaking courtroom drama. Hallelujah.

---

[8] Job 1:8. Matthew 3:17, Mark 1:11, Luke 3:22 and 2 Peter 1:17.

[9] The Hebrew word *hinnām* in Job 2:3 is also used in Psalms 35:19, 69:4 and 109:3. See John 15:25.

[10] Compare Job 2:4 with John 10:17–18, Job 2:11 with Mark 14:33, and Job 7:21 with Psalm 22:15.

[11] Isaiah 53:12, Romans 8:34, 1 Timothy 2:5, Hebrews 7:25, 8:6, 9:15 and 12:24, and 1 John 2:1.

Prayer in a Minor Key
(Job 10:1–22)

"Does it please you to oppress me, to spurn the work of your hands?"

(Job 10:3)

"The God of the Old Testament is arguably the most unpleasant character in all fiction... a vindictive, bloodthirsty ethnic cleanser, a misogynistic, homophobic, racist, infanticidal, genocidal, filicidal, pestilential, megalomaniacal, sadomasochistic, capriciously malevolent bully."[1] I remember cringing the first time that I read those words from Richard Dawkins in his book, *The God Delusion*. Like Eliphaz or Bildad, I half expected a thunderbolt from heaven to smite both him and his publisher. I feel the same way about Job when I read the prayer he prayed in Job 10. In his anguish, he makes no effort to hide his bitterness.[2]

Job's suffering has brought him a long way with God. As we saw in the ninth chapter, it has granted him insights into the Gospel that the Hebrew patriarchs never saw. But it doesn't feel that way to him. He feels as if he's going nowhere. Isn't that how we normally feel in the midst of suffering? We don't appreciate being told that *"God works in mysterious ways His wonders to perform."*[3] We don't respond well to encouragements that sound like the Christian equivalent of "every cloud has a silver

---

[1] Richard Dawkins in *The God Delusion* (2006).

[2] Job responded to Eliphaz's speech with one chapter replying to his friend, then one of prayer. He responds in the same way to Bildad's speech. His complaint in Job 10 is therefore a prayer to God.

[3] This well-known phrase doesn't come from the Bible. It is a paraphrase of the first two lines of the William Cowper hymn, *God Moves in a Mysterious Way* (1774).

lining". And yet, Job is genuinely getting to know God through his suffering, even if he doesn't feel it. That's one of the things that the writer wants us to see here as we eavesdrop on Job's prayer. The Bible insists that times of suffering can be major breakthrough moments for our soul.

> *We know that in all things God works for the good of those who love him, who have been called according to his purpose.* (Romans 8:28)

> *Therefore we do not lose heart. Though outwardly we are wasting away, yet inwardly we are being renewed day by day. For our light and momentary troubles are achieving for us an eternal glory that far outweighs them all. So we fix our eyes not on what is seen, but on what is unseen, since what is seen is temporary, but what is unseen is eternal.* (2 Corinthians 4:16–18)

Job is too distressed to believe that this is true. Concluding that the Lord must have turned down his request for a spiritual go-between, he launches into a tirade against the Lord in verses 1–7 for treating him unfairly – a tirade that wouldn't look out of place in a book by Richard Dawkins. *"Does it please you to oppress me ... while you smile on the plans of the wicked?"* he fumes. Nobody is innocent in your heavenly courtroom, are they? Then why am I suffering on my own? Haven't you heard what my three friends are saying about you? Aren't there some Sabean and Chaldean raiders who ought to be suffering with me too? Job essentially says to God: *I can't stand another day of living. Don't just tell me that I'm guilty. Spell out the charges so that I can see what kind of Judge you are!*[4]

Job is making far more progress than he knows, but the

---

[4] The word *rīb* in 10:2, means *to press charges*, and the word *'ēd* in 10:17, means *witness* – both words from the Hebrew legal courtroom. They continue the theme of Job 9. In chapter 10, Job isn't backtracking on his confession of sin. He is just insisting that, heaven's courtroom aside, he is blameless on earth in comparison to his peers.

fact that he can't see it serves an important purpose in the drama. The writer of the book of Job is trying to teach us how to pray. I feel shocked by the way Job speaks to God in this chapter, but I really shouldn't. If we want a real friendship with God then we have to get real with God. The worship leader Tim Hughes reminds us that:

> There has to be a place for expressing pain in our churches. We need a bigger picture of what worship is. Questioning God doesn't mean we are disobeying Him. Expressing doubt doesn't mean we are lacking faith... Expressing anger and pain to God is a beautiful and intimate act... In our everyday lives, the people that we are most likely to share our deepest fears and hurts with are those we love and trust the most. True intimacy can be experienced when we choose to share honestly and vulnerably.[5]

In verses 8–12, Job reminds the Lord that he is one of the creatures that the Lord has made.[6] This sounds a bit more like the sort of prayer we expect to see modelled for us in the Bible but then, in verses 13–17, Job accuses God of only doing so in order to be able to stalk his creature like a cantankerous old schoolmaster, waiting for him to put a foot out of line so that he can take delight in punishing him.[7] Job accuses the Lord of preying on him like a ravening lion and of pummelling him like a general commanding a vicious invasion army. Job's prayer is honest and emotional. It is as raw as his peeling skin. It is meant to teach us how to express our true feelings to God in prayer.

---

[5] Tim Hughes in *Holding Nothing Back: Embracing the Mystery of God* (2007).

[6] Job likens the Lord knitting his body together in his mother's womb to an ancient dairyman curdling cheese in a clay pot. This is a vivid way of declaring that the Lord was as active in creating him as he was in creating Adam. It is also a declaration that a foetus has life that belongs to God, long before it is born.

[7] The Hebrew word for *unpunished* in 10:14 is linked to the word *nāqī*, which meant *innocent* in 9:23 and 28. The Hebrew word for *innocent* in 10:15 is *tsādaq*, which was used in 9:2, 15 and 20.

The Christian psychologist Dan Allender argues that learning to do so is more vital than we know.

> *Christians seldom sing in the minor key. We fear the sombre; we seem to hold sorrow in low esteem. We seem predisposed to fear lament as a quick slide into doubt and despair; failing to see that doubt and despair are the dark soil that is necessary to grow confidence and joy... To sing a lament against God in worship reveals far, far greater trust than to sing a jingle about how happy we are and how much we trust him... Lament cuts through insincerity, strips pretence, and reveals the raw nerve of trust that angrily approaches the throne of grace and then kneels in awed, robust wonder.*[8]

In verses 18–22, Job certainly knows how to pray in a minor key. He echoes his previous lament, in chapter 3, when he tells the Lord that he wishes he had never been born.[9] He slips back into the language of his lament in chapter 7 when he repeats his inversion of Aaron's high priestly prayer, asking the Lord to turn his face away from him to bless him with a brief moment of joy![10] He even expresses his doubt that what he said in chapter 9 about the afterlife is true. He describes life beyond the grave as a land of deep gloom and utter darkness and disorder. Job is not afraid to pray in a minor key.

Dan Allender continues by pointing out the unintended consequences of our own failure to do so.

> *How much of the current counselling frenzy is due to an absence of opportunity to confess our hurt, anger and*

---

[8] Dr Dan Allender in an article entitled *The Hidden Hope in Lament*, in the *Mars Hill Review* (vol 1, 1994).

[9] Don't be surprised that Job echoes 3:11–16 here. Grief is like that. It takes three steps forward, two steps back.

[10] Job probably lived two or three centuries before Aaron, so the ironic link between 10:20 and Numbers 6:22–26 is for our benefit, not for his. The Lord really wants to teach us to pray in a minor key ourselves.

confusion to God in the presence of others of like mind? In many ways, one role of counselling is to legitimise pain and struggle and focus the questions of the heart towards God. How much better it would be if in concert with others we passionately cried out to God with the energy that is often expressed only in the privacy of the counselling office. [11]

So let's get real with God in our prayers. Let's not be afraid to tell him precisely how we feel. Let's believe that God wants to hear the overflow of our soul, even on our darkest days. He delights in our honest prayers, even when we offer them in a minor key.

---

[11] Dan Allender, as above.

Unreasonable
(Job 11:1–20)

Then Zophar the Naamathite replied...

(Job 11:1)

We can tell that Zophar is the youngest of Job's three friends from the fact that he speaks last.[1] He also prides himself on being the most progressive. Whereas Eliphaz spoke from "experience" and Bildad spoke for "tradition", Zophar claims to be the voice of "logical reasoning". His first speech betrays, however, that he is in fact even more unreasonable than his friends.

In verses 1–6, we discover that Zophar is the rudest of the three friends. He accuses Job of being a *"talker"* who has spouted too much *"idle talk"* already.[2] He wishes that God would speak up and rebuke Job to his face – but then he is more than happy to do the talking for him![3] It quickly starts to dawn on us that, although Zophar claims to speak on behalf of reason, it is a ruse. He uses logic to tear down other people's opinions so that he can replace them with some very unreasonable assertions of his own.[4]

---

[1] Elihu, who is even younger than Zophar, has to wait even longer for the same reason (32:4).

[2] In 11:2, Zophar literally calls Job a *"a man of lips"*. The word he uses in 11:3 can be translated *"babbling"*.

[3] The Lord never rebukes Job – but he does rebuke Zophar in 42:7–9! Let's be confident that if we keep on clinging to God's Word in the face of flawed secular logic, then the Lord will vindicate us in the end.

[4] Zophar clearly sees his own words as a response and correction to those spoken by Job. The Hebrew word that Zophar uses in 11:2 for *vindicated* is *tsā daq*, just like 9:2, 9:15, 9:20 and 10:15.

In verses 7–9, Zophar extols the wisdom of God.[5] He rightly points out that the Lord can out-think every one of us. His ways are higher than the clouds above and deeper than the deepest ocean floor.[6] But note his duplicitous application. He uses genuine truth about God to make Job doubt his understanding of God's Word and the conscience God has given him, while making bold and unsubstantiated assertions of his own.[7] He accuses Job of being so steeped in evil that *"God has even forgotten some of your sin."*[8]

In verses 10–12, Zophar says that Job is right to fear to stand in the courtroom of heaven. The Lord can spot a liar and a sinner like him a mile away. Zophar then accuses Job of being as stupid as a donkey, unable to understand the ways of the Lord. This would be rude enough if Zophar were including himself in that comparison, but he doesn't say it out of humility. He does it in order to present himself as the only one who truly understands!

In verses 13–20, Zophar challenges Job to repent. It seems only reasonable to Zophar that Job's suffering is due to his stubborn refusal to come clean with God about his sin. Zophar is staggeringly insensitive towards the death of Job's ten children when he tells his friend to cheer up because, a quick prayer of repentance later, *"You will surely forget your trouble, recalling it only as waters gone by."* Zophar approaches the problem of suffering differently from Eliphaz and Bildad, but he arrives at

---

[5] The Hebrew word that Zophar uses in 11:6 for the *secrets* of God's wisdom is linked to the word for a *virgin* daughter, a young girl *hidden away* from the world. The inference is that the Lord protects his secret wisdom from impure eyes and only brings it out for the one who can be trusted to guard it faithfully.

[6] Zophar uses the Hebrew word *she'ôl* in 11:8, which strictly speaking refers to the depths of the *grave* or the depths of *hell*, rather than the depths of the ocean.

[7] The Hebrew word *leqah* in 11:4 means more than simply *beliefs*. It means *learning*, and in some cases means biblical *doctrine* or *instruction* (Deuteronomy 32:2, Proverbs 1:5 and 4:2, and Isaiah 29:24).

[8] Zophar's point here in verse 6 seems to be that God isn't unfair to cause Job to suffer – Job is actually getting less than he deserves! Note how Zophar uses logic to deny the validity of our asking questions about suffering.

the same old hackneyed answer. He uses logical reasoning in the same way that his friends used experience and tradition – to avoid having to think too hard about the problem – reasoning that, if Job is suffering, then it must mean Job is sinning. Zophar's speech is shorter than the other two, but he leaves nobody wishing that he had given us a little more.

Readers often struggle to know what to do with the speeches made by Job's three friends. Are we to accept all that they say as authoritative Scripture, or are we to go to the other extreme and dismiss everything that they say? The writer actually wants us to do a bit of both. We mustn't swallow their arguments hook, line and sinker (after all, God rebukes them for much of what they say in 42:7–9!), but nor must we forget that these Scriptures are included in Paul's assertion in 2 Timothy 3:16 that *"All Scripture is God-breathed and is useful for teaching, rebuking, correcting and training in righteousness."* These chapters take up far too much space in the Bible for us simply to skim read them. Instead, we need to read them at each of Paul's levels – for teaching, rebuking, correcting and training.

We need to study these speeches carefully for *teaching*. Some of what they say is entirely true. Job notes what Eliphaz tells him in 5:9 and repeats it in 9:10. The apostle Paul notes what Eliphaz says in 5:13 and quotes it back to us in 1 Corinthians 3:19. Even this speech from Zophar, which definitely feels like the weakest of the three, contains some stunning insight into the character of God and into the Gospel. He is quite right to remind us that the intellectual gap between a human and a donkey (both creatures) is far smaller than the intellectual gap between a human and God (a creature and its Creator). That ought to teach us some humility. By contrasting the heavens above with *she'ōl* below in verse 8, he also gives us some basic teaching on the reality of heaven and hell.[9]

We also need to study these speeches carefully for *rebuking*.

---

[9] Also, Zophar's reference to *a dying gasp* in 11:20 means literally a *"breathing out of the soul"* – not so much a fight to breathe in one final lungful of oxygen, but a final breathing out of the spirit into the life to come.

Much of what Job's friends say is true in general (God blesses those who obey him and curses those who don't) but not true in every case (since God has a better view of what blessing means than we do). So these speeches rebuke us whenever we twist Scripture to offer people easy answers, instead of grieving with them, reflecting with them and offering to pray for them.[10]

We also need to study these speeches carefully for *correcting* and *training*. The Lord has included them in the Bible to make us wise in our own discussions about faith with our friends. He wants us to spot that Zophar's claim to speak for reason is in fact an insidious attempt to avoid logical reasoning at all. He doesn't approach faith with a blank sheet of paper and a calculator. He rubbishes Job's trust in God's Word to make room for unreasonable speculations of his own.[11] Zophar's speech therefore exposes the lie that secularism thinks logically while Christianity takes a blind leap of faith into the dark. The real reason why our culture doubts Christianity is that it holds an unprovable belief in something else. Secularism demands a greater leap of faith than trust in God.

So allow these speeches to teach you not to be wowed too easily by other people's bold assertions. Let them teach you to doubt other people's doubts, to be cynical about their cynicism, and to spot the intellectual fig leaves that they often hide behind to avoid listening and submitting to the answers that God gives them in his Word.

---

[10] Romans 12:15. In all of their speeches *about* God, Job's friends never once offer to pray with him *to* God.

[11] Job 1–2 tells us that Job *isn't* suffering due to his sin, but because his virtue has put him on Satan's radar!

Better Friend
(Job 12:1–13:19)

"Though he slay me, yet will I hope in him..."

(Job 13:15)

In 1871, Horatio Spafford wrote in a letter to one of his friends that he felt as if he were *"sitting on top of the world"*. Everything was going right for him. He had a loving wife, four beautiful daughters, a successful law firm and a profitable business portfolio. How quickly things can change. In a matter of a few hours in October of that year, the Great Chicago Fire destroyed his law firm and most of his portfolio. Financially ruined, he sent his wife and daughters across the Atlantic to stay with family in Europe while he set about rebuilding their family fortune. Seven days later, he received a telegram from his wife informing him that their ship had sunk and that their four daughters had been drowned. Her two-word telegram read simply: *"Saved – alone."*

Horatio Spafford booked a cabin on the next ship across the Atlantic to comfort his grieving wife in Britain. As it passed the spot where the ship's captain told him the disaster had occurred, instead of weeping inconsolably for his four daughters, he picked up his pen and notebook and wrote what has since become a very famous hymn:

When peace, like a river, attendeth my way.
When sorrows, like sea-billows roll;
Whatever my lot, Thou hast taught me to say,
It is well, it is well with my soul.

Though Satan should buffet, though trials should come,
Let this blest assurance control;
That Christ hath regarded my helpless estate
And hath shed His own blood for my soul.[1]

Zophar's speech to Job was the shortest of the speeches so far. Job's reply to Zophar is the longest. This is partly because he addresses all three friends in his response, and partly because he is regaining some of the same confidence that stirred Horatio Spafford.

In 12:1–6, Job tells his friends exactly what he thinks of them. He is brimming with sarcasm as he effectively says to them: Wow! You are so wise that when you die I'm really worried that there won't be anyone as wise as you left in the world to help me! He lays into them as lousy friends who have told him nothing that he didn't already know before. They have accused him of sin, though he is righteous and blameless.[2] They have laughed at his pain instead of comforting him. But he isn't about to buckle under the pain. He has found a better Friend than them to help him. *"I called on God and he answered"* (verse 4).

In 12:7–12, Job calls the fish and birds and animals to bear witness that the one he calls his Friend is the Sovereign Ruler of the universe. It doesn't matter that God's judgment has not yet fallen on the wicked in verses 5–6. For the first and only time in all these speeches, Job refers to him as *Yahweh*. He recognizes that he is the Lord, the Eternal One, the great I AM. That's all Job needs to know to be able to say that it is well with his soul.

In 12:13–25, Job spells out what this means for him in the midst of his suffering. It means that he can see past their false friendship and their fake formulae to keep believing that God's sovereign hand is at work behind the terrible calamities that

---

[1] *It is Well with My Soul* (1873) became a favourite hymn at D.L. Moody's Gospel crusades.

[2] The Hebrew word *tsaddîq* in 12:4 means *righteous* or *justified*. The word *tāmîm* means *blameless* or *perfect*.

have befallen him.[3] It stops him from embracing easy excuses that sidestep the question: *Why does God allow suffering?* He knows he isn't suffering because God lacks the strength to protect him (12:14–16) or because God lacks the wisdom to know how to protect him (12:16–25). *"To God belong wisdom and power; counsel and understanding are his."*[4] Job doesn't know what God is doing in the darkness, but he takes solace in the fact that he knows the God who is doing it. Job's three friends have failed him, but he has found a better Friend.

In 13:1–12, Job makes up his mind that he will seek an answer to his questions about suffering from God and God alone. He tells his friends that they are of no comfort to him. Their proverbs are like burnt wood that the wind quickly blows away as ash, and their formulae are as fragile as the broken piece of clay pottery that he is using to scratch the festering sores on his skin. Why don't they shut their mouths and pretend to have wisdom instead of opening their mouths and removing all doubt that they haven't?[5] They purport to speak for God, but anyone can see that they are each pursuing their own private agenda. Job has had enough of their lies. *"I desire to speak to the Almighty and to argue my case with God."*

In 13:13–19, Job feels a sudden surge of faith to do whatever it takes to gain proper answers to his questions about suffering. He will press God for those answers, regardless of the dangers of confronting the Almighty.[6] This leads Job to utter one of his greatest confessions of faith in all his speeches: *"Though he slay me, yet will I hope in him; I will surely defend my ways to his*

---

[3] Job tells his friends that he knows how to test words with his ears, not just how to test wine with his palate (12:11). He is old enough to see through their false formulae (12:12). He knows what lousy friends they are.

[4] God judges churches by preventing their leaders from making good decisions (12:17, 20 and 24) and from preaching effective sermons (12:20). The Hebrew word *lēb* in 12:24 can mean *courage* as well as *reason*.

[5] This is essentially what Job says to his three friends in 13:5. It is one of his wittiest ripostes.

[6] Compare 13:15 with Esther 4:16 and Daniel 3:16–18. Job's promise to keep hoping in God even after death signifies recovery from his doubts in 10:18–22. He is freshly convinced that there is life beyond the grave.

face."[7] Gone is the despairing lament of chapter 10. Back is the glorious courtroom language of chapter 9.[8] Job has determined to risk whatever is left of his life to ensure that the Lord declares him righteous in that courtroom before he dies. *"Indeed, this will turn out for my deliverance,"* he declares, *"for no godless person would dare come before him!"* Job sees his willingness to gamble everything on God as a massive sign that, even in the midst of his agony and suffering, it remains well with his soul.

It is easy for us to read the book of Job and to conclude that the Lord treated him rather harshly. It is easy to read about his sufferings and to wonder why God didn't deliver him as soon as he responded with faith at the end of chapter 2. But Job himself is starting to suspect why. The Lord is becoming a better Friend to him in the darkness than he ever used to be in the light. As a result, Job assures us, it is well with his soul.

J.I. Packer says:

> *God in his wisdom means to make something of us which we have not attained yet, and is dealing with us accordingly... We may be frankly bewildered at things that happen to us, but God knows exactly what he is doing, and what he is after, in his handling of our affairs. Always, and in everything, he is wise; we shall see that hereafter, even where we never saw it here. Job in heaven knows the full reason why he was afflicted, though he never knew it in his life.*[9]

---

[7] Although the Hebrew text here can also be translated, *"He will surely slay me, I have no hope"*, that would make no sense within the thrust of what Job is saying. The majority translation is better.

[8] The courtroom language here includes the words *rîb* meaning *to plead a case* (13:8 and 19), *mishpāt* meaning *judgment* or *justice* or *case* (13:18), and *tsādaq* meaning *to vindicate* or *to justify* or *to declare righteous* (13:18).

[9] J.I. Packer in his book, *Knowing God* (1973).

Glimpses of Glory
(Job 13:20–14:22)

"If someone dies, will they live again? ... I will wait for my renewal to come."

(Job 14:14)

My nephew loves doing jigsaws. He will work on one for days and days. Each time I come back into the room, he has made a bit more progress and it starts becoming clearer what the completed picture will eventually be. When I listen to Job's prayer in these verses, it feels a lot like watching my nephew do one of his jigsaws. Through the agony and the tears, Job is beginning to piece together some glimpses of glory.

In this first cycle of speeches, Job responds to each of his three friends, first by speaking back to them, then by speaking to the Lord in prayer.[1] We saw in the twelfth chapter that his response to Zophar was full of confidence that the Lord would prove to be a better Friend than any of them, resolving to get some answers from that Friend, come what may. These verses tell us what he discovered when he then turned to prayer.

Job has already found the edges of his jigsaw. He has declared that God is real. He has referred to him as *Yahweh*. He has confessed him to be the all-powerful and all-wise Ruler of the universe, who knows what he is doing even in the midst of our suffering. He has confessed that the Lord is far too holy for even a man who is blameless on earth to look him in the eyes in his heavenly courtroom. Job has cried out for a Go-Between to

---

[1] Job's three friends are happy to talk endlessly, but they never once pray. Job talk backs to them (6:1–30, 9:1–35 and 12:1–13:19), but his bigger instinct is to pray (7:1–21, 10:1–22 and 13:20–14:22).

mediate between himself and God. He has even caught a glimpse of that Go-Between's death and resurrection, crying out as Jesus would effectively cry out in the Garden of Gethsemane, *"Though he slay me, yet will I hope in him."*[2] Job has already pieced together some great glimpses of glory. Now, in his third prayer, he pieces together a few more.

In 13:20–28, Job begins his prayer with fresh insight into his own sinfulness. He still believes that he is blameless in comparison to the people who live around him. This isn't just his own self-assessment, but what we have been told once by the writer and twice by the Lord himself.[3] Job's new insight is that godly living *now* cannot atone for ungodly living *back then*. He confesses that the Lord can see his spiritual footprints stretching back to all his sins as a young man. God still has a written record of them, so Job uses three different Hebrew words in verse 23 to come clean about his trail of sin.[4]

In 14:1–6, Job gains fresh insight into his need for a Saviour. He confesses that his life is brief and fragile.[5] In only a moment he will find himself standing in God's heavenly courtroom to receive his spiritual pay cheque from the Lord, and he knows he will not like what he finds inside that envelope.[6] Job needs a Saviour and he needs one fast. But who can save him? Every man and woman on earth is in the same boat as he is, a boat that is sinking fast. Suddenly, Job receives a glimpse of glory. He foresees the incarnation of Jesus, the Son of God, born to a virgin, when he

---

[2] Job was probably unaware of much of what he prophesied, but compare 13:15 with Psalm 16:7–11, Luke 22:41–44 and Hebrews 5:7.

[3] Job 1:1, 1:8 and 2:3. Job isn't flip-flopping here, influenced by the foolish thinking of his friends. He is recognizing a distinction between being blameless on earth and being declared righteous in heaven.

[4] The Hebrew word *'āvōn* means iniquity, *hattā'āh* means sin (twice), and *pesha'* means transgression.

[5] Job's insight in 14:5 is later echoed in Psalm 139:16, Matthew 6:27, Luke 12:25 and Acts 17:26.

[6] Job's talk of payday for a *hired labourer* is echoed in 34:11, Psalm 62:12, Proverbs 24:12, Jeremiah 32:19, Matthew 16:27, Romans 2:6 and 6:23, 2 Corinthians 5:10 and Revelation 22:12.

cries out that God alone can save him: *"Mortals, born of woman...*
Who can bring what is pure from the impure?" (verses 1 and 4).[7]

In 14:7–12, Job begins to gain fresh insight into the promise
of resurrection from the dead. At first glance, there doesn't seem
to be much hope in these verses. Job complains that, while the
stump of a tree that has been chopped down can put out fresh
shoots and grow again, a dead person has no stump from which
to do the same. They are chopped down, laid in the grave and
heard from no more. But don't miss the glimpse of hope at the
end of these six verses, when Job declares that they will only
remain in the grave *"till the heavens are no more"*. We might have
missed this hint of hope were Job not more explicit in verse 14,
crying out, *"If someone dies, will they live again? ... I will wait for
my renewal to come!"* I love that Hebrew word *hālaph*. It is used
elsewhere to describe Jacob changing his clothes to express his
fresh commitment to follow God, to describe Jesus changing
the earth when he comes back at the end of time to recreate it
as it was always meant to be, and to describe God changing our
weakness into strength as we wait on him.[8] Job uses it here to
describe Jesus changing our dead bodies into their resurrected
glory when he finally comes back in answer to Job's prayer.

In 14:13–17, Job gains fresh insight into what will happen on
that Judgment Day. He declares that he will not remain in *she'ōl*,
the home of the dead, forever. The Lord will merely hide Job away
there until he has found a way to divert his righteous anger from
him. On the Day of Judgment, when the Lord will command the
dead to rise up from the grave, he will take his written record of
Job's filthy footprints and he will seal it up in a parcel.[9] He will
hide it and plaster over it so that nobody can read the record of

---

[7] The Hebrew word for *mortals* in 14:1 is the name *Adam*. See 1 Corinthians
15:45 and Romans 5:12–21. We do not sin and become sinners; we are sinners
and so we sin! Yet Jesus was born without our Original Sin.

[8] Genesis 35:2, Psalm 102:26 and Isaiah 40:31. The Hebrew word *hālaph* is
also used to describe the tree stump *sprouting* in 14:7.

[9] Job uses the exact same words in 14:16–17 that he used in 13:23 – *hattā'āh*
meaning *sin*, *pesha'* meaning *transgression*, and *āvōn* meaning *iniquity*.

his sin.[10] Then he will finally declare Job righteous in his heavenly courtroom.

In 14:18–22, Job shows us that he still needs further insight. He hasn't completed the jigsaw, because he still had no idea how God is able to do this. Judges who deliberately hide evidence don't get praised – they get fired! The Lord must therefore know a way *both* of being seen to be just *and* of being merciful to sinners.[11] Job can't yet imagine how, so he slides back into pain and confusion at the end of his prayer. He has seen glimpses of glory, but the whole jigsaw picture of the Gospel is not yet fully formed before him.

Job has seen enough, however, to show us what to do whenever we go through periods of intense suffering ourselves. He looked forward to Jesus; we are to look back to Jesus. He is always our greatest source of hope and comfort in our pain. Feelings yo-yo up and down, but in Jesus we find God's stable, definitive answer in the midst of our suffering. *"I am the resurrection and the life. The one who believes in me will live, even though they die."*[12]

It's just like the apostle Paul says at the end of Romans 8, having just assured us that we can trust God to use absolutely everything that happens to us for our good.

> *If God is for us, who can be against us? He who did not spare his own Son, but gave him up for us all – how will he not also, along with him, graciously give us all things? ... Christ Jesus who died – more than that, who was raised to life – is at the right hand of God and is also interceding for us.* (Romans 8:31–34)

Job only saw glimpses of glory, but we can see the full picture. Praise the Lord.

---

[10] The Hebrew word *tāphal* in 14:17 means *to smear* or *to glue* or *to plaster over*. God hides our sin in Jesus, covering over its ugly brickwork with the beautiful rendering of his Son.

[11] God's desire to vindicate his justice in the eyes of his heavenly courtroom is not just a big theme of Job. It is Paul's big theme in Romans 3:26. Through the death of Jesus, God saves us by *right*, not just by *might*.

[12] John 11:25 is Jesus' resounding answer to Job's question in 14:14.

Here We Go Again
(Job 15:1–35)

Then Eliphaz the Temanite replied…

(Job 15:1)

Here we go again. The same old answers. Just when we thought that one set of speeches might have settled the matter, the same cycle suddenly starts all over again. It won't be the last time, either. That was just the first of three long cycles of speeches.

Introduction:	Job's lament (3)
The first cycle of speeches:	Eliphaz (4–5) Job's reply to Eliphaz (6–7) Bildad (8) Job's reply to Bildad (9–10) Zophar (11) Job's reply to Zophar (12–14)
The second cycle of speeches:	Eliphaz (15) Job's reply to Eliphaz (16–17) Bildad (18) Job's reply to Bildad (19) Zophar (20) Job's reply to Zophar (21)
The third cycle of speeches:	Eliphaz (22) Job's reply to Eliphaz (23–24) Bildad (25) Job's reply to Bildad (26–27)

In verses 1–13, it becomes clear that we're going to get more of the same old answers from Job's three friends. Eliphaz still uses his old age to claim he is the voice of experience. He still claims to speak for *"the grey-haired and the aged... men even older than your father."*[1] His second speech is a re-run of his first – except that this time he is considerably ruder! He accuses Job literally of spouting *"windy knowledge"* from a belly full of the *"hot east wind"*. He dismisses all that Job has said so far as *"useless words... speeches that have no value."* Then he restates his own hackneyed formula:

> People who do evil + A loving, powerful God = People who are cursed
> People who do good + A loving, powerful God = People who are blessed

Eliphaz is convinced that Job has proved his formula to be true. Job has claimed to be blameless, so his own mouth has condemned him. He has spoken angrily towards God, so his sin is plain to see. Eliphaz is so self-deluded that he truly believes that his words are *"God's consolations"* rather than his own pontifications.[2] He truly believes that they were *"words spoken gently to you."* Sure, he was a bit less rude than Bildad and Zophar the first time around, but he is certainly making up for that now.

We must not judge Eliphaz too harshly here. Simplistic though it is, his cause-and-effect formula seems pretty hardwired into our thinking. The disciples of Jesus instinctively assumed that wealth was proof of godliness and that suffering was proof of sin.[3] So do any Christians today who succumb to a false prosperity gospel. John Piper warns us that:

---

[1] Eliphaz is right. Old age ought to bring wisdom (12:12). But he is wrong to assume it always does (32:6–9).

[2] God's consolations *were* enough for Job. It's just that he couldn't hear them in the words of Eliphaz! Eliphaz speaks about *"God's council"* in 15:8, but he knows precious little about it. Psalm 25:14 and Amos 3:7 use this same Hebrew word *sôd* to say that God does indeed invite us into his council. Job also uses the word in 29:4.

[3] For example, in Matthew 19:23–25 and John 9:1–2.

The prosperity gospel is no gospel because what it does is offer to people what they want as natural people. You don't have to be born again to want to be wealthy, and therefore you don't have to be converted to be saved by the prosperity gospel. When you appeal to people to come to Christ on the basis of what they already want (First Corinthians 2) it makes no sense. "The natural man does not receive the things of the Spirit; they are foolishness to him." Therefore if you offer to people what they do not consider foolishness in the natural man, you are not preaching the Gospel. And the prosperity gospel offers people what they desperately want as long as people get to do things and grow churches. And we export it to Africa and the Philippines, flying in with our jets, milking up their money and going back to our condos, worth $3 million. It is horrific what we export as Americans! I can't believe what we tolerate in the church! So I'm on a crusade to crucify the prosperity gospel. I hate the prosperity gospel because I love the glory of God.[4]

This is one of the reasons why we need three cycles of speeches, rather than just one. The writer takes us through the wringer three times because these foolish formulae are deeply rooted into all of us, and because he is determined to root them out.

In verses 14–35, Eliphaz essentially trots out the same old answer as before. *"Listen to me... let me tell you what I have seen."* Verses 14–16 are entirely a rehash of what he said in 4:17–19.[5] Eliphaz insists that his experience proves that anyone who suffers must be wicked, and that anyone who loses their herds

---

[4] John Piper said this in a sermon at the *Resolved* conference in Palm Springs, California, in June 2008. Cited from: https://www.desiringgod.org/messages/god-is-the-gospel--2.

[5] Eliphaz is not completely wrong. What he says in 4:18 and 15:15 is echoed by 2 Peter 2:4 and Jude 6. He is also correct that Job's sufferings have something to do with *"God's council"* (15:8). His formula fools us because it contains elements of truth. Compare 15:35 with Isaiah 59:4, Galatians 6:7–9 and James 1:14–15.

to marauding raiders must have shaken their fist at the Lord.[6] Anyone whose children die in a windstorm, like a vine untimely stripped of its unripe grapes, ought to view the windstorm as *"the breath of God's mouth"* (verse 30).[7] These insensitive words add nothing to what Eliphaz has already said before. Good things happen to good people and bad things happen to bad people.

Eliphaz misses the mark this second time around because his formula still fails to engage with our real question about suffering. It merely restates the problem. The fact is: the world is full of nice people who don't seem to deserve what they are suffering, and full of sinful people who seem to be living in ease and comfort. And yet, in spite of this, the rabbis who created the Jewish Talmud still fell for the neatness of this tidy formula. They knew that the book of Job says three times in its first two chapters that Job was blameless, but they claim in the Talmud that Job was one of the wise men of the East who served at the court of Pharaoh, and who failed to stop him from murdering all of the Hebrew baby boys. *That's* the reason why he suffered. It's total poppycock but, that's the whole point. The prosperity gospel always is.[8]

So don't be surprised at this point in the book of Job to be presented with a second cycle of speeches. The writer knows how much the fake formulae of these three false friends are hardwired into our own thinking. He wants to get rid of them, so here we go again.

---

[6] The reference in 15:27 to the sinner having a *fat face* and *fat waist* is not a warning against overeating. It's a warning that prosperity leads to self-reliance (Deuteronomy 32:15, Psalm 119:70 and Isaiah 6:10).

[7] In the Hebrew text, Eliphaz says *"the breath of **his** mouth"*, but most translators think he means the Lord.

[8] Sotah 11a. Some scholars believe that the rabbis were also provoked by Christian claims that Job prophesies a lot about Jesus. They were therefore happy with the myth of "the blasphemer Job".

What Suffering Achieves
(Job 16:1–17:16)

"Even now my witness is in heaven; my advocate is on high. My intercessor is my friend as my eyes pour out tears to God..."

(Job 16:19–20)

The Christian apologist Michael Ramsden points out something rather surprising about the question: *Why does God allow suffering?* It's a question that people tend to ask a lot less in poorer countries than they do in the relatively comfortable Western world.

> *I have never been asked questions about God and suffering when I am travelling in countries riddled with the realities of it. In fact, when I visit churches in parts of the world where they are faced daily with the horrific realities of suffering, I normally leave inspired. They trust God in everything, even when things are going well. When times are hard, they cling on to Him because they have already learned to trust Him. God hasn't changed, even though the circumstances have. Maybe we struggle with suffering so much in the West because we are so comfortable most of the time that we feel we don't need God. We don't rely on Him on a daily basis, and so we don't really know Him as we should. When suffering comes along, therefore, it is not so much that it takes us*

*away from God, but that it reveals to us that we haven't
really been close to Him in the first place.*[1]

In 16:1–5, it is clear that Job's faith will only survive if he has
truly been close to the Lord. Unlike his first three replies,
where he responded first to his friends and then turned to the
Lord in prayer, these two chapters reveal a man very close to
the end of his tether. Instead of replying in an orderly way, he
flits back and forth between talking to his friends and crying
out in pain to God. These first five verses are some of Job's
rudest. He accuses his friends of being *"miserable comforters"*
(verse 2) and claims that he would be a much better friend to
them if the roles were reversed. He asks in desperation, *"Will
your long-winded speeches never end?"* (verse 3). Job was first
to ask that question, but he wasn't the last. These speeches
are long, but the writer is far from finished. He wants us to
feel some of Job's endless misery in order to teach us what
suffering achieves.

In 16:6–14, Job cries out to God in front of his friends,
sometimes speaking to God directly and sometimes turning to
his friends and expressing how he feels about God. He feels
worn out by the way that God has treated him. He feels that
the Lord has scratched him, bitten him, glowered at him,
abandoned him, shattered him, strangled him and taken out his
arrows to do some target practice on him.[2] He feels as though
God is attacking him like a fully armed warrior running into
action against the enemy.[3] Eliphaz warned in 15:27 that happy
times promote a dangerous self-sufficiency that mitigates
against genuine relationship with God, so Job now retorts in
16:8 that happy times are but a dim and distant memory to

---

[1] Michael Ramsden wrote this on the UK Evangelical Alliance blog on 1st
July 2004. https://www.eauk.org/church/resources/theological-articles/how-
can-i-believe-in-god-when-theres-so-much-suffering.cfm.

[2] Job repeats in 16:12–14 what he claimed earlier in 6:4 and 7:20.

[3] It is hard to read 16:10–11 without thinking of John 19:1–16, or to read 16:13
without thinking of John 19:32–37. Job's complaint hints at how much it will cost
Jesus to become the Advocate he glimpses in 16:19–21.

him. He isn't spiritually fat. He is spiritually gaunt, emaciated and shrivelled up. He is starving to death in a hurry.[4]

I don't know if you have ever felt like Job does in these chapters. Maybe you are feeling that way now. Maybe *Why does God allow suffering?* is more than just an intellectual question. Sometimes we scream it from the very deepest pit of our hearts, which is why we need to believe the Bible when it says that every single stab of pain we suffer, every single tear we shed and every single trial we bear in the path of obedience towards the Lord is totally meaningful.[5] The Lord assures us in 2 Corinthians 4:17 every single one of them is *"achieving for us an eternal glory that far outweighs them all."*

In 16:15–21, Job begins to discover what that means. Had he not spent the good times developing a close walk with God, getting up early to offer sacrifices in 1:5, he would certainly have crumbled under the sheer weight of his calamities now. But because he trained himself during the good times to worship God, it comes naturally to him in the bad times to look up and to seek his answers in God, rather than looking down at his own life and giving up on God. Job instinctively prays to God in the manner of the ancients – fasting, heaping dust on his head and wearing clothes made of sackcloth, despite how painful it must feel on his red-raw skin. He instinctively weeps and prays for God to grant him the missing pieces in his Gospel jigsaw puzzle. As a result, in these verses he suddenly receives one of the biggest glimpses of glory in the entire book of Job.

"Even now my witness is in heaven," Job gasps, with a sudden conviction from the Holy Spirit that the Lord has heard his prayer for a Go-Between to stand by his side in the heavenly courtroom. *"My advocate is on high. My intercessor is my friend as my eyes pour out tears to God; on behalf of a man he pleads with God as one pleads for a friend!"* Don't skim

---

[4] The Hebrew word for Job's skinny body being a *witness* against him in 16:8 is the same word as in 16:19.

[5] This is what Psalm 56:8 means when the writer says literally, *"You have collected all my tears in your bottle."*

over those words too quickly. Note what Job actually says. He declares that he received this life-changing revelation as *his eyes poured out tears to God*. His suffering was not incidental to the revelation. The revelation was the result of his suffering! It is only as a result of the calamities that have befallen him that he finally grasps God's plan to be both just and the one who justifies sinners, saving people by *right* and not just by *might*.

Job's suffering initially propelled him to despair that there would ever be a Go-Between to help him. Then his suffering drove him to confess to God, in some distress, that unless God provided him with such a Go-Between then he would not survive a second in his courtroom. Now his suffering opens a door to faith that God has answered his prayer. He uses the technical language of a Hebrew courtroom as he rejoices that he indeed has a *Witness*, a *Defence Lawyer*, an *Intercessor*, preparing his legal brief in heaven.[6]

None of this makes Job's suffering go away. Job still feels on the brink of death (16:22–17:2). He still longs for God to grant him some token of proof that what he says in his speeches is right and what his friends say is wrong (17:3–5). He still has to endure the sound of people mocking him and he still feels that his life is intensely unfair (17:6–12).[7] But in his suffering he has learned to view these things as light and momentary. Not only will they pass, but his Advocate in heaven has infused every one of them with deep, deep meaning. Even the grave can't steal from him the eternal weight of glory that

---

[6] The Hebrew word 'ēd means *witness* or *evidence*; sāhēd means *witness* or *advocate* or *defence barrister*; and mēlīts means *interpreter* or *ambassador* or *intercessor*. None of these words is the one that Job used in 9:33. All are echoed in Isaiah 53:12, Romans 8:34, 1 Timothy 2:5, Hebrews 7:25, 8:6, 9:15 and 12:24, and 1 John 2:1.

[7] Job feels it is acutely unfair that his hopes and plans for the future have been stolen from him (17:11). He does not yet know that God has far greater plans for his future than any of his own (42:7–17, Ephesians 3:20).

his suffering is producing in and for him at the resurrection from the dead (17:13–16).[8]

Job has come to know the Lord far more deeply amidst his misery.[9] Praise God, that's what our suffering often achieves.

---

[8] Job's argument in 17:13–16 is essentially: God did not create me to decay and be eaten by worms. He made me to know him, so he will not leave my hope in the grave! The Hebrew word he uses for grave in 17:13 and 17:16 is *she'ôl*. His words are echoed by Psalm 16:9–11 and Acts 2:22–32.

[9] Job still hasn't completed his Gospel jigsaw puzzle. He will receive the next big jigsaw piece in 19:25–27.

Slot-Machine God
(Job 18:1–21)

"The lamp of a wicked man is snuffed out..."

(Job 18:5)

Bildad's second speech is one of the emptiest in the book of Job. It is also one of the most tragic. Job has just given him a whole host of jaw-dropping insights into the Gospel, and he doesn't even mention one of them. That's because he claims to speak on behalf of tradition. He is more interested in ancient formulae than in Job's new theology.[1]

Getting real with God in prayer? That's not part of Bildad's tradition. Resurrection from the dead? That's not part of his tradition either. A friend who will stand with us in the courtroom of heaven? Bildad doesn't want a friendship that will enable him to enjoy God. He wants a formula that will help him to get what he wants out of God.

There is very little structure to Bildad's second speech. He begins with anger that Job hasn't just accepted what he said the first time around. He asks impatiently, *"When will you end these speeches?"* – to which the answer surely has to be: *Hey, Bildad, we were going to ask you the same question.*[2] He then launches into a long accusation, which is essentially the same old answer that he trotted out before. If Job's light is being snuffed out, then that must mean Job is a sinner. Job has brought his suffering

---

[1] Bildad doesn't mention God until the very final word of his speech. Like those who follow slot-machine religion today, the religious formula takes centre stage. God himself is an afterthought, at best.

[2] Bildad is unfair in 18:3 to accuse Job of regarding his friends as stupid. But that's often the way with traditionalists. They treat refusal to accept their point of view as a personal rejection.

down on his own head. Bildad repeats his formula in case Job has forgotten it:

> A God who is just + A person who is suffering = Clear proof of sin
> A God who is just + A person who isn't suffering = Clear proof of virtue

Bildad's speech is extremely repetitious. It's about lights and lamps and torches. It's about nets and meshes and traps and nooses and snares. He hopes that by multiplying words he will mask the fact that he actually has very little to say. He just can't see that, by focusing on a formula, he is robbing himself of an opportunity to really know God. He can't see that his formula completely misses why God allows suffering.

Bildad has never really considered what it would mean for our relationship with God if his formula were actually true. It would make a real relationship with God impossible. If a sure-fire way of getting whatever we wanted was to do whatever God asks us to do, then how would he (or for that matter *we*) ever know for certain that we were doing what God asks because we love God, and not because we love whatever we imagine he will be forced to give us if we do? How would anybody ever know whether they prized God for the sake of God or whether they merely liked to use God as the means to an end? In the days when Europeans were much richer than their Chinese counterparts, Western missionaries to China used to talk about the problem of "rice Christians" – locals who converted to Christ for the benefits of friendship with white Westerners, rather than to enjoy friendship with God. If Bildad's formula were true, then there could only ever be "rice Christians". Slot-machine religion can only ever create spiritual consumers.

The early anthropologist Bronisław Malinowski explored this idea in his seminal essay *Magic, Science and Religion*, first published in 1925. He defines magic as a human attempt to find some supernatural mechanism which gains control over spiritual forces and manipulates them to achieve human ends. Religion, on the other hand, he defines as human submission to spiritual forces, renouncing manipulation to rely on supplication alone. Based on Malinowski's definition, slot-machine religion is therefore no religion at all. It is magic, pure and simple. One man offers a plate of food to his god to ensure a blessing. Another man sacrifices a goat. Still another offers a collection of good works – and then gets angry about suffering because he feels that his slot-machine god has reneged on the deal.[3] Isn't this, then, a major reason why the Lord allows us to suffer? He wants to reveal, not just to his heavenly council, but to us, whether we love him for the sake of loving him, or for the sake of what we think that we can get out of him.

I love reading the biographies of Christians who have been blessed with fruitful ministry. One of the things that strikes me most when I read them is that almost all of them started out with a long period of what seemed like failure. It's as if the Lord needs to refine our hearts before we are ready to be entrusted with what he wants to give us.

One of my favourites is the story of how David Wilkerson began the *Teen Challenge* ministry that would see thousands of drug addicts and gang members saved and set free. He writes very honestly about his disastrous first visit to New York City to engage with the gangs. He was arrested by the police and his photo was plastered on the front pages of the national newspapers. He became a laughing stock and almost gave up entirely. Then he concluded:

> *I have been humbled and humiliated. Perhaps it was to teach me a lesson.*[4]

Less than a week later, he felt God speak to him as he prayed:

> *Go back to New York.*

---

[3] Comparing Bildad's formula with such pagan practices is helpful. A slot-machine view of God insults him by shrinking him down to be a puny, tribal god who cuts deals with people to grow his following on earth.

[4] David Wilkerson shares his story in his bestselling book *The Cross and the Switchblade* (1963).

After three days of resisting God, he went back to visit the gangs. Suddenly he found that the doors which had been slammed in his face during his first visit now opened up to him right across the city.

> *"What do you mean, I'm one of you?", I asked. Their logic was simple. The cops didn't like me; the cops didn't like them. We were in the same boat, and I was one of them... Suddenly I caught a glimpse of myself being hauled up that courtroom aisle, and it had a different light on it. I felt the little shiver I always experience in the presence of God's perfect planning.*

So if you are suffering in your attempts to do what God wants, don't be surprised and don't get angry. God wants real friendship far too much to pander to our magic formula. He allows us to suffer in order to test whether we want him for his own sake, or for the sake of something else. Whatever that something else is, is our real deity.

Thank God that Bildad's formula isn't true. The Lord refuses to be a slot-machine god. He offers us real friendship, not an impersonal religious formula.

Price Tag (Job 19:1–29)

*"I know that my redeemer lives, and that in the end
he will stand on the earth."*

(Job 19:25)

I would really love to be able to play the guitar like Eric Clapton
or Brian May. Except I wouldn't. If I really wanted it, then I would
spend a lot more time practising my guitar. I would really love
to be able to run the London Marathon in less than three hours.
Except I wouldn't. I think you get the idea. How much we love
something isn't proved by how much we say we want it, but by
how much we are willing to pay the price tag for it.

Job's reply to Bildad's second speech betrays his doubt
about how much God loves him. That's what happens to us when
we experience persistent suffering. It's hard to keep believing
in the glimpses of glory that the Lord has given us when there
are few signs to confirm his future promises in the here-and-
now. We can tell how upset Job is from the fact that this is the
first of his speeches so far in which he doesn't pray. In the first
cycle of speeches, Job responded first to each of his friends and
then to the Lord in prayer. In his last response to Eliphaz, he
flip-flopped in and out of prayer. In this response to Bildad he
doesn't pray at all. Job is a man on the edge here.

In verses 1–6, Job feels as though God may not love him
at all. He pleads with his friends to stop tormenting him and
attacking him and using his misfortunes to lord it over him.
He confesses to them that it feels as though the Lord has dealt
craftily with him, luring him in like a fish with a promise to
bless him, only to use that bait in order to trap him in a net.[1] He

---

[1] The Hebrew word *'āvath* in 19:6 means to *deal crookedly* or *to trick*. Job is
so distraught that he comes even closer to accusing the Lord of wrongdoing

simply cannot understand why the Lord would treat him quite so badly. Is this what God's love is like? Is God as unwilling to pay the price tag of real love as I am whenever I talk about how much I'd love to run a marathon or to play the guitar?

In verses 7–12, Job gets even more honest about his doubts that God loves him.[2] He doesn't try to hide his feelings from his friends. He hasn't fallen for the lie that spiritual maturity means putting a brave face on how we really feel. Job is honest that, right now at least, God seems to be ignoring his cries for help like a lazy policeman, seems to be blocking his path ahead of him like a violent highwayman, and seems to be stripping everything good away from his life like a conqueror turfing a defeated king off his throne.[3] It feels as though the Lord is demolishing him like a dilapidated building, tearing him out of the ground like an unwanted tree stump and encircling him like a general laying siege to a city. There once was a time when he was certain that he was God's friend, but now it feels as if the Lord has numbered him among his enemies.

In verses 13–20, Job confesses that he feels utterly alone. It is verses like these that drew the American novelist Thomas Wolfe to Job as one of the greatest tragic figures in all literature, claiming that *"The most tragic, sublime, and beautiful expression of human loneliness which I have ever read is the Book of Job."*[4] Job admits to his friends that his surviving friends and family have abandoned him. His wife, who has said nothing at all to comfort him since she failed so badly in chapter 2, takes one sniff of his breath and pushes him away. Even his closest friends have forgotten him – that's why he is still sitting in the dust with such miserable comforters as the three of them! His handful of surviving servants no longer respect him enough even to

---

than he did in 7:20–21 and 9:21–24. The writer doesn't censure him for this. He wants us to get real with God too.

[2] Don't judge Job for his vivid language here. He knew nothing of the conversation in God's council that we were told about in Job 1–2. He had no idea that his body was the battlefield in a great celestial battle.

[3] The language in 19:9 is similar to that of 2 Samuel 12:29–31.

[4] Thomas Wolfe in his *Anatomy of Loneliness* (1941).

respond to direct summons. The little boys in the street sing sarcastic ditties about him.[5] His peeling skin, his thinning hair and his rotting teeth are all signs that his body is abandoning him too.[6]

In verses 21–22, Job therefore pleads with his three remaining friends to have pity on him. If he is right that *"the hand of God has struck me"*, then theirs is the last love he has left in the world. He longs for them, at least, to pay the price tag of loving a loser like him.

Don Carson argues that:

> *One of the major causes of devastating grief and confusion among Christians is that our expectations are false. We do not give the subject of evil and suffering the thought it deserves until we ourselves are confronted with tragedy. If by that point our beliefs – not well thought out but deeply ingrained – are largely out of step with the God who has disclosed himself in the Bible and supremely in Jesus, then the pain from the personal tragedy may be multiplied many times over.[7]*

But praise God, that's not Job. As he teeters on the brink of despair, we discover that his walk with God during the good times yet again comes to his aid. He is a man who has studied such Holy Scriptures as are available in his day. He isn't governed by his feelings, but by the truth of God's Word. He speaks with far more insight than he knows when he wishes that his own

---

[5] See 30:9. The honour that the ancient world held for the aged made this even more galling (15:10 and 32:4).

[6] *"I have escaped only by the skin of my teeth"* (verse 20) either means that Job's teeth are literally falling out and he is down to his gums, or it is a metaphor, a bit like saying, *"I am only hanging on by my fingernails."*

[7] D.A. Carson in his book *How Long, O Lord? Reflections on Suffering and Evil* (1990).

troubles might become part of Scripture too. *"Oh, that my words were recorded, that they were written on a scroll"* (verse 23).[8]

It doesn't take much faith to turn around our situations. The mere thought of God's Scripture promises is all it takes for Job here. In verses 25–27, he lifts his eyes up to God and is rewarded by another amazing piece in his Gospel jigsaw puzzle. He suddenly grasps that the Lord has planned a way to be able to declare that sinners are saints in his heavenly courtroom without undermining his own absolute commitment to justice. In the ancient world, any down-and-out could turn to a loving relative and plead with them to act as their *redeemer*. A slave or a convicted criminal or a prisoner-of-war could ask the relative to pay the price tag of their freedom.[9] A widow could ask the relative to pay the price tag of her restoration – usually by stepping up and marrying her.[10] Suddenly Job grasps that his Advocate in heaven is planning to be more than a defence lawyer to him. He will come to earth to live as the only truly blameless man, so that his own righteous lifestyle can become "Exhibit A" in heaven's courtroom. He will lay down his life on behalf of the accused, paying the ultimate price tag to prove his love for them by making his own sacrificial blood "Exhibit B". This changes everything. Job no longer feels alone. *"I know that my redeemer lives,"* he gasps in wonder, *"and that in the end he will stand on the earth. And after my skin has been destroyed, yet in my flesh I will see God; I myself will see him with my own eyes – I, and not another. How my heart yearns within me!"*[11]

In verses 28–29, Job therefore finishes his response to

113

---

[8] It is possible that Job is longing for his troubles to be recorded in the Book of Life (Revelation 20:12), but the most natural interpretation is that he feels so alone that he at least wants future generations to pity him.

[9] Exodus 21:29–30 and Leviticus 25:47–49. The Lord uses this as one of his main Gospel pictures throughout the Old and New Testaments. For example, in Exodus 6:6, Galatians 3:13 and 1 Peter 1:18–19.

[10] The Hebrew word Job uses in 19:25 is *gō'ēl*, the same word used throughout the book of Ruth to describe Boaz as her kinsman *redeemer*.

[11] Hold that thought. Job 19:25–27 is such an important piece of Job's Gospel jigsaw picture that we will devote the whole of the next chapter to unpacking in much more detail what he actually saw.

Bildad's speech by warning his three friends to get ready for that Judgment Day themselves. He no longer doubts the Lord's love for him. He now understands how God is planning to be both just and the one who justifies the wicked. Job knows that his Redeemer – the one who will pay the price tag – lives.

Afterlife (Job 19:25–27)

*"After my skin has been destroyed, yet in my flesh I
will see God…"*

(Job 19:26)

The people of Job's day did not know much about what lay
beyond the grave. They were certain that there was an afterlife
of some sort, but they had very little clue what kind of afterlife it
might be.[1] One of the most remarkable aspects of Job's spiritual
journey of discovery is therefore that his suffering taught him
answers which were many centuries ahead of his time. Let's
take a moment, while we still hold the magnificent jigsaw piece
of 19:25–27 in our hands, to cast our eyes back over some of the
most important jigsaw pieces that Job has been given about the
afterlife so far.

Job's lament in chapter 3 reveals that he started out with
many of the assumptions that were prevalent in the land of
the East in his day.[2] Our best window into those assumptions
is the ancient Akkadian epic poem, *The Descent of Ishtar into
the Underworld*, which describes a *"land of no return, the land
of darkness,"* where everybody goes after they die, regardless of
whether their deeds in life are judged to have been good or bad.[3]
The Underworld is a gloomy place where *"dust and clay are their
only food"* and where *"they have no light, in darkness they dwell."*
It is a *"house without exit for whoever enters in."* Knowing this

---

[1] The Ancient Egyptians were more sophisticated and certain, but Job lived in
the land of the East (1:3), a world away from Egypt and much more dominated
by Mesopotamian ideas about the afterlife.

[2] The patriarchs shared something of Job's limited understanding too (Genesis
15:15, 25:8 and 37:35).

[3] The poem refers to the Underworld as *Irkalla*, which means *The Great Below*.
Ishtar is also known as Inanna.

background helps us to understand why Job was so very gloomy in his first lament in chapter 3. He believes that there is one eternal home for everyone, both good and bad, and that it isn't a very nice place for anyone. We'd feel pretty gloomy too.

Job derives some small encouragement from what Eliphaz says to him in chapters 4–5, that there are spirits who might be persuaded to help him in his journey to the Underworld, if only he knew to which one of them he ought to turn.[4] Having referred to the Underworld as *she'ol* for the first time in 7:9, Job dares to start believing in 9:33 that there might be a spirit in God's heavenly courtroom who will mediate for him and secure him a better afterlife than the gloomy shadows described in *The Descent of Ishtar*. Job slips back into a very negative view of the Underworld in 10:20–22, but he is encouraged by Zophar's declaration for the first time in 11:8 that there are in fact *two* destinations for those who die – either the heavens above or the grave below.[5] This leads to Job's own confession in 13:15–16 that his hope in the Lord is stronger than death and that he believes God will ultimately vindicate him in his heavenly courtroom on that day.

Slowly it begins to dawn on Job in the midst of his sufferings that this is why he needs the Lord to provide him with a spiritual Defence Lawyer, and to do so fast. In 14:13–17, he expresses his hope that the Lord will find a way to cover over all his sins and to transform his life into something beautiful beyond the grave. He pleads with God to conceal his body in the grave until that way has been prepared for him. In 16:19–21, he later comes to faith that God is lining up that Way-Maker for him. He sees a vision of a Witness, an Advocate, an Intercessor on high, who is already preparing his legal papers. He intends to vindicate Job in God's courtroom and to secure his entrance into

JOB 3–27: THE SAME OLD ANSWERS

116

[4] Job 4:15–19 and 5:1. This is why we need to read these speeches carefully. Job's friends are not all-wrong.

[5] Again, this is why we need to read all of these speeches carefully. Even Zophar gets some things right. In the Hebrew text of 11:8, he talks about *shamayim* and *she'ol*, later the Old Testament words for *heaven* and *hell*.

the glorious heaven above instead of the gloomy hell that he has heard about below.

Following Job on this spiritual journey reminds me of the time I did a team-building exercise at work. We had to get from one side of a field to another using ropes and various stepping stones, without touching the ground. Much of what Job and his friends say in their speeches is quite depressing, but there are glorious stepping stones of hope along the way. Perhaps the greatest of all is the one we have arrived at here in 19:25–27:

> I know that my redeemer lives, and that in the end he will
> stand on the earth. And after my skin has been destroyed,
> yet in my flesh I will see God; I myself will see him with
> my own eyes – I, and not another. How my heart yearns
> within me!

Job is speaking greater truth about the afterlife in these verses than anyone has ever spoken before him in the whole of human history. What he says here is massive. He declares that the wise men of the East are all wrong: there is a far greater hope for the afterlife than any of them has imagined. The grave is not something to dread. Life in heaven will be so much better than earth that Job's heart even yearns for it to begin now!

Job sees by faith that God has not only appointed a Redeemer for him but that, even now, the Redeemer is alive and getting ready for the task in heaven.[6] He is going to come down to live on earth as a man.[7] He will take on flesh and blood and conquer death so completely that, even after Job's flesh has decayed in the tomb, he will be raised to new life through faith

---

[6] Under ancient law, a person's *gō'ēl*, or *redeemer*, would not only rescue them (Ruth 4:1–13) but would also avenge them against their foes (Deuteronomy 19:12). Job's Redeemer would therefore not only deal with his sin, but also vindicate his cause by dealing with the people who had wronged and abandoned him.

[7] Job predicted this obliquely in 14:1–4, but now he states it more explicitly. The Hebrew word *'aharōn* means *later* and refers to the first coming of Jesus as much his second. See Acts 2:17, Hebrews 1:2 and James 5:3.

in his Redeemer.[8] He will see that Redeemer with his own eyes through the resurrection body the Redeemer purchases for him. There are still gaps in Job's picture. He still knows little about the cruel crucifixion through which his Redeemer will satisfy the demands of justice to save him by *right*, as well as by *might*. But he has seen much more than any man or woman who has ever lived before him. Even in his suffering, he can hardly contain his joy. *"How my heart yearns within me!"*

When the German composer George Handel wrote his famous *Messiah* in 1741, he turned Job's vision in these verses into one of its most powerful arias. He intermingles what Job saw in these verses with the words of 1 Corinthians 15:20 – *"For now is Christ risen from the dead, the first-fruits of them that sleep."* What Job saw partially in the distance looking forwards, we can now see in detail looking backwards. Jesus has now come as our Redeemer. He has performed his great work of redemption. It is finished.

So take a moment to reflect and to say thank you. Sing a *Hallelujah* chorus of your own.

---

[8] Job prophesies literally in 19:25 that his Redeemer will stand on the *dust* of the earth – perhaps linking to 2:12, 7:21, 10:9, 16:15 and 17:16.

Beyond Reason
(Job 20:1–29)

"My understanding inspires me to reply."

(Job 20:3)

The French philosopher Blaise Pascal observed that *"The supreme function of reason is to show man that some things are beyond reason."*[1]

Zophar had never read Pascal, and in his second speech it shows. Once again he claims to speak for reason, and once again he is unreasonable. Like Eliphaz's second speech based on experience and Bildad's second speech based on tradition, Zophar's second speech based on logical reasoning is nothing more than a rehash of the same old answer.

In verses 1–3, Zophar plays the victim card. It's remarkable how easily people who claim to speak for reason get emotional instead. Zophar is terribly offended that Job has suggested that he and his friends need to prepare themselves for God's Judgment Day. He feels dishonoured, so he rushes back to his safe place. He retreats inside his mind palace, then rushes back out on the offensive: *"My understanding inspires me to reply."*[2]

In verses 4–29, Zophar shows us how little those who claim to be governed by reason actually are. He doesn't argue from logic at all. He claims that everybody knows that what he says is true, but then states things that are patently false. The wicked are *not* always swiftly judged by the Lord. Bad things *don't* always happen to evildoers. They often *do* happen to those

---

[1] This is the 267th of Blaise Pascal's *Pensées* (1670).

[2] Zophar refers literally to *"the spirit of my understanding"*. Like many secular thinkers, he is quasi-religious in his faith that the goddess Reason will guide him into all truth.

who try to live good lives. The reason we are still discussing the question *Why does God allow suffering?* twenty chapters into the book of Job is precisely because things *don't* always work out as we expect them to in a well-ordered world.

If somebody sent a film script to Hollywood that reflected the world we actually live in, the Hollywood producers would send it back. They would insist on an ending where good things happen to the goodies and where bad things happen to the baddies. Zophar's repetitive clichés fail to grapple with this problem. It doesn't make sense for a world that is run by God to feel less fair than a movie made by a media mogul.

Those who claim to speak for reason tend to see this problem as the killer blow for faith in God. I've lost track of all the times that my nonbelieving friends have shrugged their shoulders and asked me "Where was God during that terrorist attack?" or "If God is so great then why doesn't he end world hunger?", before turning away as if they have asserted an open-and-shut case for atheism. But we need to be careful not to allow people to be as disingenuous as Zophar is in these verses. If we really think about the question of suffering logically, then we quickly see that it poses an even bigger problem for the atheist than it does for the believer.

C.S. Lewis reflects on this as a key factor in his own conversion to Christ while at Oxford University. His commitment to atheism had been strongly based on a pithy maxim by the Roman poet Lucretius:

> Had God designed the world, it would not be
> A world so frail and faulty as we see.[3]

And yet, as he reflected afresh on his position, C.S. Lewis became convinced logically that the problem of suffering was a far bigger problem for his atheism. If he refused to believe in God because the world seems cruel and unjust, then where did this idea of "just" and "unjust" come from? Nobody calls a line

---

[3] *On the Nature of Things* (5.198–199). Lucretius was a devotee of Epicurus.

crooked unless they have some idea of a straight line – so who put this sense of injustice within us?

> If the whole show was bad and senseless from A to Z, so to speak, why did I, who was supposed to be part of the show, find myself in such violent reaction against it?

For a while, C.S. Lewis tried to give up on his idea of justice altogether, treating it as nothing but a private idea of his own. But soon he discovered that his argument against God collapsed with it, since his argument against the existence of God depended upon the world truly being unjust, not just seeming so to him. In the very act of trying to prove that God cannot exist, because the world is senseless, he was therefore forced to admit that at least one thing – his own idea of justice – was full of sense.

> Consequently atheism turns out to be too simple. If the whole universe has no meaning, we should never have found out that it has no meaning: just as, if there were no light in the universe and therefore no creatures with eyes, we should never know it was dark. "Dark"'would be a word without meaning.[4]

C.S. Lewis had originally assumed that the Christians around him were naive and that he and his secular friends based their own beliefs on logical reasoning. But now he found himself waking up to the fact that many of his arguments were like this speech from Zophar. There are many shoddy arguments in the book of Job, but there are few worse than Zophar's bluster here, hoping to use a dramatic, *"Surely you know...?"* as a distraction tactic to mask the utter unreasonableness of what he says.

The atheist has no basis to be outraged by all the suffering in the world. If it evolved, in the words of Tennyson, from *"Nature, red in tooth and claw"*, then we would feel no

---

[4] C.S. Lewis remembers this in his book *Mere Christianity* (1952).

instinctive revulsion against its unfairness of suffering.[5] We would instinctively rejoice in it as our mother's voice, for our very existence through natural selection would be a result of it. But we don't. We do something which is only logical if the God that Job discovered in his suffering truly is our Creator and truly wants us to discover him too.

We instinctively ask the question: *Why does this world appear faulty?* Answer: because the Lord created it very good. We instinctively respond: *Then what ruined it?* Answer: our sin did, at the Fall. We instinctively wonder: *Is there any way to fix it?* Answer: yes, but only through the Redeemer that Job saw. He is the one who did more than complain about our suffering. He is the one who came to earth and embraced the worst of our suffering. He took it so seriously that he paid the price tag of fixing it.

As he reflected on the unreasonableness of unbelief, C.S. Lewis came to faith:

> *You must picture me alone in that room in Magdalen [College, Oxford], night after night, feeling, whenever my mind lifted even for a second from my work, the steady, unrelenting approach of Him whom I so earnestly desired not to meet. That which I greatly feared had at last come upon me. In the Trinity Term of 1929 I gave in, and admitted that God was God, and knelt and prayed.[6]*

---

[5] This is a line from Alfred, Lord Tennyson's poem *In Memoriam* (1850).

[6] C.S. Lewis remembers this in his book *Surprised by Joy* (1955).

True Love (Job 21:1–34)

"Nothing is left of your answers but falsehood!"

(Job 21:34)

Job is no longer on the defensive. He has listened to two cycles of speeches from his three friends and he is determined to end their empty pontificating right here. We can tell he is still upset from the way that his response to Zophar is again all talk and no prayer, but at least he is now getting clearer about why God allows such suffering.

In verses 1–3, he asks his three friends to shut up and listen. He has heard them out and he has spotted that they have trotted out the same old answer six times in six different guises. Now it is their turn to listen to him. This will at least offer him some small consolation in his suffering. After that, they can mock on if they please.

In verses 4–16, Job tells his friends that his gripe isn't with them. If their formulae were true then, as a good man, he would be happy. No, his real gripe is with the Lord for not running the universe as it ought to be run. The wicked live to a ripe old age in safety. Their families and their fortunes flourish. They live happy and they die happy, boasting, *"Who is the Almighty, that we should serve him? What would we gain by praying to him?"* (verse 15).

Even as Job complains about their arrogant boasting, he begins to stumble on the answer to his question. Their boasting proves that the Lord hasn't created a race of virtual assistants who are pre-programmed to do as they are told. He has given them real choice as to whether or not to serve him.[1] If God

___

[1] The Hebrew word *hāphēts* in 21:14 means *to take delight in* or *to take pleasure in* or *to strongly desire*. It is not a word that speaks about enforced duty, but

judged them immediately for rejecting him, then there would be no such thing as a real worshipper. Everyone would serve the Lord, not out of love for him, but out of begrudging self-interest. Job is angry in this chapter that his friends have fed him a pack of lies, but in his anger he stumbles upon the truth.

Job's reply echoes what we reflected upon earlier. The Lord is not a slot-machine God. He wants us to pursue friendship with him for his own sake. Otherwise, he would prefer that we didn't pursue it at all. He allows good things to happen to those who reject him, and bad things to happen to those who worship him, because both scenarios are better than the alternative. He refuses to underwrite a world full of hypocrisy, where everybody claims that he is their God while using him as a means of acquiring what they truly cherish as a god. He either wants true love from us, or nothing.

After C.S. Lewis got up from his knees at Magdalen College, Oxford, he went on to experience much grief and sorrow. He reflected that God allows this because he wants a true love relationship with us. Suffering is how he first draws us into that relationship.

> *The human spirit will not even begin to try to surrender self-will as long as all seems to be well with it... Every man knows that something is wrong when he is being hurt... We can rest contentedly in our sins and in our stupidities... but pain insists upon being attended to. God whispers to us in our pleasures, speaks in our conscience, but shouts in our pain: it is His megaphone to rouse a deaf world.*[2]

Suffering is often how God first gets our attention and draws us into friendship with him. Unless he spoke to us through his megaphone, all of us would stay asleep, too self-centred in our

---

about freely given desire and delight.

[2] The quotations from C.S. Lewis in this chapter come from his book *The Problem of Pain* (1940).

ease ever to answer his call. Once we have answered it, God often continues to lead us through times of suffering to transform our lives into something better. Pain chisels away at the canker of sin that disfigures the beauty he has placed within us. That's what the Christian hip-hop artist Lecrae means when he sings that being broke made him rich.[3]

As C.S. Lewis reflects on this further in his book *The Problem of Pain*, he recognises the great difference between mere kindness and God's love. Kindness wants its object to escape suffering at any terms. That's why we offer it to those we care for the least. We do not offer mere kindness to those we truly love – to our spouses, our friends, our children, our brothers, and our sisters. Our care for them is so much deeper that, at times, we would rather see them suffer than see them happy in contemptible circumstances. C.S. Lewis concludes that *"If God is Love, He is, by definition, something more than mere kindness."*

When the Bible says that God loves us, it means that he truly loves us. He does not merely feel kindness towards us, in a detached and disinterested sense. He does not offer us senile benevolence or a shallow platitude that "it doesn't matter what you choose in life, just so long as it makes you happy in your own way". Gods feels a love towards us that is as deep as the oceans and as terrible as a raging forest fire. Reconciling human suffering with the existence of a God who loves us is only impossible if we mistake love for mere kindness. We wanted a loving God, so we must not complain about what the existence of a God who truly loves us truly means.

Job is stumbling upon this truth here but, in verses 17–21, he isn't satisfied with how it works out in practice. It makes sense that the Lord allows his worshippers to suffer in order to reveal his beauty in their lives, but it makes no sense for him to pamper those who reject him. That's a recipe for anarchy. Job has heard it said that God sends calamities on the children of

---

[3] Lecrae sings this in his song *Broke* (2017).

those he pampers, but of what use is that?[4] By definition, self-centred evildoers don't care about what happens to anybody but themselves. Job wants to see the judgment of God fall on them personally![5]

In verses 22–26, Job therefore throws up his hands in exasperation that the world is not run as he feels it ought to be. It appears to be run badly, which is frustrating because Job knows it is impossible for him to teach God anything. He can only complain about him.[6]

In verses 27–33, Job therefore ends this second cycle of speeches by telling his three friends not to bother giving him a third one. He says he knows what they will say, cooking up some bogus case study about a certain good man who has prospered and a certain evildoer who has been struck down. But as anyone who didn't fall off the turnip truck yesterday knows full well, such case studies are the exceptions, not the rule. Job effectively tells his friends in verse 29: *If you think that's true then you need to get out more!*

In verse 34, Job therefore brings the second cycle of speeches to an end by telling his friends to stop talking nonsense. Their theories are nothing more than a pack of lies.

---

[4] Job seems particularly riled that their children flourish while his own ten children have been killed (21:8). He also seems particularly to resent their herds growing while his own herds have been stolen (21:10).

[5] In talking about *she'ōl*, or the *grave*, in 21:13, Job forgets what God has taught him about the Final Judgment and about heaven and hell. In the heat of his anger, he contradicts his own words in earlier chapters.

[6] Job's suggestion that both the good and the wicked lie down next to each other, unjudged, in the grave denies much of what he has learned so far in the book of Job. Anger is a poor teacher. It causes us to forget.

How Not to Pastor People
(Job 22:1–30)

> *"Will you keep to the old path that the wicked have trod?"*

(Job 22:15)

Walter Mallory felt sorry for his old friend Thomas Edison. Time and time again, the inventor's experiments had failed to create a lightbulb or a battery that could power one. After his nine-thousandth failure, Walter Mallory tried to comfort him over his lack of results. Quick as a flash, Thomas Edison retorted, *"Results? Why, man, I have gotten plenty of results! I now know several thousand ways in which it definitely won't work!"*[1]

That's why I'm glad that God inspired the writer of the book of Job to record at great length the speeches of Job's three false friends. As we move into the third and final cycle of their speeches, I'm not getting bored with them. I view these speeches in the same way that Thomas Edison viewed his experiments. They may feel foolish and frustrating, but they are also fruitful. These speeches teach us how not to pastor people.

In verses 2–3, Eliphaz teaches us not to pastor people *by seeking to downsize God.* We do this far more often than we realize.[2] Eliphaz believes that he is helping Job by reassuring him that the Lord is not his enemy, since he is far too great to think about a puny creature such as him, but don't miss how much this cheap comfort will cost Job in the end. Whenever we answer people's questions about the suffering in their lives by

---

[1] Quoted by Frank Lewis Dyer and Thomas Commerford Martin in *Edison: His Life and Inventions* (1910).

[2] Eliphaz calls God *Shaddai* – the *Almighty* – five times in this chapter, even as he downplays the Lord's power.

downplaying God's total sovereignty over it, we peddle a false god to them.[3] We offer them a superficial comfort that robs them of a proper view of God's character. We may well make them smile in the short term, but only by cheating them out of the only true source of comfort that can sustain them for the long term.

Eliphaz offers easy answers that sidestep the crucial question which began this drama way back in Job 1:9: *"Does Job fear God for nothing?"* He fails to reflect on what true friendship means between God and people, and on how much his facile formula undermines true worship. He gives no consideration to the Lord's desire to vindicate the righteousness of his rule before his heavenly council. The truth is, the Lord *does* place great value on the life of Job. The truth is, he *does* delight so much in Job's blameless life that he actually singled him out to Satan. Eliphaz thinks that he can comfort Job by bringing God down to his level, but downsizing God never upsizes our faith in him. Easy answers to complex questions always end up robbing us of real comfort.[4]

In verses 4–11, Eliphaz teaches us not to pastor people *by seeking to downsize the problem*. Instead of listening to Job's reply to his first two speeches, Eliphaz simply repeats the same old answer: Job is suffering so Job must have sinned. Eliphaz refuses to engage with the real problem – that Job is the kind of person whom God ought to be blessing in a well-run world – and instead he becomes very accusatory. Having weaponized the gift of prophecy to claim superior spiritual insight to Job in his first speech, he now does so again here. He has no evidence that Job has sinned in any of the ways that he describes. It is pure speculation, based on a prophetic hunch, which Job refutes entirely in chapter 29. The writer wants us to grasp that we

---

[3] Note how Paul comforts his Jewish readers, in Romans 9–11, over the fact that their nation has largely rejected Jesus as its Messiah. He doesn't downplay God's sovereignty. He preaches divine predestination.

[4] The Hebrew word for *wise person* in 22:2 is *maskîl*, the same word that is used in the title of thirteen of the Psalms to denote a *teaching psalm*. The only way to comfort people long term is to teach them what God is truly like.

can never truly comfort people unless we identify their true problem. Pastoring people means listening to them.

In verses 12–20, Eliphaz teaches us not to pastor people *by downsizing their faith in God*. In his first two speeches, he was gentler than Job's other two friends, but he certainly makes up for it here. He accuses Job of walking the same path as the wicked, who reassure themselves that the Lord will neither see nor judge their evil actions. Instead of commending Job for trusting God in the midst of his misfortunes, he accuses him of being the architect of his own suffering. He doesn't love Job, so he is deaf to Job's pain and agony. He pours the petrol of condemnation onto the flames of Job's misery.

Recently I discovered that a fourteen-year-old boy at one of the churches that I serve has been diagnosed, out of the blue, with both testicular and lung cancer. His parents are leading members of the church. You would love them. They are godly. They are fun. They are vibrant witnesses to the Lord. And now they have been struck down by sudden tragedy. Some of their friends have suggested that, if they have a bit more faith in God, their son will be healed. We need to be very cautious about such quick-and-easy fixes. The truth is, Job was not suffering because of his sin, but because he was less sinful than any of his neighbours! The writer wants these speeches to train us to affirm people's faith in the midst of their suffering, not to criticize it and to tear it down.[5]

In verses 21–30, Eliphaz teaches us not to pastor people by *seeking to downsize the Gospel*. He may be ruder and more callous in this third speech than in his first two speeches, but his message is essentially the same.[6] There is an air of unreality and

---

[5] We pastor people by reassuring them that their willingness to suffer loss for Christ is proof they are true believers. The Christian who remains single rather than marry a nonbeliever and the Christian who is ridiculed for being open about their faith have not done something wrong. They are doing what is right.

[6] *Ophir* was the far-off land from which King Solomon's fleet brought back gold (1 Kings 9:28 and 10:11). Probably modern-day Yemen or Oman, its gold was viewed as the best on the market (28:16, Psalm 45:9, and Isaiah 13:12). Eliphaz accuses Job of only owning such fine gold as the fruit of his wickedness.

of dishonesty to his words that reveals a heart more attached to his slot-machine formula than to the truth:

> People who do evil + A loving, powerful God = People who are cursed
>
> People who do good + A loving, powerful God = People who are blessed

Eliphaz is the archetypal preacher of the prosperity gospel. He is convinced that the Lord guarantees certain benefits to anyone who obeys his Word.[7] He will make them rich (verse 20). He will answer their prayers (verse 27).[8] He will make them successful (verse 28). He will make them evangelistically fruitful (verses 29–30). It's all a quid pro quo. *"Submit to God and be at peace with him; in this way prosperity will come to you"* (verse 21). If we do what God wants, then God will do what we want. But such a view of God is two-dimensional. Of course he wants what is best for those who love him, but he also knows what is truly best for them. Eliphaz has no humility to accept this.[9] He has no room in his simplistic formula for the truth of Acts 14:22, that *"We must go through many hardships to enter the kingdom of God"*.

Eliphaz has failed in his three speeches. We shall hear from him no more. He has merely served to teach us how not to pastor people.

---

[7] The Hebrew word that Eliphaz uses for God's *instruction* in 22:22 is *tōrāh*, which would later become the Jewish name for the *Law of Moses*. God's Word makes us wise but it doesn't exempt us from suffering.

[8] The prosperity gospel is dangerous because it is partly true. God really does answer the prayers of the righteous more than the prayers of the wicked (Proverbs 28:9, Isaiah 1:13, 1 Timothy 2:8, James 5:16 and 1 Peter 3:7). But that isn't the same thing as declaring that our righteous acts force God to answer our prayers.

[9] Don't miss the staggering arrogance in Eliphaz's words in 22:21. By "submit to God", he actually means "confess that my own formula is true"!

No Way (Job 23:1–17)

"If only I knew where to find him; if only I could go to his dwelling!"

(Job 23:3)

There is a medical name for the anxiety that I feel whenever I leave my house without my mobile phone. They call it *nomophobia*. What if my wife needs to get hold of me? What if one of my children gets ill at school? What if my car breaks down? What if a crisis kicks off at the church I lead? It's a very twenty-first-century type of suffering.

Job lived almost 4,000 years before the invention of the mobile phone, but in this chapter we find him suffering from nomophobia too. He listens to the third speech of Eliphaz, then replies: *No way!* He longs for better answers to his questions from the Lord himself, but he has no way of reaching him. He feels disconnected from God.

In verses 2–7, Job tells Eliphaz that he longs to stand before the Lord in his heavenly courtroom.[1] *"If only I knew where to find him; if only I could go to his dwelling!"* Gone is the fear that Job expressed about God's courtroom in chapter 9. It has been blown away by his glorious vision of God's Redeemer in chapter 19. Job is convinced that the Lord has a Saviour for him who will be his Witness, his Advocate, his Intercessor, his Mediator and his Defence Lawyer in the courtroom of heaven. Job is no longer

---

[1] These verses are full of Hebrew courtroom language. The words for Job's *case* and Job's *judge* in 23:4 and 23:7 are the sister words *mishpāt* and *shāphat*. The words for *oppose* and *upright* in 23:6 and 23:7 are *rīb* and *yāshār*.

afraid of standing in God's presence. He just confesses that he doesn't have a clue how to get there.[2]

In verses 8–12, Job acts as we do in our worst moments of nomophobia. His eyes dart around for a way to connect with God. He looks to the east, to the west, to the north and to the south, but he looks around in vain. He looks to God's Word as the very best place for us to look for God whenever he feels distant, but even there Job fails to find the connection that he craves.[3] He has come a long way in these first twenty-three chapters. He knows that there is one true God who has appointed a Day of Judgment when everyone will stand in his courtroom.[4] He knows that God has prepared a Redeemer who will do something that enables him both to be just and to justify sinners on that great day. He knows that God has appointed a Mediator, a Bridge-Builder, a Way-Maker, but he doesn't yet know how to get hold of God in the midst of his suffering.

In verses 13–17, Job becomes even more anxious in his nomophobia. If the Lord is hidden from him, then the Lord's purposes are hidden from him too. If the Lord's purposes are hidden from him, then the Lord can do whatever he pleases without any comeback from the likes of Job. If the Lord can do whatever he pleases, and if it has pleased him to decree such misery, then Job is terrified of the plans that God still has in store for him![5] He feels more desperate than ever to stand before the Lord and to receive some answers about what is happening to him, but he has lost all connection with God. He feels as if

---

[2] In 23:2, Job essentially complains that his anguished prayers seem to be falling on deaf ears.

[3] Job's hunger for the Word of God in 23:12 is echoed in Deuteronomy 8:3 and Matthew 4:4. Those who truly love the Lord would rather hear him speak than they would eat. They prize the Bible more than their food.

[4] Job is full of anguish in this chapter but he is also full of faith. In a polytheistic, pagan nation, he declares in 23:13 that the Lord is not one God of many. *"But he stands alone"* and *"does whatever he pleases."*

[5] The Hebrew word *hōq* that is used for God's *decree* in 23:14 was also used for Job's *daily bread* in 23:12.

his face is covered by thick darkness which prevents him from finding any way to God.

I love Job's faith in his suffering. I can see why James 5:11 tells us to learn patience from him. But I have to confess that I get confused when Christians point to Job as the great example of how we are supposed to suffer faithfully today. I find it odd that people this side of the Day of Pentecost point to Job and say that we should bear our suffering like a man who lived before God poured out his Holy Spirit on all of his followers. We don't need to feel the same nomophobia as Job in this chapter. God has sent his Son to earth to do away with our nomophobia towards God by becoming the answer to Job's anguished plea. He declares that *"I am the way and the truth and the life. No one comes to the Father except through me... [but] Anyone who has seen me has seen the Father."*[6]

We don't have to feel disconnected from God, like Job, because our lives have been united with the one King David sang about in his famous twenty-third psalm: *"The Lord is my shepherd, I lack nothing... Even though I walk through the darkest valley, I will fear no evil, for you are with me; your rod and your staff, they comfort me."*[7] Job bore his pain brilliantly with the little insight he was given into God's plans and with the limited connection he could feel with God before Christ came. We are called to bear our own pain with far greater faith than Job, because we live on the other side of the death and resurrection of Jesus. Even in our darkest days, we live on the sunny side of history. We go through many valleys, but we never go through any of them alone. We sometimes lose our sense of closeness to God, but we never truly lose our connection with him. If we have put our faith in Jesus, then the New Testament assures us we are now *in Jesus* forever. We have died with him, we have been

[6] John 14:6–9 corresponds to Job 23:3 in the same way that John 11:25 corresponds to Job 14:14. The way to God is not found in some secret place. It is found in his Son, Jesus of Nazareth, our great Redeemer.

[7] Psalm 23 points towards John 10:11. The reference to the Lord's *rod* reminds us that we can even take comfort in his discipline towards us (Hebrews 12:5–11). Job hints at this comfort in 23:10.

buried with him, we have been raised to new life with him and we have been exalted to sit with him in heavenly places with God.[8] We have something to support us in the midst of our own suffering that Job could only long for in this chapter. We know Jesus, the Way-Maker, the Friend who will never let go of us.

The New Testament encourages us to shake off all sense of spiritual nomophobia. Hebrews 10:19–23 commands us to live in the good of all that Jesus has done for us:

> *Therefore, brothers and sisters, since we have confidence to enter the Most Holy Place by the blood of Jesus, by a new and living way opened for us through the curtain, that is, his body, and since we have a great priest over the house of God, let us draw near to God with a sincere heart and with the full assurance that faith brings, having our hearts sprinkled to cleanse us from a guilty conscience and having our bodies washed with pure water. Let us hold unswervingly to the hope we profess, for he who promised is faithful.*

---

[8] Romans 6:1–14, Galatians 2:20, Ephesians 2:4–6 and Colossians 2:20–3:4.

The School of Suffering
(Job 23:10)

"He knows the way that I take; when he has tested me, I shall come forth as gold."

(Job 23:10)

There is a Calvin and Hobbes cartoon in which the six-year-old Calvin shouts at the top of his lungs: *"I don't want to go to school! I hate school! I'd rather do anything than go to school!"*[1]

That's how most of us feel when God enrols us in his School of Suffering. Job shouts as loudly as Calvin about how much he hates it here. He is suffering *physically* through the sores on his skin. He is suffering *emotionally* through a sense of shame and failure that is compounded by the harsh words of his wife and friends. He is suffering *mentally* as he struggles with the dark depression that he feels over the loss of his ten children and of his herds. He is suffering *spiritually*, believing that God has abandoned him or, worse, become his bitter enemy. And yet, in the midst of his agony, Job makes such an astonishing declaration of faith in verse 10 that we ought to pause and reflect on it for a moment. Job declares to Eliphaz that none of his misery is meaningless. Since God is the architect of his suffering, Job is confident that God will work it all out for good in the end. Amidst his agony, Job insists the Lord knows what

---

[1] Bill Watterson's first published this particular cartoon on 12th March 1992. Watterson published this particular cartoon in various US newspapers on the same day, since by then his comic strip had become so successful that it was widely syndicated.

he is doing: *"He knows the way that I take; when he has tested me, I shall come forth as gold."*[2]

It is easier to recognize the loving hand of God in the suffering of others than it is to recognize it in our own. That's why God uses the life of Job to teach us this important principle, and why he came in person as the Suffering Servant to lead the way for us to follow. God doesn't just enrol us in the School of Suffering. In Jesus, he has personally become its head boy. He didn't try to squirm his way off the hook of our question: *Why does God allow suffering?* He placed himself very firmly on the hook by enrolling in our same school. Jesus embodied what Job teaches us here when he learned earthly obedience through his flesh-and-blood sufferings.

This is a particular theme of the New Testament book of Hebrews. In Hebrews 2:10, the writer echoes the words of Job 23:10 when he says that *"In bringing many sons and daughters to glory, it was fitting that God, for whom and through whom everything exists, should make the pioneer of their salvation perfect through what he suffered."* Jesus didn't hide from this world's pain, like a Buddhist monk.[3] He embraced it, like Job. He became *"a man of suffering, and familiar with pain."*[4] He suffered more than Job *physically* when he was whipped and beaten and nailed to a cross by his hands and feet until he died. Job's friends struggled to recognize him in 2:12, but by the time the Romans finished with Jesus people could barely even recognize that he was human.[5] Jesus suffered more than Job *emotionally* when one of his closest friends betrayed him and the rest abandoned him. Jesus suffered more than Job *mentally* in the Garden of Gethsemane, and more than Job *spiritually* in the darkness of Calvary. Jesus had always lived in unbroken

---

[2] Job uses a different Hebrew word for gold in 23:10 than the two words that Eliphaz used in 22:24–25. Nevertheless, it is hard to see this as anything other than a defiant reply to Eliphaz's unfounded accusations.

[3] In verse 83 of the *Dhammapada*, the Buddha reflects aloofly, "Wise men rise above all pleasure and pain."

[4] Isaiah 53:3.

[5] Isaiah 52:14.

fellowship with God as his Father (John 1:18), yet he cried out in agony in Matthew 27:46, *"My God, my God, why have you forsaken me?"*

John Stott reflects on how significant it is for us that God has graduated from his own School of Suffering: *"I could never myself believe in God, if it were not for the cross... In the real world of pain, how could one worship a God who was immune to it?"* He contrasts statues of the Buddha, with a remote look upon his face, with depictions of Jesus on the cross, twisted and tortured, nails through his hands and feet, his back lacerated, his forehead bleeding, his mouth deathly dry as he is plunged into God-forsaken darkness, and then John Stott concludes: *"That is the God for me! He laid aside his immunity to pain. He entered our world of flesh and blood, tears and death. He suffered for us. Our sufferings become more manageable in the light of his. There is still a question mark against human suffering, but over it we boldly stamp another mark, the cross that symbolises divine suffering."*[6]

Hebrews 5:8 informs us that Jesus *"learned obedience from what he suffered"*. The reality of his worship was proved in the furnace of his suffering. How much more, then, must ours? Jesus enrolled in the same school as Job so that he can help us when we tread the same path as Job, trusting that God *"knows the way that I take; when he has tested me, I shall come forth as gold."*

If you feel that God has enrolled you in the School of Suffering, then the writer of Hebrews is not seeking to downplay your pain. He is simply trying to help you to see God in the midst of it. He is assuring you that Jesus attended the School of Suffering *for you* during his life on earth, and that he wants to attend it *with you* in your own suffering today. He is rejoicing that Job was right, the Lord does much of his best work in the worst moments of our lives, and he is pointing out that those painful seasons cost us far too much for us to squander them on bitterness and complaining.

---

[6] John Stott in his book *The Cross of Christ* (1986).

So take a moment now to thank God for accepting you as a student in his School of Suffering. Rejoice with the same faith as Job that the Lord knows what he is doing. Hear the echo of Job's words here in verse 10 when Hebrews 12:5–11 encourages us:

> *"My son, do not make light of the Lord's discipline, and do not lose heart when he rebukes you, because the Lord disciplines the one he loves, and he chastens everyone he accepts as his son." Endure hardship as discipline; God is treating you as his children. For what children are not disciplined by their father?... [Our fathers] disciplined us for a little while as they thought best; but God disciples us for our good, in order that we may share in his holiness. No discipline seems pleasant at the time, but painful. Later on, however, it produces a harvest of righteousness and peace for those who have been trained by it.*[7]

---

[7] For other verses that echo this major theme of Scripture, see Genesis 41:52, Deuteronomy 8:2–5, Acts 14:22, Romans 5:3–5, 2 Corinthians 1:3–7 and 12:7–10, Philippians 3:7–11, James 1:2–12 and 1 Peter 1:6–7.

You're Fired! (Job 24:1–25)

*"Why does the Almighty not set times for judgment?
Why must those who know him look in vain for such
days?"*

(Job 24:1)

In the movie *Bruce Almighty*, Jim Carrey's character gets fired from his dream job. Outraged that the Lord should allow such an injustice, he shouts towards the sky in anger, *"Fine, the gloves are off, pal! Come on and let me see a little of your wrath. Come and smite me! The only one around here who should be fired for failing at his job is you!"*[1]

Jim Carrey isn't the only person to have shouted that kind of angry prayer at God. Most of us at one time or another have shouted at the sky in frustration after watching tragedy on the TV news or after hearing about something that has happened to a friend. People who perform their job badly generally get fired. On that basis, if it were up to humans, God would have been fired many times over. In this chapter, a third cycle of speeches finally pushes Job over the edge, and he shouts a similar angry prayer at God. He cries out that the Lord isn't doing what he ought to be doing in a well-run world.

In verses 1–12, Job complains that God has failed to deliver on his job description. He is the Almighty, so why doesn't he use his power? He is the Judge, so why doesn't he deal with those who defy his laws? He is the one that righteous people worship, so why does he make them wait in vain for his Day of Judgment? Job has witnessed people stealing land and animals from their

---

[1] Paraphrased from the movie *Bruce Almighty*, Universal Pictures (2003).

neighbours.[2] He has seen the rich and powerful oppressing the poor and the needy.[3] Hasn't the Lord noticed that many hungry and homeless people are that way because the rich have cheated them out of their wages? Doesn't he care that those whose wardrobes are full of clothes enslave those whose wardrobes are empty? If you are shocked that Job should question whether or not God is up to his job, then you need to read the Bible a bit more slowly. God never rebukes Job for speaking these words, and the psalmists pray to the Lord in a similar way.[4] The Lord would rather have us speak out how we truly feel about him, even if we feel confused and angry, than have us speak religious niceties which mask the turmoil that we feel.

In verses 13–17, Job doesn't hold back. He complains that the Lord has failed to judge those who hate the light – those who treat midnight as their morning, hiding away during the day so that they can get up and use the cover of darkness to steal and kill and commit adultery with their neighbours' wives. Don't skim over these verses and miss how much Job is questioning whether or not the Lord is up to his job. These verses are like the moment in the movie when Bruce finally meets with God and follows up his angry prayer by shouting in frustration words along the lines of: *Well, nice to meet you, God. Thank you for the Grand Canyon and everything. Oh, and by the way, you SUCK!*

One of the reasons why the Lord encourages us to vent our anger towards him in prayer is that the very act of speaking out our feelings helps us to process them. Western culture tends to

---

[2] Moving a boundary stone was the ancient equivalent of moving your fence in the middle of the night in order to steal part of your neighbour's garden. After Job 1, it is natural that he feels furious towards those who steal another person's flocks and herds, but perhaps the Lord feels the same sense of outrage towards church leaders who seek to poach Christians from other churches instead of obeying the Great Commission.

[3] What Job describes in 24:3 and 24:9 was perfectly legal. However, God demands more from us than honouring the rules of free-market capitalism. There are times when pressing home our legal rights is wrong.

[4] The Hebrew words used for the Lord *charging no one with wrongdoing* in 24:12 are the same Hebrew words that are used for Job not *charging God with wrongdoing* in 1:22. This is deliberate on the part of the writer.

be vocal about happiness and success, but to bottle up sadness and confusion. We self-medicate with alcohol, drugs, sex or bingeing out on Netflix boxsets. Anything to take our minds off how we actually feel. People become violent or depressed if they never learn to voice their anguished pain, so note what happens to Job as he is honest with the Lord in prayer. In verses 18–25, he bows his head and lets go of his anger. He admits that, of course, the Lord knows what he is doing. If he is big enough to blame for our suffering, then he is big enough to trust in the midst of it too.

Job recognizes that time is running out for the wicked. He also recognizes that God's scariest judgment doesn't come in the form of swift punishment, but in the form of silence. The English Puritan Thomas Watson warned that:

> *The greatest judgment God lays upon a man in this life is to let him sin without control. When the Lord's displeasure is most severely kindled against a person, he does not say, I will bring the sword and the plague on this man, but, I will let him sin on.*[5]

As Job vents his anger, he finds himself trusting that God's failure to judge the wicked swiftly isn't a sign that he is a pushover, but a sign that he has handed them over to their sin. He has made up his mind to judge them, not to save them.[6]

Job recognizes that, even if the wicked prosper in this world, they will not escape the wrath of God in the world to come. Who is the lucky one in the Parable of the Rich Man and Lazarus in Luke 16:19–31? It isn't the rich man who lives his life free from trouble. It's the beggar Lazarus, whose earthly misery provokes him to cry out to God. God's blessing on the wicked therefore proves to be a curse, because it stops them

---

[5] Thomas Watson in *The Doctrine of Repentance* (1668).

[6] We don't like to think of this because it is quite frightening, but it is the clear teaching of Romans 1:24–28. Job says in 24:23 that one of God's greatest judgments is letting people rest in a false sense of security.

from considering the dreadful fate that awaits them.[7] Suffering often proves to be an act of grace through which God readies our hearts for the great Day of Judgment that is to come. Those whose prosperous lives make them laugh at the idea of a day of reckoning will not have the last laugh. The apostle Paul warns us: *"The sins of some people are obvious, going before them into judgment, but for others, they show up later."*[8] Whatever God appears to overlook now, he will make obvious to all when his Judgment Day arrives.

So if you feel angry at the amount of suffering in the world then take comfort from Job's honest prayer. God is inviting you to tell him how you truly feel. If you feel so angry that you feel like questioning whether God is up to his job, then he invites you to tell him that too. Unless you are honest with the Lord in prayer, you will never grasp what comforted the English Puritan preacher Stephen Charnock in his own suffering:

> *Presume not upon God's patience. The exercise of it is not eternal... You know not how soon His anger may turn His patience aside, and step before it. It may be His sword is drawn out of the scabbard, His arrows may be settled in His bow, and perhaps there is but a little time before you may feel the edge of the one or the point of the other, and then there will be no more time for patience in God to us, or petition from us to Him.[9]*

---

[7] Job uses the Hebrew word *she'ol* in 24:19 to mean more than just *the grave*. He is echoing the words of Zophar in 11:8, recognizing that Judgment Day will admit some to heaven and damn others to hell.

[8] 1 Timothy 5:24 (*New English Translation*). This is why God's fiercest judgment is to stay his hand.

[9] Stephen Charnock in his *Discourses upon the Existence and Attributes of God* (1682).

Half-Truth (Job 25:1–6)

"How then can a mortal be righteous before God?
How can one born of woman be pure?"

After ordering his cannon to open fire on the British lines, Napoleon Bonaparte sent an urgent message to Marshal Grouchy, six miles away. He was to come quickly with his 33,000 men to help his master win the Battle of Waterloo. Fortunately for the British, Marshal Grouchy misread the second half of the message. Instead of *"La bataille est engagée"* (meaning *"The battle has begun"*), Marshal Grouchy misread it as *"La bataille est gagnée"* (*"The battle is won"*). Instead of marching to help his master, he celebrated victory until Napoleon had been driven from the battlefield. He would protest until the day he died that it was not his fault France lost the Battle of Waterloo, but he only kept protesting because so many Frenchmen were convinced that it was.[1]

Marshal Grouchy found out to his cost that half-truths are also half-lies. So do the three friends of Job. It's clear that some of what they say to Job is true from the fact that the apostle Paul uses the words of Eliphaz to back up one of his arguments in 1 Corinthians 3:19, but it's equally clear that much of what they say to Job is false from the fact that God rebukes them in 42:7: *"you have not spoken the truth about me."* Bildad's third speech is therefore more than just the last of their speeches in the book of Job. It is more than just the shortest chapter too. It is meant to serve as a reminder that half-truths are every bit as dangerous to our spiritual well-being as outright lies.

Bildad is aware of God's transcendence but unaware of

---

[1] See Paul O' Keefe's *Waterloo: The Aftermath* (2014).

God's immanence. In other words, he tells the truth about the greatness of God but downplays the nearness of God. He is quite right that the Lord possesses all dominion and awe. He is correct to point out that even the light of the moon and stars appears dark and impure alongside God's utter holiness. He is right to observe that the difference between a man and a maggot, both of them creatures, is far smaller than the gulf between a man and his Creator.[2] But Bildad is wrong to extrapolate from these truths that there will never be a righteous person born to a woman. He hasn't listened to Job's prophecies about the Redeemer who is coming into the world. Bildad is only half-right in what he says, so his conclusions are all-wrong.

Bildad is aware of human sin but unaware of the divine Saviour. His third speech is so much shorter than the other speeches because Job interrupts him in frustration, but we can already see where his speech is headed from these six opening verses. He is about to rebuke Job for being so confident of his own blamelessness that he feels he can rejoice about what God's Day of Judgment holds in store for the wicked. This is ironic, given Bildad's complete confidence in the correctness of his own formula, based on tradition:

A God who is just + A person who is suffering = Clear proof of sin

A God who is just + A person who isn't suffering = Clear proof of virtue

Bildad is aware of God but unaware of the Devil. He knows nothing of the demons that are watching the Lord in his heavenly council to decry the righteousness of his rule. We cannot blame him for his ignorance, but we need to be more aware than he is of our own relative ignorance about the spirit world. We are like the crowd that surrounded Jesus in Matthew 13, frustrated that the Lord seems slow to root out all of the suffering in the world. Jesus replied in his famous Parable of the Weeds that we have an enemy who has sown evil into our hearts. If God were to root out all sin and suffering today then he would destroy those

---

2 Isaiah 41:14 also points out that this is true.

he plans to save alongside those he plans to punish on his final Judgment Day. God's patience is therefore a mark of his mercy, but since Bildad is unaware of the spirit realm his half-truths lead him to a conclusion that is all-wrong.

Bildad is aware of God's judgment but unaware of God's patience. This is partly because he is running out of patience himself. He was rude to Job in his first two speeches, but he is even ruder here, calling Job a maggot and a worm. By only seeing half of what is happening, he rubs salt into Job's wounds when he ought to be consoling him with talk about God's mercy and his love. This is what provokes Job to interrupt him and to bring this third cycle of speeches to an end. Job is sitting in the dust covered in sores. He has been bereaved of his children and dispossessed of his wealth. He has been rejected by society and feels disconnected from the Lord. The last thing that he needs to be told is that his life means nothing to God! Bildad's third speech is a sobering lesson for anyone engaged in pastoral ministry. Half-truths can be even more hurtful than outright lies.

Bildad is aware that the Lord blesses those who love him, but he is unaware that he calls them to bear a cross too. We cannot blame him for not understanding that the Messiah would have to walk the death-and-resurrection road to redeem God's people, or that the Messiah would call his followers to walk that same road too: *"If anyone comes to me and does not hate father and mother, wife and children, brothers and sisters – yes, even their own life – such a person cannot be my disciple. And whoever does not carry their cross and follow me cannot be my disciple."*[3] We cannot blame Bildad for his ignorance, but we on the other side of Calvary must not be as ignorant as he is. We must recognize that his prosperity gospel is in fact no Gospel at all. It is a half-truth, a cross-less Christianity, which is every bit as fatally misleading as an outright lie.

Hudson Taylor, the British missionary who laid the

---

[3] Luke 14:26–27. See also Matthew 10:38 and 16:24–26, Mark 8:34–37 and 10:21, Luke 9:23–25, John 12:24–25 and 2 Timothy 3:12.

foundations for the massive move of God that swept through China at the end of the twentieth century, warns us that:

> *Fruit-bearing involves cross bearing "Except a corn of wheat fall into the ground and die, it abideth alone." We know how the Lord Jesus became fruitful – not by bearing His Cross merely, but by dying on it. Do we know much of fellowship with Him in this? There are not two Christs – an easy-going one for easy-going Christians, and a suffering, toiling one for exceptional believers. There is only one Christ. Are you willing to abide in Him, and thus to bear much fruit?*[4]

Eliphaz tells half-truths based on experience, Bildad tells half-truths based on tradition, and Zophar tells half-truths based on reason. All of their speeches show us that half-truths can be every bit as deadly to our hearts as outright lies.

---

[4] He said this to the conference of the China Inland Mission in May 1890. Quoted by Howard Taylor in *Hudson Taylor and the China Inland Mission* (1918).

Don't Miss the Obvious
(Job 26:1–4)

Then Job replied… "What great insight you have displayed!"

(Job 26:1, 3)

Sydney is proud to be one of the first cities in the world to usher in the New Year. Being so close to the International Date Line means that the city's New Year's Eve celebrations hit the news all around the world. To celebrate the start of 2019, the city spent £3.2 million on a colossal firework display over the harbour. There was just one tiny problem. At the end of the celebrations, having burned almost nine tons of fireworks, a miskeyed message was projected onto Sydney Harbour Bridge. Sydney celebrated the start of 2019 with a message broadcast all around the world: *"Happy New Year 2018!"*

Somebody in Sydney missed the obvious, and it made a massive difference, so let's make sure that we don't miss the obvious here. We have reached the end of all the speeches given by Job's three false friends, so have you spotted the two big things that ought to be obvious to us? I'll give you a clue about the first one:

Introduction:	Job's lament (3)
The first cycle of speeches:	Eliphaz (4–5) Job's reply to Eliphaz (6–7) Bildad (8) Job's reply to Bildad (9–10) Zophar (11) Job's reply to Zophar (12–14)
The second cycle of speeches:	Eliphaz (15) Job's reply to Eliphaz (16–17) Bildad (18) Job's reply to Bildad (19) Zophar (20) Job's reply to Zophar (21)
The third cycle of speeches:	Eliphaz (22) Job's reply to Eliphaz (23–24) Bildad (25) Job's reply to Bildad (26–27)

That's right. Zophar contributes to the first two cycles of speeches, but he doesn't get to deliver a third speech. Job gets so frustrated that he interrupts Bildad after only six verses and declares that he has had enough of hearing the same old answers. His friends' speeches are over. Job ended the first cycle of speeches with heavy sarcasm in 12:2, effectively exclaiming: *Wow! You are so wise that when you die I'm really worried that there won't be anyone as wise as you left in the world to help me!* Now he ends the third cycle of speeches with even heavier sarcasm. He effectively says to his friends: *Wow! What would I ever have done without you? How can I thank you enough for your breakthrough insights? What divine revelation did you receive to be able share such life-changing pearls of wisdom?*[1] Bear in mind that these three friends represent the very best insights that the

---

[1] Job is caustic, but his friends deserve it. The Hebrew word he uses for *spirit* in 26:4 is not *rûach*, which often refers to the Holy Spirit. It is *neshāmāh*, more often used to refer to the breath of mortal men and animals.

pagan ancient world had to offer. The world respected them, but Job tells them: *I've had enough of your human half-truths. From now on, I want some proper answers from the Lord.*

You may or may not have spotted the other obvious thing about the speeches that are delivered by Job's three false friends. It's not about what they say and do. It's about what they *don't* say and do. They speak for nine chapters and for 211 verses in total, but never once does any of the three friends offer to pray for Job. They speak about theology but never turn to God mid-speech, in the way that Job does, to ask him questions. They pontificate about Job's suffering but they never attempt to relieve it by partnering with him in tender-hearted prayer.[2] This may be obvious, but let's not miss it like a Sydney fireworks operator. It is one of the most important lessons that these speeches are meant to teach us.

This matters because one of the main reasons why the Lord lets us pass through periods of suffering is to draw us into fervent prayer. The eighteenth-century revivalist Jonathan Edwards observes that:

> *It is very apparent from the Word of God that he often tries the faith and patience of his people, when they are crying to him for some great and important mercy, by withholding the mercy sought for a season; and not only so, but at first he may cause an increase of dark appearances. And yet he, without fail, at last prospers those who continue urgently in prayer with all perseverance and "will not let him go except he blesses."*[3]

Jonathan Edwards argues that God often withholds his blessing from us in order to provoke us to pursue a deeper relationship with him, and the book of Job suggests that he is right.

This also matters because the speed with which we turn to

---

[2] In 1 Samuel 23:16, Jonathan strengthens David by helping him to pray. Don't miss the obvious, that Job's friends ought to have done the same.

[3] Jonathan Edwards in *A Call to United Extraordinary Prayer* (1747).

God in prayer reveals how deep our friendship truly runs with him. Are we like Job's three friends, quick to talk *about* God but slow to talk *to* God; or like Job himself, instinctively moving in and out of prayer? The nineteenth-century bishop J.C. Ryle was convinced that:

> *Of all the evidences of the real work of the Spirit, a habit of hearty private prayer is one of the most satisfactory that can be named. A man may preach from false motives. A man may write books, make fine speeches, and seem diligent in good works – and yet be a Judas Iscariot. But a man seldom goes into his closet and pours out his soul before God in secret, unless he is in earnest. The Lord Himself has set His stamp on* prayer *as the best proof of a true conversion.*[4]

So, let me ask you: Is prayer your first port of call or your last resort? Your answer matters deeply.

It matters because prayer is how God turns things around. It is how he links our earthly problems to the power of heaven. Trying to solve our problems without praying is like trying to row a boat on the beach: totally impossible. Praying to God makes the tide come in and lifts the boat off the beach, enabling us to row it anywhere with ease.[5]

So don't miss the obvious in these speeches. Pray. If you struggle to pray by yourself then get with others and pray together. There is only one thing that my children love more than jumping on their trampoline. It's jumping on their trampoline with me. I weigh more than them, so they have worked out that they can jump higher whenever I jump with them. What is true for trampolines is also true for prayer. Find some praying friends who don't just know how to talk *about* God, but who know how to talk *to* God.

---

[4] J.C. Ryle in *A Call to Prayer* (1840).

[5] In Luke 22:31–32, when Jesus warns Peter that he is about to go through a period of suffering, his solution is something far better than a pep talk or a coaching session. He tells Peter, *"I have prayed for you."*

Natural Conclusions
(Job 26:5–14)

"And these are but the outer fringe of his works; how faint the whisper we hear of him!"

(Job 26:14)

Very few people have examined God's creation as closely as Sir David Attenborough, the host of many of the BBC's best nature documentaries. However, his studies haven't given him a deep faith in God as the Creator. Quite the opposite. He complains that:

> *When Creationists talk about God creating every individual species as a separate act, they always instance hummingbirds, or orchids, sunflowers and beautiful things. But I tend to think instead of a parasitic worm that is boring through the eye of a boy sitting on the bank of a river in West Africa, that's going to make him blind. Are you telling me that the God you believe in, who you also say is an all-merciful God, who cares for each one of us individually – are you saying that God created this worm that can live in no other way than in an innocent child's eyeball? Because that doesn't seem to me to coincide with a God who's full of mercy.*[1]

Many Christians are afraid of such natural conclusions. A recent survey found that 38 per cent of people who believe in Jesus also believe that modern science does more harm than good.[2] That's

---

[1] Sir David Attenborough said this in an interview on BBC Radio Five on 2nd December 2005.

[2] Taken from the *British Social Attitudes* survey in 2019.

why I find it fascinating how Job responds to the foolish chatter of his friends. He isn't afraid of science. He enlists it as an ally in his refusal to accept simplistic answers to complex questions. Job appeals to God's world, and not just to God's Word, as proof that the Lord knows how to rule in righteousness. His reply to Bildad teaches us that we don't just need good answers to people's difficult questions about suffering. We also need good questions to challenge their easy answers.

Job brings Eliphaz, Bildad and Zophar's three cycles of speeches to an end by rebuking them for trotting out the same old answers to his suffering. Since the Hebrew language makes a clear distinction between *you* (*singular*) and *you* (*plural*), we can tell that he addresses chapter 26 to Bildad and chapter 27 to all three friends.[3] Job therefore starts by rebuking Bildad for merely looking back to the lessons of human tradition. He needs to look far further back in time to draw conclusions from the Lord's creation.

In verses 5–6, Job moves on from his sarcasm in verses 1–4. He urges Bildad to yield to some natural conclusions about the limitations of human knowledge. Job uses three key Hebrew words to point out that, while every human dies, God alone stands immortal. Most English translations take the word *repha'īm* to mean *the spirits of the departed*, although the translators of the Greek Septuagint saw it as a reference to the Rephaites, a race of giant-sized men also known as the Nephilim, who were largely wiped out by Noah's Flood.[4] Either way, Job's point is that even the greatest humans die in the end, while the Lord lives on forever. *She'ōl* means *the grave* or *hell*. *'Abaddōn*

---

[3] We can also tell this from the break that the narrator inserts between the two halves of Job's speech in 27:1. He inserts similar breaks between Elihu's four speeches (Job 32–37) and the Lord's two speeches (Job 38–41).

[4] The Septuagint reading makes more sense of Job's assertion that they lie dead *"beneath the waters"*. Noah's family evidently carried some Rephaite genes into the ark in their own bodies, because a few final Rephaites emerged from their gene pool after the Flood. See Genesis 6:4 and 14:5, and Deuteronomy 3:11.

means *destruction* or *hell*.[5] All three Hebrew words therefore proclaim the same natural conclusion. Mortal humans shouldn't pretend to understand the world as well as the immortal God.

In verses 7–8, Job steps up his rebuke of Bildad for merely looking back to human tradition. Does he understand how water, although heavier than air, hangs in the sky in clouds instead of falling to the ground? Does he understand how the earth remains stable in its orbit instead of plummeting through space like a giant meteor? If he does not know the answer to such basic questions about life on earth, then how dare he be so confident about his answer to the great question of human suffering? If God is so powerful that our natural conclusion is to blame him when things go wrong, then he is also powerful enough for us to trust him to know what he is doing in our suffering.[6]

I find Job's approach wonderfully refreshing. He doesn't fear science. He enlists it as a natural ally of the Gospel. He is like Sir Isaac Newton in his seminal scientific textbook, the *Principia*, when he concludes that *"This most beautiful System of the Sun, Planets and Comets, could only proceed from the counsel and dominion of an intelligent and powerful being."*[7] He is like the leading modern geneticist, Francis Collins, who concludes that *"The God of the Bible is also the God of the genome. He can be worshipped in the cathedral or in the laboratory. His creation is majestic, awesome, intricate, and beautiful."*[8]

In verses 9–13, Job reminds Bildad that chaos ruled over the world before God proclaimed *"Let there be light!"* in Genesis 1.[9]

---

[5] *'Abaddōn* is also used to describe *hell* in Job 28:22 and 31:12, Psalm 88:11 and Proverbs 15:11. Its sister word *'abaddōh* is used for *hell* in Proverbs 27:20.

[6] The apostle Paul states something similar, in Romans 1:18–20 and 8:28, that God's world echoes the truth of God's Word: *"we know that in all things God works for the good of those who love him"*.

[7] Sir Isaac Newton in Book III of his *Principia* (1687).

[8] Francis Collins in *The Language of God: A Scientist Presents Evidence for Belief* (2007).

[9] God's proclamation comes in Genesis 1:3. Before that, we are told that *"the earth was formless and empty"* and that *"darkness was over the surface of the deep"*.

When God spoke, he defeated Rahab, the demonic power behind that chaos, which also goes by the name of Leviathan.[10] We must not allow the fact that the Devil is still at his chaotic work in the world to blind us to the truth of Genesis 1:31: *"God saw all that he had made, and it was very good."* We mustn't be short-sighted, like Sir David Attenborough, and blame the fallenness of God's creation on its Creator. It was humans listening to the Devil who brought sin and suffering into the world, so we mustn't listen to the Devil ourselves and begin blaming God for problems of our own making. God is so great that he divides the bright sky from the murky sea on the horizon. He is so great that he can hide the light of the moon behind his clouds. He is so great that his earthquakes even make mountains tremble.[11] God's world echoes God's Word, that we can trust him in the midst of our suffering.

In verse 14, Job therefore urges Bildad to recognize that *"these are but the outer fringe of his works; how faint the whisper we hear of him!"* The greatest scientific discoveries reveal only the tip of the iceberg of God's wisdom. The greatest scientific papers contain only the whispered echo of God's greatness. The greatest scientific minds can only come to the same natural conclusion as Sir Isaac Newton:

> *I do not know what I appear to the world, but to myself I seem to have been only like a boy playing on the sea-shore, and diverting myself in now and then finding a*

---

[10] *Rahab* is also mentioned in 9:13 and means *Proud* or *Insolent* or *Arrogant*. It is another name for *Leviathan*, mentioned in 3:8, 7:12 and 41:1, and described literally in Hebrew in 26:13 as *"the fleeing snake"*. Both names refer to the Devil and his demons, who sought to keep the world in chaos before the Lord defeated them with the proclamation, *"Let there be light!"* See also Psalm 89:9–10 and Isaiah 51:9.

[11] Job is a poet before he is a scientist, referring to the mountains in 26:11 as the *"pillars of the heavens"*.

*smoother pebble or a prettier shell than ordinary, whilst
the great ocean of truth lay all undiscovered before me.*[12]

Job invites us to take a good look at creation and to find ourselves
similarly humbled. If this is but the echo of God's wisdom, *"Who
then can understand the thunder of his power?"* (verse 14).

---

[12] Quoted by Sir David Brewster in his *Memoirs of the Life, Writings, and Discoveries of Sir Isaac Newton* (1855).

Enough! (Job 27:1–23)

"Why then this meaningless talk?"

(Job 27:12)

You have now reached the end of Act One of the book of Job. Well done. It is by far the longest section of the book and by far the hardest-going. From this point onwards, we emerge into a brighter view. We are given clearer answers, first by Job and by another of his friends, and then ultimately by God himself. The basic structure of the book of Job is:

Chapters 1–2	Prologue: Job's Suffering
Chapters 3–27	Act One: The Same Old Answers
Chapters 28–37	Act Two: Some New Answers
Chapters 38–41	Act Three: God's Own Answers
Chapter 42	Epilogue: Job's Comfort

By this stage in the book of Job, most people feel more than ready to leave behind the three cycles of speeches between Eliphaz, Bildad, Zophar and Job. Don't feel ashamed if you do too. It is how we are meant to feel. Job feels even readier to move on than we do. In this final chapter of Act One, he effectively calls the curtain down by shouting: *Enough!* Job calls time on the simplistic speeches and the facile formulae of his three friends.[1]

---

[1] The narrator is doing more than reminding us who is speaking in 27:1. That verse divides a first speech directed to Bildad (*you, singular* in Hebrew) from a second speech directed to all three friends (*you, plural*).

In verses 2–6, Job declares that he has had enough of their trying to cajole him into confessing that he is the architect of all of his sufferings through his own sin. He insists that God alone is the author of his misery.[2] Since he is the Almighty, he could deliver his servant Job in a moment if he wanted. He has chosen not to do so, and Job refuses to reframe the problem any other way.[3] Job uses the same courtroom language that he used in his earlier speeches when he tells his three friends that he has had enough of their unfounded theories.[4] He is certain in his heart that he is blameless and righteous.[5] He will not accept that he deserves his misery, when he sees it entirely as an act of God.

In verses 7–12, Job declares that he has had enough of those he counts as his friends acting like enemies towards him. If Eliphaz, Bildad and Zophar are correct that the Lord always judges the wicked, then they had better watch out themselves! Anyone can see that Job is innocent, so their speeches are full of *"meaningless talk"*. They simply kick a good man while he is down. From now on Job will do the talking. From now on Job will do the teaching.[6] With the time they save on preparing speeches, they can prepare their souls to stand before the Lord. They can repent of acting as Job's enemies and adversaries,

---

[2] Job even uses the Hebrew word *rûach* in 27:3, insisting that the breath in his nostrils is the *Spirit of God*.

[3] Having been commended in 1:22, Job comes perilously close to accusing the Lord of wrongdoing in 27:2. These verses lead God to rebuke him in 40:8 for *condemning me to justify yourself*, along with 7:20–21, 9:21–24 and 19:6.

[4] In 27:2, Job accuses God of denying him *mishpāt* meaning *judgment* or *justice*. In 27:5, he refuses to *tsādaq* his friends – that is, *to vindicate* or *justify* or *admit the rightness* of what they say. In 27:6, he refuses to let go of his *tsedāqāh* – his own sense of *righteousness* or of *innocence* or of *being justified* by the Lord.

[5] The Hebrew word *lēbāb*, which is translated *conscience* in 27:6, is simply the normal Hebrew word for *heart*. The word used for *integrity* in 27:5 is *tūmmāh*, the same word that is used for Job's integrity in 2:3 and 2:9.

[6] The Hebrew word that Job uses for *teaching* his friends about the power of God in 27:11 is *yārāh*, the root of the noun *tôrāh*, which means *instruction* and which would become the Jewish name for the *Law of Moses*.

when they ought to have brought comfort to their innocent friend.

In verses 13–23, Job declares that he has had enough of human wisdom altogether.[7] As we have noted, Eliphaz, Bildad and Zophar represent the very best answers that the wise men of the ancient world had to offer in response to the question: *Why does God allow suffering?* Job therefore points out that they are all at least agreed on one thing – that God has prepared a Day of Judgment for the wicked. Those who take many wives will not outwit the Almighty on that day. They will merely multiply the number of their widows.[8] Those who father many children will not preserve their inheritance on that day. They will merely increase the number of their family funerals. Those who store up silver and fine clothes in their palaces will not protect themselves from God's judgment.[9] They will simply stockpile blessings to be enjoyed by those who put their trust in the Lord.[10]

So enough of these three cycles of speeches from Job's three false friends. Enough of their meaningless talk and their simplistic formulae. Enough of human speculation. Enough of pontificating about God in our pride.[11] Enough of attributing Job's suffering to anybody but the Lord, and enough of viewing suffering as a reason to reject the Lord.

158

---

[7] Job calls God *Shaddai* – the *Almighty* – four times in this chapter. That's over 8 per cent of all the times God is called by that name in the Bible. Job has had enough of human wisdom and now wants answers from the Lord.

[8] The Hebrew text of 27:15 says that *his* widows will not weep. Polygamy was normal practice for the wealthy magnates of the ancient world.

[9] Job is a poet, comparing the mighty mansions in which a rich man puts his trust to a moth's fragile cocoon and to the shack a watchman quickly builds out of old pieces of wood to hide from the sun.

[10] Job 27:16–17 is echoed by Proverbs 13:22 and 28:8, and by Ecclesiastes 2:26. It is also echoed by the words of Jesus in Luke 12:20, as part of his Parable of the Rich Fool.

[11] Job commends humility in 27:19. If God is powerful enough to turn a prisoner into prime minister in a single night (Genesis 41:14 and 39–45) then he is also powerful enough to do the reverse in a single night too (Esther 5:9–7:10, and Daniel 4:29–33 and 5:30–31).

Enough of Act One of the book of Job. We have heard the same old answers too many times. We need to hear new answers in Acts Two and Three.

It is time for the curtain to fall on the first act of the drama and for the interval to begin.

Act Two – Job 28–37:

Some New Answers

Interval (Job 28:1–28)

"The fear of the Lord – that is wisdom, and to shun evil is understanding."

(Job 28:28)

Act Two of the book of Job begins with an interval. Instead of rushing into further speeches, we are invited to take a step back and to look at Job's predicament with fresh eyes. If we are looking for some new answers, then we need to find a fresh perspective.

Although it's possible that the speaker in chapter 28 is Job, there are two big clues that the writer who narrated the prologue in chapters 1-2 and who will narrate the epilogue in chapter 42 also delivers this speech as a halftime team talk that prepares us for new insights in the second half of the book of Job. For a start, the tone is different. It is reflective, not combative. It makes no specific reference to Job's troubles, but instead speaks in much more general terms about the human search for wisdom. What is more, the great crescendo of this chapter is a verse that refers to the Lord as *Adōnāi*, one of the main Hebrew words for the Lord, which is never used anywhere else in the book of Job other than here. These two factors convince me that chapter 28 is not the words of Job, but a halftime interval during which the writer prepares us for some new answers in Act Two of the drama. He says:

28:1–11	Search for wisdom – it is glorious!
28:12–19	Confess that wisdom can't be found
28:20–28	But don't give up – true wisdom is found in the Lord!

In verses 1–11, the writer seems to go off at a tangent by asking us to consider the mining industry. It isn't initially clear why he starts talking about men digging for gold, silver, iron, copper and precious stones, until we spot that the Hebrew word he uses in verse 11 for *hidden thing* is the same word that Zophar used in 11:6 to extol the glories of the uniquely human quest to learn *secrets of wisdom* from the Lord.[1] The writer likens that quest here to mining the earth for treasures in order to warn us not to be satisfied with superficial answers to our questions. He wants us to dig deeper, taking part in the great human endeavour that is described in Proverbs 25:2: *"It is the glory of God to conceal a matter; to search out a matter is the glory of kings."* A hawk has far better eyesight than we do, but it never gets to see what human miners see. A lion is a far better hunter than we are, but it never gets to pounce on the jewels that are hidden beneath the ground. The hunt for answers to the meaning of the universe is therefore a uniquely human pursuit. It may be difficult and dangerous and lonely, but it is worth our while.[2]

In verses 12–19, the writer laments that he is sending us on a wild goose chase. The wisdom of God cannot be grasped by our mortal human minds. There is no mine beneath the earth or at the bottom of the sea where miners can harvest insight into the things of God. They come back instead with fine gold and silver, with precious stones and gemstones, or with coral – very useful for purchasing the things of this world, but totally useless when it comes to obtaining the heavenly wisdom that belongs to God alone.[3]

---

[1] This link is deliberate, since the only other place in the Bible where the word *ta'alŭmmāh* is used is in Psalm 44:21. It appears in its plural form in 11:6 and in its singular form here, referring to *Wisdom* itself.

[2] Think about it. There is no reason why God had to hide precious metals and jewels underground. He forces us to work hard to lay hold of them in order to create a picture that urges us on to do whatever it takes to lay hold of true spiritual treasure. See Matthew 13:44–46, Luke 13:24 and 2 Peter 1:3–8.

[3] The writer echoes 22:24 by treating the gold of *Ophir* – probably modern-day Yemen or Oman – as the finest gold in the world (1 Kings 9:28 and 10:11, Psalm

Nevertheless, in verses 20–28, the writer urges us to press on in our quest. Wisdom may be hidden from the eyes of every living thing on earth and from those who have passed on into the realm of the dead.[4] But God knows the way to wisdom.[5] It was by wisdom that he created the world, and he still holds the key to that same wisdom now.[6] That leads towards the great crescendo of this halftime team talk. The final verse of this chapter stands out because it isn't poetry, but prose. It doesn't follow the rhythm used throughout the speeches because it contains truth that transcends all the speeches. The final verse also stands out because it is the only verse in the book that refers to the Lord as *Adōnāi*. The writer warns us that we will never discover wisdom if we seek it as a stand-alone commodity, but that we surely succeed if we seek to find it in a relationship with our Creator. *"The fear of the Lord – that is wisdom, and to shun evil is understanding."*

This is one of the biggest themes of the entire Bible. Adam and Eve sin by seeking to possess wisdom independently from God through eating from the Tree of the Knowledge of Good and Evil.[7] King Solomon becomes wise by renouncing their folly, asking the Lord in 1 Kings 3:9 to give him, literally, *"a hearing heart"* so that he can learn true wisdom through friendship with the Lord. That's not to say that human reason

---

45:9 and Isaiah 13:12). He also treats the topaz mined in *Cush* – on the border between modern-day Egypt and Sudan – as the finest topaz in the world.

[4] We have already noted that *'abaddōn* means *hell* in Job 26:6, 28:22 and 31:12, Psalm 88:11 and Proverbs 15:11.

[5] The statement in 28:23, backed up by an appeal to what the forces of nature teach us about our Creator, serves as a precursor to chapters 38–41, where God answers our questions about suffering in a similar way.

[6] The Ancient Greeks referred to this divine Wisdom, which overcame Chaos at the dawn of time and which still holds the universe together, as the *Logos*, or the *Word*. Heraclitus taught that *"all things come to be in accordance with the Logos"* (fragment DK 22B1). That's why John heralds Jesus as the true *Logos* in John 1:1–5.

[7] The Lord had enabled them to know right from wrong by listening to his voice in their consciences (Romans 2:14–15), but they were tempted by the Devil to seek such knowledge on their own.

is unhelpful. Quite the contrary. Common sense should have taught Eve to believe the words of God above those of a talking snake in the Garden of Eden! The Spanish artist Francisco Goya was right to argue that *"The sleep of reason produces monsters."*[8] Solomon simply points out that reliance on man-made wisdom produces many monsters more.[9]

Solomon unpacks this further when he echoes Job 28:28 in Proverbs 3:19 and 8:1–9:12. He tells us that Wisdom is a person we can know: *"By wisdom the Lord laid the earth's foundations"* and *"The fear of the Lord is the beginning of wisdom, and knowledge of the Holy One is understanding."*[10] The apostle Paul unpacks this further in New Testament language when he tells us in 1 Corinthians 1:24 and 30 that Jesus is *"the wisdom of God"*, and when he explains in Colossians 2:2–3 that this makes Jesus the hidden thing that is described in Job 28:11, since in Jesus *"are hidden all the treasures of wisdom and knowledge."*

Do you see, then, why the writer calls an interval before diving into the second half of the book of Job? If we want to find new answers to our questions about why God allows suffering, then we need to take a fresh perspective on the nature of true wisdom. We will never find new answers if we continue to treat wisdom as a stand-alone commodity. We will only find them if we fall face down before God and allow human investigation to give way to divine revelation. So let's make the most of this interval to accept the limitations of our human reason. Let's ask God to answer our deepest questions

[8] Goya etched this proverb on the forty-third of his eighty prints known as *Los Caprichos* (1799).

[9] Solomon warns against the limits of human wisdom in Proverbs 14:12 and 16:25. He also describes God's wisdom as the true *Tree of Life* in Proverbs 3:18, as opposed to the Tree of the Knowledge of Good and Evil.

[10] Proverbs 3:19 and 9:10, In addition to these verses, we find echoes of Job 28:28 in Proverbs 1:7, 3:7 and 8:13, and in Psalm 111:10. In many ways, this verse summarizes the second half of the book of Job. It is the first time that God has spoken since Job 1–2, and the first time that he has spoken directly to humans. The new answers that we seek are not to be found in philosophy or in human speculation, but in a personal relationship with the Lord.

about suffering in the person of Jesus, who alone is the true Wisdom of God.[11]

---

[11] Jesus has returned to heaven, but he gives us his Spirit of Wisdom to teach and to guide us into the Wisdom that only comes through knowing God. See Deuteronomy 34:9, Isaiah 11:2 and Ephesians 1:17.

The Righteous One
(Job 29:1–25)

*"I put on righteousness as my clothing; justice was
my robe and my turban."*

(Job 29:14)

The interval is over. Act Two of the book of Job has begun. But
still the final words of the writer's halftime team talk hang in
the air. The message of the interval was that we can only find
true wisdom if we develop a close friendship with the Lord and
that the proof that we have such a relationship is not found in
what we say. It is found in whether or not we fear the Lord – that
is, in whether or not we take him seriously – and in whether
or not our lives proclaim that we hate wickedness and love
righteousness.[1]

In verses 1–6, Job claims that he epitomizes what we were
taught during the interval.[2] All of the wisdom he possesses
stems from his relationship with the Lord. Back in the days of
his prosperity, he walked in the light of God's Word and was
blessed with *"God's intimate friendship"* (verse 4).[3] The Hebrew
word he uses in verse 4 is *sôd*, the very same word that Eliphaz
used to ask him mockingly in 15:8, *Do you listen in on God's
secret conversations?* Job said nothing at the time, but now he

---

[1] Fearing the Lord means trembling at his Word (Isaiah 66:2) and giving sin the
cold shoulder (Exodus 20:20). In this sense, fearing God lies at the heart of our
relationship with him (Exodus 18:21 and Acts 9:31).

[2] If Job 28 is spoken by the narrator, then 29:1 is meant to indicate that Job is
back. Act Two has begun.

[3] Job has lost everything yet it appears that the blessing he misses most is his
deep friendship with the Lord. Can we honestly say that we prize the richness
of our prayer life more than any of our other riches?

answers: Yes, that's exactly what I did! If anybody ever learned true wisdom from friendship with God, then it was Job.[4]

In verses 7–17, Job claims that his close friendship with God was obvious from the righteous manner in which he lived. Many people claim to fear the Lord but disprove it by disobeying his clear commands to them in Scripture, but not Job. When he sat down with the other elders in the gateway of his city, everybody recognized him as a man of integrity.[5] He was respected by both young and old. He was honoured by both poor and rich. He was praised, not just by the needy widows and orphans and beggars of his city, but also by the wealthy noblemen.[6] The only people who didn't praise him were the wicked scoundrels that he hauled before the law courts, so Job isn't exaggerating when he claims that *"I put on righteousness as my clothing; justice was my robe and my turban"* (verse 14).[7] If anybody in the ancient world could claim to be righteous, it was Job.

In verses 18–25, Job claims that he has not departed from this path of righteousness. He expected that his close friendship with God and his complete obedience to God's Word would ensure continued blessing right up until the day he died. He expected people to keep on listening expectantly to his words of wisdom, for nobody else personified the writer's halftime team talk as well as him. *"The fear of the Lord – that is wisdom, and to shun evil is understanding"* (28:28). Job expected the people of his city to continue looking to him as their leader. He expected them to keep on longing to see his smile and hear his words of comfort. He never imagined that his words of wisdom would

---

[4] Job is a poet. Cream oozing from his every footstep and olive oil gushing out of rocky places for him are both vivid metaphors for how easily his business turned a profit in the good old days with God.

[5] The elders of an ancient city would sit down to conduct their discussions together in the public square at the gateway in and out of their city. See Genesis 19:1, Deuteronomy 21:19, Ruth 4:1–2 and Amos 5:10.

[6] This is what makes Job's sufferings all the harder for him to bear, since even little children have now taken to despising and taunting him (19:18 and 30:1).

[7] I love the authenticity of the book of Job. The great men of the ancient Middle East dressed in robes and turbans, so that is precisely the get-up which Job describes here. See Ezekiel 23:14–15 and Daniel 3:21.

be rejected or that he would find himself being lectured to, not listened to, by sinners.

Job is not bragging in this chapter. He is introducing us to some new answers to our question: *Why does God allow suffering?* The structure of Act Two of the book of Job is:

29:1–25	Job's new answer #1: The Righteous One
30:1–31	Job's new answer #2: The Suffering Servant
31:1–40	Job's new answer #3: The Curse-Bearer
32:1–33:33	Elihu's new answer #1: God Knows What He is Doing…
34:1–37	Elihu's new answer #2: … and What You are Doing
35:1–16	Elihu's new answer #3: God Doesn't Need You…
36:1–37:24	Elihu's new answer #4: … but You Need God

Therefore, far from bragging here, Job is prophesying. His words are meant to be read in three different ways. He is talking about himself, about Jesus, and about you and me.

First, Job is presenting himself as the righteous one, the fulfilment of all that the writer's halftime team talk encouraged us to be. Job uses the words *I* and *me* and *my* fifty times in these twenty-five verses in order to fix our gaze on himself because he believes that his own life can teach us what wisdom looks like day-to-day. He isn't suffering as a sinner, but as the righteous one.

Second, Job is prophesying in this chapter about the heavenly Redeemer that he spoke of in his speeches in Act One. The truth is, Job shared some of the blind spots of his culture. The most blatant example is that we are told he owned *slaves* in chapter 1.[8] Job was righteous among the people of the ancient world, but not before God's courtroom. He could not complain about his sufferings, because he was not the real Righteous One.

---

[8] The servants who tend Job's flocks and herds are listed among his possessions in 1:3.

Jesus alone would walk in true unbroken fellowship with his Father. Jesus alone would truly take his nation by storm, the crowds hanging on the wisdom of his every word.[9] Jesus alone would truly make the widow's heart sing. Jesus alone would truly save the blind and the lame and the needy and the dying. Jesus alone would be hailed by God's heavenly courtroom as the truly Righteous One.[10] Jesus alone is the true and better Job.

Third, Job is prophesying about you and me, as followers of Jesus. It isn't enough for us to say that we believe in him. We need to take the words of 28:28 to heart and prove the reality of our belief by fearing Jesus and by doing what he says.[11] The apostle Paul picks up on 29:14 when he commands us in Romans 13:14 to *"clothe yourselves with the Lord Jesus Christ, and do not think about how to gratify the desires of the flesh."*[12] If a relationship with Jesus is the only way to know God's wisdom, then we ought to dig down deeper into our friendship with Jesus than the greediest gold digger ever delved into his mine.

This chapter is challenging when we see it as a description of Job's lifestyle – enjoying God's company and then becoming God's agent of righteousness throughout his city. But this chapter is even more challenging when we grasp that it is also a description of Jesus, the true Righteous One, and of anybody who claims that they follow him.

I don't know about you, but I need to take a break now to get changed. There's some righteous clothing that God has given me, and I think it's time for me to put it on.

---

[9] Compare 29:4 with John 5:19–20, 12:49–50 and 14:10–11. Compare 29:21–23 with Luke 19:47–48.

[10] Compare 29:14 with Isaiah 59:17, with Acts 3:14, 7:52 and 22:14, and with 1 John 2:1. The Hebrew words *tsedeq* and *mishpāt* in 29:14 meaning *righteousness* and *justice*, are both courtroom terms.

[11] Jesus states this explicitly in Matthew 10:37–38, and in John 14:15, 14:21–24 and 15:14.

[12] We are to wear the righteousness of Jesus, both as our imputed righteousness before God (justification) and as our imparted righteousness before people (sanctification). See Isaiah 61:10, Zechariah 3:3–5, Psalm 132:9, Ephesians 4:21–24 and 6:14, 1 Thessalonians 5:8 and Revelation 19:7–8.

Looking for Trouble
(Job 29:16)

"I searched out the cause of him whom I did not know."

(Job 29:16, *English Standard Version*)

In the classic movie *Coming to America*, Eddie Murphy plays Prince Akeem, heir to the throne of a wealthy African nation.[1] Akeem is so fed up with women wanting to marry him for the sake of becoming queen that he travels to New York City in disguise and begins working as a waiter in a fast-food restaurant. He is determined to marry somebody who loves him for his own sake, not just for the wealth and status he can offer them. When the beautiful Lisa falls in love with him, in spite of his apparent poverty, he knows her love is genuine and that he has finally found a worthy queen.

Coming to America is just a movie, but the book of Job reminds us that it is also how God often acts towards us. He tests our hearts to see whether our love for him is genuine by coming to us in disguise, hidden in the faces of the poor and needy. Do we worship him for his own sake or in the hope of getting something from him? Job 29 teaches us that God answers that question by testing our hearts through coming to us in the poor.

Job's description of his righteous lifestyle begins with his devotional life with God. There are no surprises there, since reading Scripture and praying throughout the day are vital aspects of what it means for us to be children of God. But don't miss the fact that this only occupies five of the twenty-five verses in this chapter. Job says that the true test of our righteousness

---

[1] *Coming to America* (Paramount Pictures, 1988).

is not what we say to God on our knees, but what we do after we get up from our knees and head into town. There is nothing theoretical about the righteousness that Job describes in this chapter. It is exceedingly practical. He says that we are only as righteous as the manner in which we treat the lost, the least and the lonely who can offer us nothing in return. Jesus echoes this when he teaches in Matthew 22:35–40 that the true test of how much we love the God we can't see is how well we treat the neighbours all around us that we can see.[2]

Job is the first of five books of Wisdom Literature in the Old Testament, and this same theme continues throughout Psalms, Proverbs, Ecclesiastes and Song of Songs too. Proverbs 14:31 warns us that *"Whoever oppresses the poor shows contempt for their Maker, but whoever is kind to the needy honours God."* Proverbs 19:17 assures us that *"Whoever is kind to the poor lends to the Lord, and he will reward them for what they have done."* The book of James is sometimes called "the Proverbs of the New Testament" and it also echoes this key theme of all biblical Wisdom Literature. James 1:27 insists that *"Religion that God our Father accepts as pure and faultless is this: to look after orphans and widows in their distress."*[3] So we mustn't miss how much of Job's description of his righteous lifestyle revolves around how much he helped the poor.

Job didn't just help the people who knocked on his door. He went down to the public square. He became one of the elders who sat in the gateway of his city. He deliberately positioned himself in a place where he would hear *"the poor who cried for help"* and where he would be visible to *"the fatherless who had none to assist them"* (verse 12). That's what Proverbs 14:22 has in mind when it encourages us to plan our acts of righteousness

---

[2] Jesus insists that the command to *"love your neighbour as yourself"* is like the command to *"love the Lord your God"*. See also Matthew 25:40 and 45, and John 21:15–17. God's command to help the poor lies at the heart of the Law of Moses. See Leviticus 19:9–10 and 25:1–55, and Deuteronomy 14:28–29, 15:7–11 and 24:17–22.

[3] See also Proverbs 21:13, 22:9, 22:22–23, 28:27 and 29:7, and James 2:14–17 and 5:1–6.

just as diligently as wicked people plan their evil deeds. It's also why Proverbs 24:11–12 warns that ignorance of other people's poverty does not make us innocent. It isn't enough for us to deal with need as and when we chance upon it. We need to go looking for trouble.

Job explains in verse 16 that this is precisely what he did. In some English translations Job says, *"I took up the case of the stranger"*, but a more accurate translation of his words in Hebrew is *"I searched out any cause that I didn't know about."* Much of the need around us is hidden away behind closed doors, so Job says he acted like an investigative reporter, sniffing out trouble in order to confront it proactively.[4] There is a great deal of difference between doing good whenever the opportunity arises and seeking out hidden opportunities to do good everywhere. Job therefore calls us to do more than simply preach about the Kingdom of God. He also calls us to practise it by going out looking for trouble, promoting justice as a key sign to people that the Kingdom of God has come.[5]

Righteousness is not just about avoiding sins of commission (doing the things we know are wrong), but about avoiding sins of omission (neglecting to do the things we know are right). Proverbs 18:9 therefore urges us to follow Job's diligent example: *"One who is slack in his work is brother to one who destroys."* So does James 4:17 when it warns us that *"If anyone, then, knows the good they ought to do and doesn't do it, it is sin for them."*[6]

So let's make a plan to help those in need. Let's go out looking for trouble, just as Job did. Let's not be like the

---

[4] Job also appears to be saying in 29:17 that, whenever the wicked won a case and the other city elders simply moved on, he fought on tenaciously to reverse the ruling on appeal and to break the power of the wicked so that they could never push such an injustice through the law courts again.

[5] Psalm 33:5, Micah 6:8, Matthew 11:1–6, Luke 4:14–21, Acts 4:32–37, Romans 14:17 and 1 Corinthians 4:20.

[6] Confucius told his followers, *"Do not do to others what you would not want them to do to you"* (*Analects*, 15.24). But Jesus calls his followers to do something far greater: *"Do to others what you would have them do to you"* (Matthew 7:12 and Luke 6:31).

Christians that Basil of Caesarea was forced to confront in one of his sermons during the great famine of 368 AD:

> When someone steals a man's clothes, we call him a thief, so shouldn't we give the same name to one who could clothe the naked and does not? The bread in your cupboard belongs to the hungry, the coat in your wardrobe belongs to the naked, the shoes you let rot belong to the barefoot, the money in your vaults belongs to the poor. You do wrong to all those you could help but do not.[7]

Come on. Let's go looking for trouble.

William Booth, the founder of The Salvation Army, came home late one night from visiting a relative in hospital. It was the first time he had seen what happened on the streets of Victorian London after everybody had gone to bed. It was the middle of the night, but he banged on the door of one of his relatives and hauled him out of bed. The relative was surprised by his strong reaction to the sight of so many prostitutes and homeless street sleepers. He asked him, *"Why, did you not know?"* William Booth was even more surprised. He shot back, *"You mean you knew and didn't do anything?"*[8]

William Booth devoted the rest of his life to helping the poor, not just in London, but all around the world. He launched The Salvation Army with a war cry that echoed Job's description in these verses of what righteousness really looks like on the ground: *"What are you going to do? ... The great test of character is **doing**. God, the Church and the world all estimate men not according to their sayings, feelings or desiring, but according to their doings."*

---

[7] Basil preached this in his sermon *On the Rich Fool*, taken from Luke 12:13–21.

[8] Both of the quotations in this chapter are taken from Roy Hattersley's excellent biography entitled *Blood and Fire: William and Catherine Booth and Their Salvation Army* (1999).

The Suffering Servant
(Job 30:1–31)

"I cry out to you, God, but you do not answer... You turn on me ruthlessly..."

(Job 30:20–21)

In the novel, *Captain Corelli's Mandolin*, the Italian captain reflects on what he has learned about God through the horrors of World War Two. *"After this, it doesn't make any sense. If you were God, would you allow all this? ... Tell God when you see him that I want to punch him in the nose."*[1] That's pretty much how Job feels about God in this chapter too.

In verses 1–15, Job complains that God ought to honour righteous people like him. Instead, people whose fathers were not worthy to be counted among the lowest of Job's servants back in the good old days no longer even bother to pretend that they respect him.[2] They spit freely in his face. They use his name to insult one another and they sing mocking songs to taunt him. Job complains that this ought not to happen in a well-run world. He feels like Captain Corelli's friend, who prays angrily, *"Is it any wonder that I lost my faith? What are you doing up there, you idle God? ... Do you think I'm stupid? Do you think I have no eyes?"*

In verses 16–31, Job complains that this has not happened in spite of God, but because God has set himself up as Job's enemy. God is the one who has broken the bowstring of Job's

175

---

[1] Louis de Bernières in his book *Captain Corelli's Mandolin* (1994).

[2] Old age was honoured in the ancient world (15:10 and 32:4–9). Job therefore finds it particularly hurtful that his mockers are younger than he is. A literal translation of 30:12 is *"At my right hand rise up the youth!"*

life.[3] God is the one who has taken hold of his clothing and who is using it to strangle him.[4] God is the one who has thrown him down into the mud. God is the one who has failed to answer Job's prayer. God is the one who sees him yet does nothing to deliver him. In short, God is the one who has failed to treat Job as righteously as Job has treated the poor and needy of his city. Like Captain Corelli, Job complains that his sufferings seem to prove that God looks very little like the righteous ruler of the world.

Job sounds even more frustrated here than in his earlier speeches, but this has been the essence of his complaint all along. What kind of God would fail to reward the righteous? What kind of God would treat so cruelly those whose actions prove they love him?[5] What kind of God would kick a man when he is down, all the way down to the grave?[6] What kind of God would weep less for his creatures in their suffering than they weep for one another? What kind of God would give them false hope, only to dash it again and again? What kind of God would stand by when a good man's skin is so disfigured by disease that he has long forgotten how to sing anything other than a funeral song?

Job's words remind me of Ben Affleck's character's angry rant in the movie *Changing Lanes*: *"It feels like God is watching us, like he's peering down on us. Sometimes God likes to watch a love story. Sometimes he prefers a football game. So he switches*

---

[3] The Hebrew text of 30:11 can either be taken to mean that God has unstrung Job's bow (contrasting with his confidence in 29:20) or that God has loosed his own bowstring at Job (echoing 6:4, 7:20 and 16:12–14).

[4] The Hebrew text of 30:18 is not saying that God has become like Job's clothing, but that he has struck Job with such force that his clothes are torn and twisted and starting to choke him.

[5] The Hebrew word 'akzār in 30:21 means *cruel*, and not just *ruthless*. The Hebrew word sātam in 30:21 means *to hate*, and not just *to attack*. Job is therefore making a strong accusation against the Lord's behaviour.

[6] Job and his friends have already grasped that the dead go to two places after God judges them – either to heaven or to hell (11:8, 13:15–16, 14:12–17, 19:25–27 and 24:18–24). The fact that Job now talks so gloomily about *"the place appointed for all the living"* is an indicator of how frustrated he now feels.

channels. Sometimes God likes to watch a war movie, so he puts two guys in the ring together just to watch them bleed!"[7]

But we are no longer in Act One of the book of Job. This chapter can't simply be trotting out the same old answers that we have already found lead us nowhere. Job offers us two big hints in this chapter that he is beginning to point us towards some new answers.

First, Job accuses the Lord in verse 21 of attacking him *"with the might of your hand"*. That's meant to alert us to the fact that there must be an error in Job's equation, because the narrator has already told us unequivocally that the hand that struck Job was the hand of Satan, not the hand of the Lord. In 1:11–12, when Satan asked God to stretch out his hand against Job, he replied: *No. You stretch out your hand.* In 2:5–6, when Satan asked God again to stretch out his hand against Job, he gave the same reply: *No. You stretch out your hand.*[8] When we suffer, the Devil tries to play the same trick on us that he tried on Jesus in Luke 22:64. He wants to dupe us into thinking that the Lord's hand is attacking us.[9] But the shocking language of this chapter is meant to wake us up to what the writer has already taught us. It is the hand of Satan that attacks us, never the hand of the Lord.

Second, there are clues throughout this chapter that the Lord is going to allow Satan to attack him, instead of us, in order to deliver us from a mess of our own making. The truth is, Captain Corelli deserves some of the suffering that befalls him, since he is part of an invading fascist army. Ben Affleck's character deserves some of the suffering that befalls him, since it all stems from his shameful treatment of Samuel L. Jackson's character early on in the movie. We deserve some of the suffering that befalls us too, since we all play a part in the sin

---

[7] This is the gist of Ben Affleck's character's rant in a confession box in the director's cut of *Changing Lanes*, Paramount Pictures (2002).

[8] This is obscured in some English Bibles that translate the Hebrew word for *hand* as *power*, but it is vital.

[9] Job falls for this trick, not just here, but also in 6:4, 7:20, 9:21–24, 13:26, 16:7–14 and 19:21.

that has given the Devil legitimate authority to unleash his evil plans upon our world. But Jesus became a human to go to the heart of that human problem. He became the Suffering Servant who is prefigured by the sufferings of Job. He was mocked for us (verse 9). He was spat on for us (verse 10). He was surrounded by his enemies and nailed through his feet (verse 12). He was laid in the dust of death (verses 19 and 23). God's hands were pierced with nails to undo Satan's authority to lay his hands on us.[10]

Jesus is the Righteous One, yet he became the Suffering Servant to show us that God knows what he is doing when good people suffer. He became the Suffering Servant to show us that God can turn even our darkest days around for good. He became the Suffering Servant so that one day he will return to recreate the universe as it was always meant to be before Satan spoiled it, wiping every tear from our eyes.[11] Watchman Nee, who spent the final two decades of his life in a labour camp for daring to preach Jesus throughout communist China, found great solace in this. He declared that *"God will answer all our questions in one way and one way only, namely, by showing us more of his Son."*[12]

---

[10] Matthew 26:67–68 and 27:27–31, 35, 39–44 and 46.

[11] Revelation 21:1–5. We are told why that day is so long in coming in Matthew 13:24–30 and 2 Peter 3:3–9.

[12] Watchman Nee in *The Normal Christian Life* (1957).

The Curse-Bearer
(Job 31:1–40)

"If I have raised my hand against the fatherless...
then let my arm fall from the shoulder..."

(Job 31:21–22)

One of my favourite characters in the novel *Animal Farm* is a grumpy old donkey named Benjamin. George Orwell tells us that:

> *Benjamin was the oldest animal on the farm, and the worst tempered. He seldom talked, and when he did it was usually to make some cynical remark – for instance he would say that God had given him a tail to keep the flies off, but that he would sooner have had no tail and no flies.*[1]

That's how Job feels about some of the answers he has received so far to the problem of his suffering. It is one thing to talk about a Suffering Servant in the future, but that doesn't explain why *he* is suffering now. He is so frustrated in his longing for new answers that he starts calling down curses on himself.

In verses 1–12, Job curses himself if he has ever looked lustfully at a girl. These twelve verses are such a fantastic exhortation to sexual purity that we will spend a separate chapter looking at them in more detail. For now, let's simply note the way his total confidence that he is sinless in this area makes him like Benjamin the donkey, too slow-witted to spot that God created flies because they play a major part in the

---

[1] George Orwell in *Animal Farm* (1945).

ecosystem from which he derives his food. Job fails to grasp the gulf between God's holiness and his own, reasoning that, since he lives in a society where rich men take many wives, his monogamy is enough to make him righteous in this respect. But while it is remarkable that Job took only one wife (verse 10) and remained faithful towards her despite her sharp tongue towards him (2:9–10), it is a huge leap from comparing ourselves with our neighbours to declaring ourselves totally sinless before the Lord. We are meant to wince as Job calls down curses on his farmlands and on his marriage bed if God doesn't find him squeaky clean in terms of sexual purity.[3] He is drafting his own death warrant.

In verses 16–23, Job curses himself if he has ever failed to help a neighbour in distress. If he is not as righteous as he claimed in chapter 29, he urges God to keep him languishing forever in the misery that he lamented in chapter 30. If there is any servant in his household who bears an unheard grievance against him, Job urges the Lord to deny him justice too. If he has failed to help a single pauper or widow or orphan in the land of Uz, then he urges the Lord to ignore him too.[4] If he has raised his hand against one of them, then he asks the Lord to snap his arm off at the shoulder. We are meant to find these curses shocking, because Job doesn't grasp what he is saying. The Hebrew words 'ebed and 'amah in verse 13 can be translated manservant and maidservant, but they are normally translated slave and slave girl. Job is so unaware of how far his culture falls short of God's righteousness that he boasts of treating his slaves fairly, never

---

[2] Genesis 1:26–28 and 2:18–25 teach us that God made humans male and female to walk before him together, in order to reflect the glory of the God who is three-in-one.

[3] Job uses the Hebrew word tummah to describe his integrity or blamelessness in 31:6, the same word that was used in 2:3 and 9. It is true that he is holier than his neighbours, but that doesn't make him holy before God.

[4] Note how Job repeats in 31:17, 19 and 32 what he taught us earlier about sins of omission. He insists that keeping our possessions to ourselves instead of sharing them with those in need makes us guilty of stealing from them. These verses are echoed by Matthew 25:40–46, Luke 3:11 and James 2:14–17.

stopping to consider whether he ought to be owning slaves at all! But isn't that precisely the problem whenever we compare ourselves with others? It's a very crooked ruler for gauging whether or not we are holy in the eyes of the Lord.[5]

In verses 24–40, Job looks around at some of the other sins that are being committed in the land of Uz and curses himself still further. If he has ever placed his trust in wealth instead of in the Lord, then may he die a pauper.[6] If he has ever worshipped the sun and moon as false gods, then may he go down to the place of darkness and never return. If he has ever cursed an enemy[7] or ever denied his guest room to a travelling stranger or ever exploited any of the tenants who rent his fields, then may his farmland yield nothing but weeds and brambles.[8] If he has ever failed to confess his sin for fear of what people would think of him, then may he bear the guilt of that sin forevermore.[9] These are terrifying curses for Job to call down on himself, because we know he isn't perfect. He was right to resist his three friends when they accused him of being an out-and-out sinner, but he is equally wrong to pretend he is an out-and-out saint. The Lord will rebuke him later, in 40:8, for being quicker to assume that

---

[5] Paul warns us in 2 Corinthians 10:12 that, whenever we gauge our holiness by comparing ourselves with other people, we lack wisdom. Job shouldn't be asking for justice from the Lord, but for mercy.

[6] By talking about the love of money in a stanza that is all about idolatry, Job teaches us the same thing as Matthew 6:24, Luke 16:13 and Hebrews 13:5–6. People trust in money to avoid having to trust in the God of Philippians 4:19. Job says that it is all about *my security... my great wealth, the fortune my hands had gained* (31:24–25).

[7] Gloating over the misfortune of an enemy is sinful. We are to desire good for all those around us, even for our enemies. See Proverbs 24:17–18 and 25:21–22, Matthew 5:43–48 and Romans 12:19–21.

[8] Capitalism is no excuse for cruelty. Delaying the payment of invoices and pushing up rent prices can be wholly legal and wholly sinful at the same time. Generosity matters more than exacting the maximum profit.

[9] The Hebrew word for *man* in 31:33 is *'ādām*, so Job's words can either be translated as talking about concealing his sin *as men do* or about concealing his sin *as Adam did* (Genesis 3:8–10).

God is unjust in his actions towards him than he is to confess that perhaps he isn't quite so squeaky clean of sin.

The apostle Paul responds to Job's curses in Galatians 3:10–14. Speaking about similar curses that the Israelites called down on themselves at the end of the Law of Moses, he warns that:

> *All who rely on the works of the law are under a curse, as it is written: "Cursed is everyone who does not continue to do everything written in the Book of the Law." Clearly no one who relies on the law is justified before God, because "the righteous will live by faith." The law is not based on faith; on the contrary, it says, "The person who does these things will live by them."*

Paul declares that Job, and anybody else who relies on their own righteousness before God, will come under the full weight of these curses. We need God's mercy, not his justice, since we are all found to be lawbreakers when we hold ourselves up against God's true standards, instead of foolishly comparing ourselves with one another.[10] But the apostle Paul also responds to Job's great longing in verses 35–37 where he repeats his desire for a Mediator who will listen to him and take up his cause before God in heaven's courtroom.[11]

This is the last of Job's speeches in Act Two, so he ends it with a flourish. He declares literally in verse 35, *"Behold my signature!"*, and the narrator echoes this by announcing that *"The words of Job are ended."* But Job doesn't actually get to speak the last word. God does. He has done as Job requested and put his standards down in writing. It is called the Jewish Law, and Job doesn't come out of it very well. That's why Paul rejoices that God has fulfilled the Law for us all: *"Christ redeemed us from*

---

[10] In 31:6, Job asks the Lord to weigh his deeds on scales of *tsedeq*, or *righteousness*. He doesn't know enough about God's holiness to grasp the full horror of what he is requesting.

[11] Job's words in 31:35–37 form a grand finale to the train of thought that he started in 9:33–35, 16:19–21 and 19:25–27. If he has a God-given Defence Lawyer, Job fears nothing his Accuser can ever say about him.

*the curse of the law by becoming a curse for us, for it is written:
'Cursed is everyone who is hung on a pole'"* (Galatians 3:13).[12]

Job's words are ended, but in these first three chapters of Act Two he has given us some new answers to our questions. He has pointed us to the fact that Jesus has become for us the true Righteous One, the true Suffering Servant and the true Curse-Bearer.

---

[12] Paul's Old Testament quotations are from Leviticus 18:5, Deuteronomy 21:23 and 27:26, and Habakkuk 2:4.

Eyes Right (Job 31:1–12)

"I made a covenant with my eyes not to look lustfully at a young woman."

(Job 31:1)

Job makes some mistakes in chapter 31 by comparing himself with his neighbours, but he gets a lot more right than he gets wrong. He may not be righteous enough to stand before the Lord in heaven's courtroom, but he really is the most blameless person in his generation. As a result, he shares some profound insights here into what it means for us to live in obedience to the Lord, so let's take a timeout to look at them in more detail. We'll look at one of them in this chapter and another in the next chapter.

In verses 1–12, Job teaches foundational truth about how we can overcome the temptation to sin. He says that sin follows a clear progression. It is conceived in our *eyes*, it gestates in our *hearts* and it is birthed through whatever our thoughts then inspire us to do with our *bodies*.[1] Job was the most blameless person in his generation because he had learned to cut off temptation at its root source. He tells us in verse 1 that *"I made a covenant with my eyes not to look lustfully at a young woman."* He calls a curse down on himself in verse 7 if he ever broke that covenant and *"if my heart has been led by my eyes."*

Job was a rich and popular man with an unsympathetic wife. He therefore recognized up front that he was in double danger of adultery. He took radical steps to protect his heart from what threatened to become a dangerous chink in his spiritual

184

---

[1] The Bible states this most clearly in James 1:13–15. Posting a guard over our eyes is therefore a form of spiritual contraception, which prevents temptation from ever being conceived into sin.

armour. Unless he got his eyes right, he knew he wouldn't get his thoughts right, and if he didn't get his thoughts right then he knew that he would not act rightly. He therefore made a covenant with his eyes that he would never steal a sinful glance at any of his servant girls or at any of the unmarried daughters of his friends.[2] The Hebrew phrase he uses was normally used to describe two warlords forging a military alliance with one another. Job therefore allied himself with God and declared war on sin. He resolved in his heart that he would always flee temptation and run hard after righteousness instead.[3]

A couple of years ago, during a holiday to Greece, I took my family to Thermopylae. Back in the days before modern roads, the narrow mountain pass there served as the only land route for armies to march in and out of Greece. Leonidas and his 300 Spartans famously used this to their advantage, holding off a massive Persian army long enough in the pass to enable the rest of the Greeks to muster and defeat them. Job therefore teaches us here that our eyes are like the pass at Thermopylae. If we are smart enough to guard our eyes, then the battle to resist temptation gets much easier. Paul echoes this in 1 Corinthians 10:13, where he assures us that *"No temptation has overtaken you except what is common to mankind. God is faithful; he will not let you be tempted beyond what you can bear. But when you are tempted, he will also provide a way out so that you can endure it."* The problem for many of us is that we fail to head sin off at the pass. We miss God's way out early on, then we wonder why sin so easily overruns us later.[4]

Eve sinned in the Garden of Eden when she *"saw that the*

---

[2] The Hebrew word *bethûlāh* in 31:1 means literally a *virgin*. Job didn't just guard against adultery through falling for a married woman, but also against polygamy through falling for an unmarried woman.

[3] 2 Timothy 2:22. For other examples of such a resolution, see Psalm 17:3, Daniel 1:8 and Luke 21:14.

[4] The Battle of Thermopylae took place in 480 BC. I am assuming that you grasp the difference between being tempted and sinning. Jesus was tempted like us but headed sin off at the pass every time (Hebrews 4:15).

fruit of the tree was... pleasing to the eye" and didn't look away.[5] Achan sinned when he saw beautiful objects in the plunder of Jericho and decided to keep on looking.[6] David sinned when he saw Bathsheba bathing from his palace roof and decided not to go back downstairs; more positively, Joseph successfully resisted the temptation to sleep with his master's wife by refusing *"even to be with her".*[7] What we look at with our eyes affects what we think about in our hearts, which in turn affects what we end up doing with our bodies.

The examples of Eve and Achan remind us that we need to guard our eyes from much more than sinful sexual desire. We also need to guard them when it comes to gluttony and materialism. But since Job focuses here on sexual desire, let's stay on topic and let's not miss the three big things he teaches us in these verses about lust in particular.

Firstly, Job warns us that sexual desire is far more powerful than we imagine. He says it leads to utter *"ruin for the wicked"* (verse 3). *The Message* translation vividly paraphrases verse 12 as a warning that *"Adultery is a fire that burns the house down; I wouldn't expect anything I count dear to survive it."* Lust is powerful and dangerous. We need to be as radical as Job.

Secondly, Job warns us that our sexual purity matters deeply to the Lord. We need to hear this, because our culture assures us that it is an entirely private matter. Job insists, however, that God sees our sex lives and treats sexual impurity

---

[5] Genesis 3:6. Her son Cain also failed to head off sin while it was still *crouching at the door* (Genesis 4:7).

[6] Joshua 7:21. God is the Great Designer who loves to make creation beautiful (Genesis 2:9), but the Devil is very good at tempting people to turn a good thing into a god thing.

[7] 2 Samuel 11:1–5 and Genesis 39:6–10. Solomon was the son of David and Bathsheba, yet he warns us in Proverbs 4:23, *"Above all else, guard your heart, for everything you do flows from it."* Jesus also echoes this warning in Mark 7:21–23 and Luke 6:45.

as *"wicked, a sin to be judged"* (verse 11).[8] Lust couldn't be more serious. Job says it drags people down to hellfire.[9]

Thirdly, Job encourages us that sexual purity is possible. He insists that if we truly fear the Lord then our hearts already possess a new hatred towards evil.[10] They also possess God's power to overcome temptation. Any covenant that we make with our eyes is backed up by the covenant that the Lord has made with our hearts, to fill us with his Holy Spirit so that we can resist our fleshly desires and walk in step with him. Lust is strong, but the Lord is stronger. We've got a partner in this fight. The same power that raised Jesus from the dead is now at work in us today.[11]

Make no mistake: What we look at with our *eyes* affects what we think about in our *hearts*, which affects what we do with our *bodies*. So resolve that you will only gaze at *"whatever is true, whatever is noble, whatever is right, whatever is pure, whatever is lovely, whatever is admirable"*.[12] Make a solemn covenant with your own eyes too.

---

[8] Job says literally in 31:11 and 28 that adultery and idolatry are equally *"a sin for the judges"*.

[9] Job uses the Hebrew word *'abaddon* in 31:12, which is the word used for *hell* in 26:6 and 28:22. It is also the word used for *hell* in Psalm 88:11 and Proverbs 15:11. See Mark 9:47–48.

[10] This is what the writer promised us in Job 28:28. Once we begin to fear God, our consciences become alive to how toxic sin is. See also 31:23, Exodus 20:20, Proverbs 8:13, Luke 8:17 and 1 Thessalonians 4:6.

[11] Jeremiah 31:31–34, Ezekiel 36:26–27, Galatians 5:16–25, Ephesians 1:18–23 and Philippians 2:13.

[12] Philippians 4:8. This is also what Jesus means in Matthew 6:22–23, Mark 9:47 and Luke 11:33–36.

Am I Not a Man and a Brother? (Job 31:15)

"Did not he who made me in the womb make them?
Did not the same one form us both within our
mothers?"

(Job 31:15)

Harriet Jacobs found it hard to understand her white mistress. She was kind enough while living, but very cruel to her when she died. Instead of freeing her black slave girl in her will, she bequeathed her to one of her relatives who would sexually abuse her. *"My mistress had taught me the precepts of God's Word: 'Thou shalt love thy neighbour as thyself.' 'Whatsoever ye would that men should do unto you, do ye even unto them.'"* But it was evident to Harriet that her mistress was blind when it came to putting those precepts into practice. *"I was her slave, and I suppose she did not recognise me as her neighbour."*[1]

We have already seen that Job had blind spots when it came to slave ownership. But we mustn't miss that he is much more right in chapter 31 than he is wrong. In fact, he states a principle in verse 15 which would eventually sound the death knell for slavery around the world and which is still the foundation of Christian ethics today. He declares that his love for the poor and needy is more than an expression of God's mercy. It is also an expression of God's justice, since every person that he meets is his brother or his sister in the human family. It is vital that we grasp what he is saying when he asks, *"Did not he who made*

---

[1] Using the pen name Linda Brent for fear of reprisals, Harriet recalls this in her autobiography entitled *Incidents in the Life of a Slave Girl* (1861).

me in the womb make them? Did not the same one form us both within our mothers?"[2]

The best way to spot how much this revolutionizes human ethics is to compare what Job says with great thinkers who have not been influenced by what he says. In pre-Christian Europe, the Greek philosopher Aristotle argued that *"Some men are slaves by nature; others are free. For the former, slavery is not just advantageous. It is only right."*[3] In the post-Christian Europe of today, Stephen Hawking argues that *"the human race is just a chemical scum on a moderate-sized planet."*[4] Thankfully, there remains enough Christian heritage in Western culture to prevent us from pressing Stephen Hawking's view through to its harrowing conclusion, but don't miss how much less value it places on humanity than the words of Job. It is a creed that could easily be used in the future to justify genocide or eugenics or the forced euthanasia of the disabled and the elderly.

Job locates the value of each person, not in their usefulness to him or to society, but in the fact that each person has been created by the same God. This makes us brothers and sisters. Not just chemical scum, but a big family. So helping one another isn't merely an act of charity. It is a matter of justice. James 3:9 picks up on Job's words and the words of Genesis 1:26–27, 5:1 and 9:6 to conclude that all of us *"have been made in God's likeness."* That's massive. In the same way that it is an offence under English law to deface a bank note which bears the monarch's image, it is an offence under heaven's law to despise the image of God in those around us. Since God created even the filthiest beggar to reflect something of his glory, we honour

---

[2] People only properly become children of God when they put their faith in Jesus (John 1:12 and Galatians 3:26), but Job insists that all humans are children of God in a lesser sense. Paul echoes this in Acts 17:28–29.

[3] Aristotle wrote this in the fourth century BC in his work *Politics* (1.5).

[4] Stephen Hawking said this in an interview with Ken Campbell in *Reality on the Rocks*, a British documentary first broadcast on Channel 4 on 12th February 1995.

their Maker whenever we show them human kindness and we dishonour their Maker whenever we refuse to do so.[5]

Despite the initial blindness of many white Christians to the evils of slavery, it should therefore come as no surprise that it was Christians who grasped the message of Job 31:15 that led the fight for the abolition of slavery. Grasping that slaves and their masters were alike created by God, they began insisting that the slave trade was evil and ought to be ended, and that all existing slaves should be set free.[6] Josiah Wedgwood embossed their slogan on his famous pottery medallion of a kneeling black slave: *"Am I Not a Man and a Brother?"* The historian Rodney Stark sees this as a uniquely Christian question:

> *Of all the world's religions, including the three great monotheisms, only in Christianity did the idea develop that slavery was sinful and must be abolished. Although it has been fashionable to deny it, antislavery doctrines began to appear in Christian theology soon after the decline of Rome and were accompanied by the eventual disappearance of slavery in all but the fringes of Christian Europe. When Europeans subsequently instituted slavery in the New World, they did so over strenuous papal opposition, a fact that was conveniently "lost" from history until recently. Finally, the abolition of New World slavery was initiated and achieved by Christian activists.[7]*

It should also come as no surprise that it was Christians who led the Civil Rights Movement for racial equality. Martin Luther King Jr was a church pastor who put the ethic of Job 31:15 right at the heart of his message. He argued that:

---

[5] The Bible lays this same foundational ethical principle in Proverbs 17:5, 22:2 and 29:13.

[6] 1 Corinthians 7:21, Galatians 3:28, Ephesians 6:9, Philemon 16 and 1 Timothy 1:9–11.

[7] Rodney Stark in *For the Glory of God: How Monotheism Led to Reformations, Science, Witch-Hunts, and the End of Slavery* (2003).

All men have something within them that God injected...
Every man has a capacity to have fellowship with God.
And this gives him a uniqueness, it gives him worth, it gives
him dignity. And we must never forget this as a nation:
There are no gradations in the image of God. Every man,
from a treble white to a bass black, is significant on God's
keyboard precisely because every man is made in the
image of God. One day we will learn that. We will know
one day that God made us to live together as brothers
and to respect the dignity and worth of every man. This
is why we must fight segregation.[8]

My question is, do we truly know that? Have we truly learned the lesson of Job 31:15? Have we genuinely grasped that a person's value is not derived from how strong or intelligent or independent or useful to society they are, but from the fact that we have all been created by the same God to bear the image of God together, as brothers and sisters in the human family?

If we truly grasp this, then we will not accept racism. We will not accept people being bullied for their beliefs or for their sexuality or for their disability. Nor will we accept the marginalization of the poor and the homeless. We will not accept the slaughter of innocent foetuses. We will not view it as normal that the most dangerous place for a human being in Western society is inside their own mother's womb. If we truly grasp this then neither will we accept the so-called mercy killing of the sick and elderly.

Instead, we will act like Job. We will seek out the hungry and the homeless and the voiceless in order to welcome them as long-lost brothers and sisters. We will not allow our homes or our churches or our diaries or our spending to become inward-looking. We will look at the people around us and we will see in each one of them the glory of the Lord. We will recognize the truth in their desperate cry: *Am I Not a Man and a Brother?*

---

[8] Dr King preached this in a sermon on 4th July 1965 at Ebenezer Baptist Church in Atlanta, Georgia.

God Knows What He is Doing... (Job 32:1–33:33)

Elihu son of Barakel the Buzite, of the family of Ram, became very angry with Job for justifying himself rather than God.

(Job 32:2)

The words of Job are over. Silence has fallen and we are unsure who will dare to break it. Job and his three friends are all talked out, so we find ourselves hoping that God himself might finally speak to us. It is rather disappointing, then, when a fourth friend suddenly pops up out of nowhere to deliver six more chapters of speeches. That friend is named Elihu and we can be forgiven for responding to him impatiently: *Eli-**who**?!*

But don't be impatient. Elihu is a good man who brings some new answers to the questions that we have been grappling with throughout the book of Job. If you have ever been to a rock concert, then you know that there is always a warm-up act before the headline artist takes the stage. That's how we are meant to view the four speeches of Elihu. He claims to speak for God, and for good reason, because the Lord does not rebuke him in 42:7–9 along with Job's other friends for talking nonsense at times. Elihu's four speeches are full of truth which prepares us to hear the final speeches from the Lord.

29:1–25	Job's new answer #1: The Righteous One
30:1–31	Job's new answer #2: The Suffering Servant
31:1–40	Job's new answer #3: The Curse-Bearer
32:1–33:33	Elihu's new answer #1: God Knows What He is Doing...
34:1–37	Elihu's new answer #2: ... and What You are Doing
35:1–16	Elihu's new answer #3: God Doesn't Need You...
36:1–37:24	Elihu's new answer #4: ... but You Need God

In 32:1–5, the writer introduces us to Elihu. He is descended from Buz, who was the son of Abraham's brother Nahor and who founded one of the ancient kingdoms of Arabia.[1] Elihu is not a Hebrew, but he appears to know the God of Israel far better than Job's other friends. His father's name Barakel means *God Blesses* and his own name means *He is God*. Elihu is angry that Job has been quicker to question the righteousness of God's rule than to question his own righteousness.[2] He is also angry with Eliphaz, Bildad and Zophar for correcting Job in ways that downsized God. Elihu claims to be a prophet, defending God's true character, and he is furious at speeches he considers to be blasphemous.[3] Elihu insists that God knows what he is doing through Job's suffering.

In 32:6–9, Elihu declares that he is different from Job's other three friends. For a start, he is much younger, which is why he waited to speak until now. He respected their seniority until he saw how little wisdom their many years had given them. Now he announces that he has new answers to give. They do not flow out of a formula based on experience or tradition or

---

[1] Genesis 22:20–22 and Jeremiah 25:23–24.

[2] The Hebrew words *tsaddīq* in 32:1 and *tsādaq* in 32:2 mean *righteous* and *to declare righteous*. They are courtroom terms which home in on the main theme of the book of Job: *How can a just God allow suffering?*

[3] The Hebrew text actually introduces Elihu's anger before it introduces Elihu! It says literally in 32:2 that *"The anger burned of Elihu."* It says this twice in 32:2, once in 32:3 and once in 32:5. He is an angry young man!

reason, but out of a relationship with God. Elihu claims to be full of the Holy Spirit and to speak new answers that are the result of divine inspiration.[4]

In 32:10-22, Elihu again claims that his answers are quite different from those of Job's other three friends. For a start, they are focused on a person, not on point-scoring. To show that he is more interested in helping a friend in distress than in beating a friend in a debate, he mentions Job by name – something that, remarkably, the other three friends never once do![5] Elihu is also much more focused on God's character than Job's other three friends, claiming that the Lord has given him the words he speaks and has filled him so powerfully with the Holy Spirit that he feels like champagne corked up in a bottle. Elihu claims to speak the truth and nothing but the truth, since no true prophet of God could ever dare to flatter people.[6]

In 33:1-11, Elihu begins the first of his four speeches. After claiming yet again to speak words of divine inspiration, he states his main point – that God knows what he is doing through Job's suffering. Elihu is furious that Job has been quicker to question God's righteousness than to question his own. *"But you have said in my hearing – I heard the very words – 'I am pure, I have done no wrong; I am clean and free from sin. Yet God has found fault with me; he considers me his enemy.'"* How dare Job cast such aspersions on Almighty God?

Unlike Job's other three friends, Elihu has actually listened to Job. The words that he quotes back to him in 33:9-11 are a fair summary of his speeches.[7] That's why we mustn't downplay

---

[4] The Hebrew word *rûach* in 32:8 is the normal Old Testament word for the Spirit of God (see 32:18 and 33:4). Elihu says literally in Hebrew in 33:6, *"Behold, I am as you spoke to God"* – which either means *"Look, I speak to God just like you"* or *"Look, I am here from God as you requested."*

[5] In the Hebrew text, Elihu says Job's name nine times (32:12, 33:1, 33:31, 34:5, 34:7, 34:35, 34:36, 35:16 and 37:14).

[6] If we were making a list of deadly sins, we would be unlikely to number flattery among them. However, Elihu warns us that flattery is one of the deadliest forms of lying. The Lord will judge it most severely.

[7] Job 9:16–24, 10:2–7, 13:23–28, 16:7–9, 16:17, 19:11, 23:10–16, 27:5–6, 29:14, 30:20–21 and 31:6.

the importance of what Elihu has to say, just because we were not told about him in the prologue. He may sound a bit full of himself, but he is also full of the Holy Spirit. Job is more convinced of his own righteousness than he is of the Lord's.[8]

In 33:12-33, Elihu tackles Job's complaint that the Lord has gone silent on him. He insists that the problem is never at God's end. It is always at ours. The Lord is constantly speaking to people – not just through dreams and visions and angelic visitations, but through our sufferings, which often prove to be our greatest teacher. This is the kind of Scripture that made C.S. Lewis refer to suffering in his book *The Problem of Pain* as the "severe mercy" of God towards anybody that he wants to make wise for salvation. We saw earlier that, like Elihu, C.S. Lewis argues that suffering is often the voice of God.

> *The human spirit will not even begin to try to surrender self-will as long as all seems to be well with it… Every man knows that something is wrong when he is being hurt… We can rest contentedly in our sins and in our stupidities… but pain insists upon being attended to. God whispers to us in our pleasures, speaks in our conscience, but shouts in our pain: it is His megaphone to rouse a deaf world.*[9]

Elihu argues that God allows suffering because it is better for us to suffer a little on earth than to suffer a far worse fate in hell.[10] He points out that, were it not for the agony of the past chapters, Job would never have grasped the truth about the Defence Lawyer that the Lord has prepared for him in heaven's

---

[8] Job 8:6, 11:4, 22:3, 23:7, 27:1–6, 29:14, 32:1 and 40:8.

[9] C.S. Lewis in *The Problem of Pain* (1940).

[10] This is the essence of what Elihu says in 33:18 and 28–30. Jesus also echoes this in Luke 6:20–25 and 16:19–31. The Hebrew word *shahath* meaning *pit* or *hell* is used twenty-three times in the Bible, and five of them are in this chapter.

courtroom.[11] He would not be where he is now – on the brink of surrender to the righteousness of God.[12]

Elihu argues that the Lord has used Job's sufferings to bring him to a place of surrender to the Gospel. In his second speech, Elihu will explain what surrender means.

---

[11] The Hebrew word *mēlīts*, which is translated *messenger* in 33:23, is the same word used in 16:20 to describe Job's heavenly *Intercessor* or *Ambassador* or *Defence Lawyer*. This is deliberate and is echoed in Romans 8:34 and 1 John 2:1. Elihu points out in 33:24 that, but for his suffering, Job would never have looked up and seen the Redeemer who pays a ransom for his sin.

[12] Elihu uses the Hebrew word *tsādaq* in 33:12 and 32 to tell Job that he *is not righteous* but God wants to *make him righteous*. He also uses the word *tsedāqāh* in 33:26 to say that God wants to *restore him to righteousness*.

... and What You are Doing (Job 34:1–37)

"Should God then reward you on your terms, when you refuse to repent?"

(Job 34:33)

A few years ago, my wife Ruth heard a strange clicking sound while she was driving our car. I wasn't in much of a mood to do anything about it. We were only a few days away from driving to the south of France for our summer holiday, and I had plenty of tasks to finish before we could go. The last thing that I needed was an extra trip to the garage.

But Ruth was insistent and I was finally persuaded. When I arrived at the garage and the mechanic popped the bonnet of the car, I was very glad I'd listened to her. The clicking sound that she had heard was the sound of a cambelt fraying and tearing. Had we not replaced it before driving to the south of France, we would have written off the car.

That's what Elihu's second speech is all about. He follows up his first speech, in which he claimed that God is talking but Job isn't listening, by spelling out what he believes God is saying in the midst of Job's suffering. He urges him not to do the equivalent of my turning up the car stereo to drown out the clicking sound in the engine. The message of Elihu's first speech was that God knows what he is doing. The message of his second speech is that God knows all about what we are doing too!

In 34:1–4, Elihu calls on all the wise men of the East to be his witnesses. What Job has learned from his sufferings is a lesson for all humanity, so they all need to grapple with what Elihu has to say. If wine connoisseurs know how to taste good vintage with their palates, then wise men ought to sense with their ears the rightness of Elihu's teaching.

In 34:5–9, Elihu summarizes what Job has said in his speeches. Once again it is a fair summary, reminding us that pastoral ministry is largely about listening carefully to people, then affirming the truth and challenging the errors in whatever they have said.[1] Job has claimed that he is *innocent, right* and *guiltless*, despite the fact that this forces him to conclude that God is therefore unjust and attacking him unfairly.[2] Job has even concluded that there is no point in trying to live a life that pleases God.[3]

In 34:10–15, Elihu argues that such conclusions are like the clicking of my car engine. They ought to alert Job to the fact that something is wrong. It is surprisingly powerful, when pastoring believers or sharing the Gospel with nonbelievers, simply to repeat their own words back to them. When they listen carefully to the things that they say, people often recognize that what they are saying cannot be true. Job knows deep down that it is unthinkable for the God who created our well-ordered universe out of chaos to be a perverter of justice, a secret purveyor of chaos – in which case, there is only one possible conclusion: that Job can't be quite as in the right as he assumes.

This is where many readers get confused. They remember that the writer said that Job is blameless, and that God agreed with him too, so they assume that Elihu is being unfair to Job. They dismiss him as a miserable comforter, just like Job's first three friends, but that misses the point. Elihu is not denying that Job is righteous and blameless compared to the other men and women of his generation; he is merely denying that this makes him righteous and blameless in comparison with the

---

[1] Eliphaz, Bildad and Zophar failed to listen to Job. They simply trotted out the same old answers, regardless of what he said. Elihu is different. He speaks Job's words back to him accurately in 33:9–11, 34:5–9 and 35:2–3.

[2] The Hebrew words *tsādaq* and *mishpāt* in 34:5, which mean *to be righteous* and *justice*, are both courtroom terms. Elihu's second speech sets out to challenge Job's conviction that he is righteous before God (32:1).

[3] In fairness to Job, he was actually quoting the words of the wicked in 21:15.

Lord.[4] Unlike Job's other friends, Elihu is not accusing him of behaving like the wicked. He accepts that Job is the best of men – he just insists that this means he remains a man at best! If it is unthinkable that a good God should allow bad things to happen to good people, then the only explanation left open to us is that none of us is quite as good as we like to assume.

In 34:16–30, Elihu teaches Job what theologians refer to as the "total depravity" of humankind.[5] This doctrine does not state that there is nothing good in our hearts. We saw earlier that God has stamped his image on even the most inveterate sinner. "Total depravity" means confessing that there is not a single aspect of our lives that has not been tainted by sin as a result of the Fall. Even our best actions often spring from sinful motives.[6] Elihu warns Job that there is no darkness dark enough to hide any of this from God.[7] He sees our every step. He records our every deed. He hears the cry of every person we have wronged. Elihu is not denying that Job is the most blameless person of his generation, but he is insisting that this doesn't make him righteous in heaven's courtroom. To insist that it does is to deny the truth, as is proven by Job's impossible conclusion that he is righteous and God is unrighteous. Such conclusions are like the clicking of a cambelt, warning us that some of our thinking has gone wrong.

In 34:31–33, Elihu urges Job to confess that being righteous compared to his neighbours is not the same thing as being righteous before God. He warns Job that he cannot be forgiven while he holds onto his false insistence that he is

---

[4] Job 1:1, 1:8 and 2:3. Noah is also described as *righteous* and *blameless* in his generation, but that didn't stop him from getting drunk and passing out naked! He wasn't righteous like the Lord (Genesis 6:9 and 9:20–23).

[5] The commands in 34:16 are all *you* (*singular*) in Hebrew. Elihu turns from the wise men to Job himself.

[6] Romans 3:9–20. Paul warns us in 1 Corinthians 4:5 that God does not merely judge people for their wrong actions, but also for their right actions performed for the wrong motives.

[7] Job 34:22 is echoed by Psalm 139:11–12, Jeremiah 23:24, Amos 9:2–3, Luke 12:2–3, 1 Corinthians 4:5, Hebrews 4:13 and Revelation 6:15–17.

already blameless. Even if he confesses his sin, Job will not be forgiven if he tries to draw a line under his sins and to create a righteousness of his own. That would be like being stopped for speeding and assuring the policeman that you will make it up to him by driving below the speed limit all the rest of the way home. If the law has been broken then no amount of future law-keeping can offset that fact. Repentance means more than promising to reform. It means asking for help from the Redeemer that Job saw standing in heaven's courtroom.

In 34:34–37, Elihu therefore ends his second speech by calling the wise men of the East to witness that Job is clearly in the wrong.[8] He prays that Job will suffer even more, if necessary, until he learns to see his life through Gospel glasses.[9] There are two ways that we can rebel against God, not just one. The first it to rebel by *defying* God's standards and by living as out-and-out sinners. The second is to rebel by *denying* God's standards and by acting as if we can achieve a righteousness of our own.

So let's not compare ourselves with one another. Let's respond to the Gospel message that Elihu preaches here. Let's freely confess both our sin and our need for a Saviour.

---

[8] In the Hebrew text, Elihu uses *you* (*plural*) to address the wise men in 34:2–15, then *you* (*singular*) to address Job in 34:16–33, then *you* (*plural*) again to address the wise men in 34:34–37.

[9] If this seems unduly harsh to you, bear in mind that God agrees with Elihu in 40:8 and that Job's suffering finally comes to an end when he follows Elihu's advice in 42:6.

God Doesn't Need You...
(Job 35:1–16)

*"If you sin, how does that affect him? If your sins are
many, what does that do to him?"*

(Job 35:6)

Elihu's third speech is short and to the point. His first speech
and its introduction are fifty-five verses long. His second and
fourth speeches are thirty-seven and fifty-seven verses long.
But his third speech is over and done with in just sixteen
verses.[1] Elihu keeps his message stark and simple. He tells us
straightforwardly: *God doesn't need you.*

We can tell that Elihu feels frustrated that Job has not yet
responded to his first two speeches from the way that he goes on
the attack in verses 2–3. He quotes Job's own words back at him
and demands brusquely, *Does this really sound right to you?*[2] His
summary of Job's speeches is a lot briefer and a lot less nuanced
than it was in 33:8–11 and 34:5–9.[3] He deliberately presents
Job's viewpoint in its most ridiculous form so that he can end
his third speech with a bang: *"So Job opens his mouth with empty
talk; without knowledge he multiplies his words"* (verse 16). This
is Elihu at his rudest, but don't let his clumsy style blind you to
how much of what he says to Job in this third speech is true.

---

[1] We can tell where Elihu's four speeches begin and end from the narrator's
words in 32:1–6, 34:1, 35:1 and 36:1.

[2] The Hebrew word *mishpāt* in 35:2 means *justice*, but Elihu is using it here to
mean *rightness*. He is asking Job: *"Listen to yourself – do you really think this
can be right?"*

[3] Elihu claims, literally, in 35:2 that Job has boasted, *"I am more righteous than
God."* Job has never actually put it quite this starkly, but it is a fair gist of what
he said in his most frustrated moments (40:8).

Elihu is right to challenge Job that he needs to repent of his sin. He is right that nobody, not even a man as blameless in his generation as Job, can ever claim to be righteous enough to stand before the Lord in heaven's courtroom. We may not know the full answer to why there is so much suffering in the world, but we can at least be sure of one thing: it isn't because we are perfectly righteous and the Lord is treating us unfairly.[4] Job isn't righteous next to God, and Elihu is right to tell him so.

Elihu is also right to insist that Job is far guiltier than he imagines. He gave his speeches in the days before God gave his Law to the Hebrews at Mount Sinai, so Elihu is doing for Job what the Law would do later for Israel. The apostle Paul explains the purpose of the Law in Romans 3:19–20:

> *Whatever the law says, it says to those who are under the law, so that every mouth may be silenced and the whole world held accountable to God. Therefore no one will be declared righteous in God's sight by the works of the law; rather, through the law we become conscious of our sin.*

Elihu may be clumsy in the way he tries to silence Job and to make him aware of his sin, but he is right to call out the fact that Job is terribly guilty.

Elihu is also right to warn Job that repentance means a lot more than deciding to reform our ways. We cannot find forgiveness through resolutions, but only through the Redeemer that God has given us. We need to see this third speech as a follow-on to the warning that Elihu gave to Job in 34:31–33 that self-help is no help at all. The name Elihu means *He is God*, and what he does consistently well in his speeches is to wrench our eyes away from ourselves and up towards the greatness of God. Elihu does this to convince us that God doesn't need our good works. We can't buy forgiveness from him, since he gains

---

[4] Job 35:12–16 invites us to question whether some of our frustration that God appears not to be talking to us is linked to the fact that we are not listening to him. See Proverbs 28:9 and 1 Peter 3:7.

nothing from our sin or our obedience. We can't buy our way back into God's good books when we sin, because we have no valid currency to spend.[5]

The eighteenth-century English evangelist George Whitefield issued a similar warning. He claimed that the last-ditch tactic of the Devil, whenever people are convicted of their sin, is to persuade them to work hard to make it up to God. He warned his hearers that this is one of the most dangerous pitfalls to be resisted at the moment of conversion.

> *When a poor soul is somewhat awakened... then the poor creature, being born under a covenant of works, flies directly to a covenant of works again. And as Adam and Eve hid themselves among the trees of the garden, and sewed fig leaves together to cover their nakedness, so the poor sinner, when awakened, flies to his duties and to his performances, to hide himself from God, and goes to patch up a righteousness of his own. Says he, "I will be mighty good now – I will reform – I will do all I can; and then certainly Jesus Christ will have mercy on me." But... our best duties are as so many splendid sins.[6]*

Elihu may sound harsh in this third speech, but he is motivated by deep love for Job.[7] He wants to convince him that he can never achieve true righteousness on his own. He wants to persuade him to lay hold of the Redeemer he has seen in heaven's courtroom.

Elihu is therefore right to divert Job's attention away from the empty Eastern philosophy of his friends, and from their

---

[5] Elihu is right that our sins do not affect God in his greatness. But what he doesn't say is that our sins affect God greatly in his righteousness and in his love. See Genesis 6:6, Luke 19:41 and Ephesians 4:30.

[6] George Whitefield said this in a sermon on Jeremiah 6:14 entitled "The Method of Grace".

[7] He refers to Job by name nine times in the Hebrew text of his speeches, something that Job's other friends never do at all. Elihu also tells us in 33:32 that his great longing is for Job to be made truly righteous.

formulae which present the Lord as a slot-machine God. In that sense, we are meant to see this third speech as a precursor to the final speeches that the Lord delivers personally in a few chapters' time. He is like the warm-up act that gets a stadium audience ready for the headline act to take the stage. In verses 4–7, Elihu directs our gaze towards the greatness of the heavens and the clouds above us, just as the Lord will in chapter 38. In verses 9–15, he directs our gaze towards God's loving care for the animals and birds, just as the Lord will in chapter 39.

Elihu is also right to prepare us for the Lord's speeches by telling us that we will not find an answer to the question *Why does God allow suffering?* by shaking our fists at God, but only by pouring out our hearts to God in honest prayer. Elihu urges us to stop sitting in judgment on God, and to recognize that he sits in judgment over us. He encourages us to ask ourselves, *"Where is God my Maker, who gives songs in the night, who teaches us more than he teaches the beasts of the earth and makes us wiser than the birds in the sky?"* (verses 10–11).

Songs in the night. That's a wonderful phrase which encapsulates the heart of what Elihu is trying to teach Job. He encourages him to believe that, although God doesn't need us, God still wants to forge a friendship with us. He permits suffering on his watch because he knows that he can use it for our greater good in the end, but he does not abandon us during those periods of suffering. He comes alongside us and he ministers to us as his friends. He helps us to sing bright songs in dark places. He gives us enough of a glimpse into his greatness so that we can sing sweet songs amidst our suffering.[8]

---

[8] He enabled Paul and Silas to do this in Acts 16:23–25, and he promises to enable us to do so too.

... but You Need God
(Job 36:1–37:24)

"God is exalted in his power. Who is a teacher like him?"

(Job 36:22)

One of my neighbours died a few years ago while chainsawing branches off a tree. He did something that I thought people only ever did in children's cartoons. Without stopping to think what he was doing, he put his chainsaw right through the branch on which he was sitting. In a kid's cartoon that's funny, but in the real world it is deeply tragic. My dead neighbour left behind a young wife and children.

That's the big theme of the last of Elihu's four speeches. He says that when we reject God because of all the suffering in the world, we are cutting off the branch that we are sitting on. We aren't punishing the Lord when we get angry and blame him for what we see. We are punishing ourselves. Elihu's third speech pointed out that God does not need us. His fourth speech follows on from this by pointing out how much we need him.

In 36:1–4, Elihu insists yet again that his four speeches are not his own thoughts. They are God's thoughts, since he is a prophet of the Lord. It is easy for us to dismiss Elihu as pompous for declaring that *"one who has perfect knowledge is with you"*, but he is referring to the Holy Spirit who inspires him, rather than to himself.[1] Elihu believes that God has sent him to speak words from heaven's courtroom to rebuke Job's claim that he

---

[1] 36:4. Elihu also uses this same phrase to refer to the Lord in 37:16.

would be found righteous there. True righteousness belongs to God and God alone.[2]

In 36:5-12, Elihu proclaims that God's rule over the world is entirely just. He is *firm in his purpose"* (verse 5), never failing to bring down judgment on the wicked or to uphold the just cause of those who love him. If he appears slow to judge the wicked, then it is because he is merciful enough to give them time to respond to his correction and to repent of their sin. If he appears slow to relieve the sufferings of those who love him, then it is because he is patient enough to wait for them to respond fully to his voice in the midst of their pain.[4] Elihu never completely answers the question *Why does God allow suffering?*, but he assures us that the answer is never that the earth is ruled by an unjust God.

In 36:13-15, Elihu proclaims that those who fall out with God over the suffering in the world are like my neighbour who sawed off the branch that he was sitting on. He insists that all human rebellion stems from a *polluted heart*.[5] We may give intellectual reasons for why we no longer believe in God. We may give emotional reasons for why we no longer trust in God. But those are always smokescreens for the real issue. Elihu says that people only ever resent God because they have let their hearts become contaminated by sin. Even when God puts them in chains of suffering to call them back to himself, they still refuse to listen. They cut themselves off from the only one who can rescue them.

In 36:16-21, Elihu therefore turns to Job and makes a personal appeal. The Hebrew text of these verses is all *you*

[2] Elihu uses the Hebrew word *tsedeq* in 36:3 meaning *righteousness*. He therefore literally declares the purpose of this fourth speech as, *"I will credit righteousness to my Maker"*. He won't credit it to Job.

[3] Note the Hebrew courtroom language here: *mishpāt* means *justice* (36:6) and *tsaddīq* means *righteous* (36:7).

[4] The references in 36:9–12 to God speaking and to people listening are meant to echo what Elihu taught us in 33:13–14. The fool asks: *Why does God not speak?* The wise ask: *Why do I not hear?*

[5] The Hebrew word *hānēph* in 36:13 means *polluted* or *defiled* or *corrupted*. When it refers to someone's heart, it is often translated *godless* or *hypocritical* or *profane*, since their pure worship has become contaminated by sin.

(*singular*). Elihu prophesies to Job that God has permitted him to endure such suffering because he wants to lead him into a better place than the one in which we found him at the start of the story. God has used the disasters that have befallen him to open his eyes to the Gospel. He has revealed to him the reality of God's holiness, the reality of his own sin and the reality of the Saviour who will one day come into the world to redeem God's people. Surely Job would not have preferred comfort to the discovery of all this through his suffering? Surely Job does not prefer evil to affliction? Elihu pleads with Job not to harden his heart, like the polluted hearts of the wicked.

In 36:22–26, Elihu starts preparing us for God's own speeches, which are about to begin. Although the Lord is *"beyond our understanding"*, he still teaches us a lot about his greatness by inviting us to study his work of creation.[6] The universe is a book about God's character that even the most illiterate peasant can read. Even those who can't study God's Word can study God's world.[7]

In 36:27–37:13, Elihu lists some of what creation teaches us about its Creator. All of this serves as a warm-up for the Lord's own speeches, which are just around the corner. First, Elihu zooms in on the clouds. How could anyone who studies the water cycle ever doubt that God runs a well-ordered world? Life on land depends entirely upon drops of water rising from the seas and falling on the hills and valleys, creating rivers which run into the sea.[8] Next, Elihu zooms in on the thunder and lightning, the snow and ice, and the windstorm – an interesting

---

[6] 36:26. We can know God (John 10:14, 14:7 and 17:3), but we can never fully fathom God. If we cannot even understand something as basic as God's life having no beginning or end (36:26), then how much less the mystery that surrounds his righteous rule and the role that suffering plays in his perfect plan!
[7] Job 36:22–26 is echoed by Psalm 19:1–4 and Romans 1:18–20. The wise men of the East viewed botany and zoology as mandatory modules in any study of the character of God (1 Kings 4:29–34).
[8] Job expressed the greatness of God in 9:9 by referring literally to the solar systems as God's *bedrooms*. Similarly, Elihu describes the greatness of God in 36:29 by saying that God stores thunderstorms in his *shed*!

choice, given that Job's children were killed by a windstorm back in chapter 1. Elihu declares that God keeps the windstorm *in his bedroom*, like a man who keeps spare batteries at the back of a drawer. In other words, the Lord is sovereign over all of Job's sufferings, and the ordered way in which he runs the natural world should reassure us that he knows precisely what he is doing.

So, in 37:14–24, Elihu ends with a final appeal for Job to admit that he can never be found righteous on his own in heaven's courtroom, but only by laying hold of the Redeemer he has seen standing there.[9] Since Job has no idea what makes water hang in the sky as rainclouds, although heavier than air, or what makes the lightning light up the night sky, it shouldn't be too hard for him to admit that God is far greater than he is. Since Job has to stop work whenever it rains or snows, and since he needs to take off his jumper whenever a warm wind blows, he ought not to think that he could ever stand unscathed before the one who holds the rain and snow and wind in the palm of his hand. Since Job cannot look at the sun without being blinded, he ought not to speak so boldly about the one who keeps the sun burning brightly in the sky. Job needs to face up to the fact that his request to stand before the Lord to state the case for his own righteousness was actually a request to be consumed!

Elihu has finished his four speeches. He has delivered all of the words that he believes the Holy Spirit has inspired him to say. Will Job confess that the Lord rules righteously, even if it means confessing that he himself would not be counted righteous in heaven's courtroom?[10] As the curtain falls on Act Two of the book of Job, we are dying to know.

---

[9] Elihu's command in 37:2 was *you* (*plural*) in Hebrew, addressed to anyone who was listening. But once Elihu addresses Job by name in 37:14, he returns to *you* (*singular*), as a personal appeal to Job.

[10] The Hebrew words *mishpāt* and *tsedāqāh* in 37:23 meaning *justice* and *righteousness*, remind us of Elihu's consistent purpose throughout these four speeches, as stated in 32:2, 33:32, 34:5, 34:17 and 35:2.

Act Three – Job 38–41:

God's Own Answers

Words, Words, Words
(Job 38:1–3)

"Who is this that obscures my plans with words without knowledge?"

(Job 38:2)

When Polonius asks Hamlet what he is reading, the Prince of Denmark is unimpressed. He tells Polonius that it is nothing but *"Words, words, words."*[1] That's also how the Lord feels when he finally bursts onto the stage to interrupt the human speeches in the book of Job with two final speeches of his own. *"Who is this that obscures my plans with words without knowledge?"* he demands. So whose words does he mean?

One thing that is for certain is that this rebuke encompasses the speeches given by Eliphaz, Bildad and Zophar in Act One of the book of Job. We saw earlier that their words contain sufficient truth for the apostle Paul to quote them as proof of one of his own arguments in 1 Corinthians 3:19, but we also saw that half-truths can be as misleading as outright lies. These three men represent the greatest man-made wisdom of their generation, so we ought to find it pretty sobering that the Lord sees their philosophy and formulae as worse than useless when it comes to fathoming what is really happening in the world. He declares that their human insight isn't just too incomplete to shed light on the problem of suffering; their "words without knowledge" actually obscure the truth God wants to teach

---

[1] William Shakespeare's *Hamlet* (Act II, Scene II).

us.[2] The Lord's frank assessment of worldly wisdom ought to challenge us to the core.[3]

Later, the Lord will come back to Eliphaz, Bildad and Zophar in order to deal with their shortcomings. He will tell them he is angry with them *"because you have not spoken the truth about me"* (42:7). He will command them to repent and offer blood sacrifices to atone for their sinful speculations about the righteousness of his rule. I find it hard to read God's unflattering assessment of their speeches without wondering how he must feel about our own culture's speculations about the big questions of the universe. So far in this commentary, I have quoted from Epicurus and Lucretius and *Bruce Almighty* and David Hume and Stephen Fry and *The Sound of Music* and David Attenborough and *Animal Farm* and C.S. Lewis and Richard Dawkins and *Captain Corelli's Mandolin* and *Changing Lanes*. Judging by how much our culture pontificates about whether or not God is up to his job, it seems as though we have rather a lot of repenting to do ourselves.

The Lord's rebuke may also extend towards the four speeches of Elihu in Act Two, although it isn't entirely clear. The Lord does not call him to repent of his words alongside Job's other three friends in 42:7–9, and the fact that the Lord's first speech begins where Elihu's fourth speech ends gives some credence to Elihu's claim that the Holy Spirit inspired him to prophesy wisdom into Job's confusing situation. If there is room to rebuke Elihu, it is because his speeches were not laced with as much grace as God's speeches here, warning Job to brace himself, but then speaking to him with tenderness and patience. Elihu's speeches were helpful, but they were far from perfect, reminding us that well-meaning counsellors can hurt those

---

[2] The Hebrew word *hāshak* in 38:2 means literally *to darken*. God is saying that much of what humans consider to be enlightenment is in fact endarkenment. Remember that the next time someone tells you that your Christian beliefs place you "on the wrong side of history".

[3] The Lord refers to his Word to us as *'ētsāh* in 38:2 meaning *advice* or *counsel* or *plans*. He does not force his truth upon us, but he holds it out to anybody humble enough to confess that human wisdom is a dead-end.

they hope to help if they speak God's truth without enough of God's love.

It is clearer that the Lord's rebuke encompasses the speeches of Job. The writer tells us that God spoke this rebuke *to Job* and warned him to *brace himself like a man* for correction.[4] This does not mean that what Job said in his speeches was all wrong. The Lord asserts twice in 42:7–9 that Job spoke a large amount of truth about his situation. But we can tell from 40:8 that God was as unimpressed as Elihu that Job was quicker to believe that God might rule the world unrighteously than to entertain the possibility that Job might not be found totally righteous before God in heaven's courtroom.[5]

But enough about who the Lord is rebuking in Act Three of the book of Job. The exciting thing is that our waiting is finally over. The Lord has stepped onto the stage to deliver his own answers to our question about why he allows so much suffering in his world. He drops a hint to us that we may find some of it pretty surprising by speaking to Job out of a windstorm – one much like the windstorm which caused the death of Job's ten children. The Lord is evidently not going to fob off our questions about suffering by blaming it all on the Devil or by pretending that he possesses anything less than total sovereignty over the world.

Quite the opposite. The God who has led us through thirty-seven chapters of answers so far is not about to give us shortcut answers now. We will never find a satisfactory answer to the question *Why does God allow suffering?* if we seek to bypass the journey, seeking out a Wikipedia summary to avoid the hard work of grappling with this question before the Lord. Human reason on its own fails us but, coupled with a deep relationship with God, it informs us. The Lord therefore warns us to *brace ourselves*, using a Hebrew phrase which means literally, to *gird*

---

[4] 38:3. The Hebrew text also makes this clear by using *you* (*singular*) throughout God's speeches.

[5] Job had obscured the truth about God's character in 7:20–21, 9:21–24, 12:4–9, 19:6–11, 24:1–12 and 27:2.

up our loins, like one of Job's contemporaries tucking the bottom of his robe into his belt in order to free up his legs so that he can run fast.[6] The Lord is about to step up the pace of our journey of discovery.

So let's listen to what God says to us. Let's buckle up and let's get ready as the curtain rises on Act Three of the book of Job. The Lord has finally taken centre stage and he is about to give us his own answers to our anguished questions.

---

[6] Exodus 12:11, 1 Kings 18:46, and 2 Kings 4:29 and 9:1. The Lord repeats this command in 40:7.

The Joy of Being God
(Job 38:4–7)

"Who laid its cornerstone – while the morning stars
sang together and all the angels shouted for joy?"
(Job 38:6–7)

The book of Job is not exactly a laugh a minute. I've heard it read at plenty of funerals, but never at a wedding. So it comes as a pleasant surprise, when the Lord finally takes centre stage, to discover that he is not at all the gloomy God that many people imagine. Right from the start, we discover that the Lord is the life and soul of history's party.

The Lord picks up where Elihu left off, by directing Job's gaze to the world around him. He starts at the beginning (one of the big themes of God's speeches is that of order) and by asking Job if he has any idea what it was like to start creating our complex world. Was Job there to help God to launch the earth into its orbit round the sun, so that it wouldn't simply plummet through space like a stone hitting water? Was Job there to hold the tape measure for him when he set the limits for the land and sea?[1] Was Job there *"while the morning stars sang together and all the angels shouted for joy?"* (38:7).

Now that's a very interesting turn of phrase. I have taken part in some pretty hefty building projects in my time, and I found each of them so difficult that I partied when I finished them. But God isn't saying here that he celebrated with the angels when they reached Day Seven of creation and finally

---

[1] Another wise man of the East, named Agur, asks similar questions about God's greatness in Proverbs 30:4.

took a rest together. He is saying that they rejoiced in the act of creation itself. They laughed as they took it in their stride.

This is more than just a throwaway comment. It is vital to our understanding of the character of God. The Christian writer A.W. Tozer argues that *"What comes into our minds when we think about God is the most important thing about us"* – and what comes to mind for many of us is most unworthy of him.[2] Some people imagine a severe God, aloof and invariably angry. Others imagine a loving God, who spends much of his time agonizing about how little the world seems to love him in return. I've heard God described in many ways in many churches, but I haven't often heard of him as *happy*, enjoying being God and shouting in delight over the world he has created. What's so strange about that is that the Scriptures repeatedly emphasize the Lord's great joy. A literal translation of 1 Timothy 1:11 even commands us to worship him as *"the happy God"*.[3]

One of the big themes of the Bible is that we become like whatever we worship. If we worship a vile false god, we will become vile. If we worship the Lord in his true glory, we will reflect that glory too.[4] Could this therefore be the reason why many Christians seem so miserable? Could it be that we have grasped too little of God's happiness and that we are therefore worshipping a false image of him, a puny god of our own making?

The Lord corrects this by informing Job that he delights in being God. He also delights in pursuing friendship with the creatures he has made. The Hebrew phrase he uses to refer to his angels here is *the sons of God*.[5] In other words, the Lord is not an antisocial miser when it comes to ruling the universe. He created a whole heavenly council of angels so that he could enjoy ruling through a diverse team instead of going it alone. One of

---

[2] A.W. Tozer says this in *The Knowledge of the Holy* (1961).

[3] The basic meaning of the Greek word *makarios* is *happy*, not just *blessed*.

[4] 2 Kings 17:15 and Hosea 9:10. Paul tells us literally in 2 Corinthians 3:18 that "as we behold the glory of the Lord, we are transformed into the same image, from one degree of glory to another."

[5] The writer used this same phrase back in 1:6. So do Psalms 29:1 and 89:6.

the first things that the angels did was to watch him creating our world and to rejoice with him that it would be home to a race of men and women created lower than the angels but predestined to enjoy a deeper relationship with their Creator.[6] Six times in Genesis 1 the Lord rejoices with his angels that the world he is creating is *"good"*. After populating it with the first humans, he laughs even louder in delight, declaring that the world has just got better. Now it is *"very good"* (Genesis 1:31).

The flip side of what Nehemiah 8:10 teaches us – *"The joy of the Lord is your strength"* – is that those who worship a miserable God become weak and miserable too. That's why I love the fact that one of the very first things the Lord says to Job in his speeches is that he is the happy God. It's why I love the fact that the Bible talks a lot about God laughing.[7] The Lord isn't stressed-out and overburdened by the task of ruling over a complex universe. He loves every second of it! I also love the way that the gospels emphasize the joy of Jesus. He wept over Jerusalem and suffered more than any of us at his crucifixion, but he did so *"for the **joy** that was set before him"*.[8] He did so full of the Holy Spirit, who is described as *"the oil of gladness"* and as the *"river of delights"*.[9]

I also love the fact that the Lord wants us to be as happy as he is. I know that it is easy to forget this in a world where Christian piety is often measured by our seriousness, but if a major aspect of God's glory is his happiness, then he calls us to reflect this aspect of his glory as much as any other. We are told in Luke 24:17 that a miserable face is the mark of those who do not yet grasp the wisdom of God's perfect plan. It does not honour

---

[6] Jesus, personified as Wisdom in Proverbs 8:30–31, recalls taking part in this great party: *"I was filled with delight day after day, rejoicing always in his presence, rejoicing in his whole world and delighting in the human race."*

[7] 1 Chronicles 16:27, Psalms 2:4 and 37:12–13, Isaiah 62:5, Zephaniah 3:17, Matthew 3:17, 12:18, 17:5, 25:21 and 25:23, and Luke 15:4–10.

[8] Luke 2:10 and 10:21, John 10:10, 15:11 and 17:13, and Hebrews 1:9 and 12:2.

[9] Psalms 36:8 and 45:7, Isaiah 61:3, Luke 10:21, Galatians 5:22 and Hebrews 1:9.

him when we live with our heads in our hands, lamenting all the evil in the world. It honours him when we are more aware of his eternal character than of our temporary suffering. God wants us to be more affected by his eternal purposes and power than we are by Satan's short-term successes. He wants us to *"be joyful always"*.[10]

I recently preached on this theme at the church I lead in London. Afterwards, one lady was furious. How could I talk about God being happy when there is so much suffering in the world? What kind of ogre was I presenting to people, this God who laughs with delight, even as people starve to death and battle with cancer and abuse one another? But that's precisely the point. This is our only hope amidst our suffering.[11]

The Lord tells Job that the key to living in a world where there is so much suffering is to recognize that God is unfazed by it. The Lord laughs, because he knows precisely what he is doing. He isn't panicked at being the ruler of our highly complex universe. He is powerful enough to turn even the Devil's worst attacks into our greatest blessings.[12]

The Lord assures Job that he is God, *and loving it.*

---

[10] Philippians 4:4 – *"Rejoice in the Lord always"*. Psalm 37:4, Matthew 25:21, John 15:11, Galatians 5:22 and 1 Thessalonians 5:16. If the Lord is glorified, not just by being God, but by his *joy* in being God, then we glorify him by delighting in him too.

[11] God also promises to teach us this secret of being *"sorrowful, yet always rejoicing"* (2 Corinthians 6:10). The more we get to know him, the more we find ourselves *"rejoicing in the hope of the glory of God"* (Romans 5:2).

[12] God does not mention Satan by name here, but by reminding us that he brought order out of chaos at creation he reassures us that he will also bring eternal good out of all of Satan's short-term misery. This is also the message of Romans 8:28 and 2 Corinthians 4:17–18.

Order, Order!
(Job 38:8–15)

"Have you ever given orders to the morning, or shown the dawn its place...?"

(Job 38:12)

Name-drop alert. Recently I attended a breakfast with John Bercow. If you don't remember him, he became world-famous as the Speaker of the House of Commons during the Brexit debates of 2018 and 2019. His famous catchphrase as he attempted to preside over one of the most turbulent periods of British history was: *"Order, order!"*

That's what the Lord's speeches are all about. Unless we grasp this, we will think that he is trying to duck our questions. We will see it as distraction tactics when he responds to our real questions about suffering by talking to us about oceans and rainclouds and lions and ostriches instead. Understanding that God's speeches are all about order helps us to see that he is actually going right to the heart of our questions. We have asked whether he is up to his job. We have queried whether he is running a well-ordered world. God therefore gives us a direct answer. *Okay,* he says, *let's talk about order.*

In verses 8–11, the Lord is more than simply reminiscing about bringing dry land up out of the oceans on Day Three of creation. He is giving us proof that he is the God of order.[1] Using the language of obstetrics, he reminds us that he presided over the moment when the oceans burst forth out

---

[1] Paul tell us in 1 Corinthians 14:33 and 40 that *"God is not a God of disorder but of peace."* Chaotic Christians and chaotic churches bring dishonour to him.

of the *womb*.[2] Using the language of parenting, he informs us that he gave them the rainclouds as their first set of *baby clothes* and wrapped them in the darkness as their first set of *swaddling-bands*.[3] Using the language of construction, he reminds us that his task on Day Three of creation was to fence off the oceans behind the *doors* that we call cliffs and beaches, fixing limits for the dry land and ordering the oceans: *"This far you may come and no farther; here is where your proud waves halt"* (verse 11).

We tend not to think about this too much. We are so overfamiliar with the world that we rarely notice how much it cries out with John Bercow: *Order, order!* To spell the name of the protein "collagen", you need to arrange eight letters in the right sequence. To make collagen, you need to arrange 1,055 amino acids in the right sequence. But you don't make it. It makes itself, spontaneously, without any direction – and this is where the vast unlikelihoods really begin.

The chances of a 1,055-sequence molecule like collagen spontaneously self-assembling are, frankly, nil. It just isn't going to happen. To grasp what a long shot its existence is, visualise a standard Las Vegas slot machine but broadened greatly – to about 27 metres, to be precise – to accommodate 1,055 spinning wheels instead of the usual three or four, and with twenty symbols on each wheel (one for each common amino acid). How long would you have to pull the handle before all 1,055 symbols came up in the right order? Effectively for ever... A larger number than all the atoms in the universe.[4]

Bill Bryson is right. In fact, he goes much further. Even if collagen were to create itself spontaneously, proteins are no

---

[2] Genesis 1:1–2 says that God created the earth and oceans before Day One of creation week. We will hear more on this in Job 41, when the Lord turns our attention to the ease with which he conquered Leviathan.

[3] The Hebrew word *hathullāh* in 38:9 refers specifically to the *swaddling-bands* in which the parents of the ancient world wrapped their babies. See Luke 2:7 and 12.

[4] For this illustration, I am indebted to the travel writer Bill Bryson in his book *A Short History of Nearly Everything* (2003).

good to us unless they can reproduce themselves, and proteins can't. For that, we need DNA. DNA can replicate itself in seconds, but it can do virtually nothing else. So we find ourselves in a paradoxical situation. Proteins can't exist without DNA and there is no point in DNA existing without proteins. Are we therefore to assume that they arose simultaneously and randomly, all by themselves, with the purpose of supporting each other? Believing in a glorious Creator God may seem difficult, but it's a whole lot harder to explain all of this glory in creation without any glorious Creator God.

And that's not all. Proteins and DNA could not exist for long without some sort of membrane to contain them. That's why no atom or molecule in your body can carry on living without you. Pluck them from your body and they are no more alive than a speck of dust or a grain of sand. It is only when they come together within the nurturing refuge of a cell that the atoms and molecules that form our body come alive. Without the cell, they are nothing but interesting chemicals. But without the chemicals the cell has no purpose. Bill Bryson concludes that

> It is rather as if all the ingredients in your kitchen somehow got together and baked themselves into a cake – but a cake that could moreover divide when necessary to produce more cakes. It is little wonder that we call it the miracle of life.[5]

Elihu was right when he told us in 36:13 that unbelief is a matter of the heart, not a matter of insufficient answers. Our complaint against God was that suffering makes us doubt that he knows how to run a well-ordered world. God replies by pointing out that everything, from the vast seas to the tiny cells of our bodies, cries out: *Order, order!*

In verses 12–15, the Lord invites us to take a closer

[5] Bill Bryson gives these examples in his book *A Short History of Nearly Everything* (2003).

look at the dry land.[6] Has there ever been a morning when he forgot to make the sun rise over it? Has there ever been an evening when it slipped his mind to command the sun to go back down again? The sun is 1.3 million times bigger than earth and it accounts for 99.86 percent of the total mass of our solar system. If we can trust God to run a well-ordered world when it comes to the sun, then we can surely trust him with the other 0.14 per cent of our solar system too.[7]

Using the language of a craftsman, the Lord then compares the mountains, hills and valleys to the embossed features of a seal left by the signet ring of any ancient ruler or businessman on a clay tablet. Using the language of housekeeping, he also likens them to rumpled clothes. We don't tend to think much about how crucial it is to life on planet Earth that its surface undulates up and down – both in holding back the oceans to form dry land in the first place and in forming rivers that flow downhill to stop it from becoming too dry – but just reflect for a moment. Earth is alone among the planets in having tectonics, and why this should be is a bit of a mystery. It is not simply a matter of size or density, since Venus is very similar to the Earth in these respects but has no tectonic activity. This matters massively because if the Earth were perfectly smooth, it would be covered everywhere with water to a depth of 4 kilometres.

You may still feel confused about why there is so much suffering in the world. You may still feel that God ought to be doing a better job. But it will help you if you open your eyes to the many ways in which the world around you cries out everywhere: *Order, order!* If you can trust God to run a well-

---

[6] The double reference in these verses to *the wicked* doing evil deeds in the darkness is meant to remind us that God's speeches are not primarily about geography, but about theodicy. Sinners hide in the darkness, as breadcrumbs hide in the folds of a tablecloth, but the Lord sends the dawn to shake them out of hiding.

[7] In our environmental concern, we often talk about "saving the planet". The Lord reminds us here that such language is ridiculous. The Lord alone can save and sustain our planet (Psalm 93 and Colossians 1:15–17).

ordered world when it comes to these big things, then you can trust him to know what he is doing in the midst of your own suffering too.

H₂O (Job 38:16–30)

"Does the rain have a father? Who fathers the drops of dew?"

(Job 38:28)

Water. H_2O. It's all around us, but we barely give a second thought to how glorious it is. We asked whether God is up to his job. We asked whether suffering casts any doubt on his ability to run a well-ordered world. Having pointed to the dry land as an answer to our questions, God now turns our attention to all the water in between.

In verses 16–18, the Lord exposes how little we know about the 71 per cent of the Earth's surface that is covered with H_2O. He asks Job whether he has ever *"journeyed to the springs of the sea"* – to which the answer for most of us is that we didn't even know the sea had springs! It was only recently that scientists discovered that water sinks into the sea-floor and then rises through hydrothermal vents in the sea-floor many miles away.[1]

The Lord also asks Job if he has *"walked in the recesses of the deep"* – to which, for Job at least, the answer is that he didn't even know that there were valleys on the ocean floor! The unprotected human body cannot bear the weight of water even fifty metres below the surface of the sea. At 150 metres, the water pressure is so great that our veins would collapse instantly and our lungs compress down to the size of a Coke can. That's less far beneath the waves than the Washington Monument stands above the ground, so just imagine the water pressure by the time we reach the bottom of the Mariana Trench, 11,000 metres below the surface of the ocean! If we cannot

---

[1] Other hints at the existence of such vents in the ocean floor are in Genesis 7:11 and 8:2, and Proverbs 8:28.

cope with a bit of H_2O, how can we ever hope to fathom the deep wisdom of the Lord? How dare we accuse him of injustice for allowing suffering or for sending people to hell – or for *not* sending certain people to hell, for that matter?[2] The Lord uses all of this marine geography to remind us of the limits of human knowledge. *"Tell me, if you know all this".*

In verses 19–21, the Lord moves on to marine biology. The ocean depths are so dark that the majority of marine species were still undiscovered even a century ago. Is there a smile on the Lord's face as he taunts Job again? *"Surely you know, for you were already born! You have lived so many years!"* (verse 21).[3] The truth is, it has taken us the whole of human history to learn the very little that we know. We are more likely to make the remaining undiscovered creatures extinct through our greed than to discover them in our wisdom.

Some of the creatures that we have only relatively recently discovered in the oceans are a group of microscopic algae known as *diatoms*. A teaspoon of water can contain a million of them, yet they are so small that for millennia we didn't even know that they were there. Nevertheless, they account for almost half of the organic matter in the oceans and they produce around 20 per cent of all the oxygen in the world! Just think about that for a moment. Job didn't know about them. You may not have known about them. Yet all life on planet Earth depends on them. It's just one of the ways that science urges us to trust God with the many other things we cannot see.

In verses 22–28, the Lord turns our attention to the water in the rainclouds. We rarely think about the fact that 97 per cent of all the water in the world is saltwater, and therefore undrinkable, or that most of the remaining 3 per cent exists in ice sheets at the North and South Poles. Only the tiniest fraction – 0.036 per cent of all the H_2O on earth – is drinkable, found

---

[2] God uses the ocean depths to make reference to hell in 38:17, just as he did in 26:5–6, in order to remind us of the stakes that we are playing with whenever we accuse him of injustice for the way he rules the world.

[3] The Lord uses *you* (singular) throughout the Hebrew text of his speeches. They are a personal reply to Job.

in lakes and rivers and reservoirs, and this only exists because water evaporates but the salt in it does not. Were it not for this fact of physics, we would all die.

Only the tiniest fraction of all the water in the world – a mere 0.001 per cent – exists in the clouds at any given time, but we rarely stop to consider how vital those rainclouds are. Every day the world experiences about 45,000 thunderstorms, each one of which drops an average of 100,000 tons of water on the land. Without this, the dry land would become unbearably dry, eventually becoming an uninhabitable desert. The Lord therefore asks us to mark him out of ten for how he's doing with the rain. Does it feel as though we are living in a well-ordered world? The water that we drink today has evaporated and fallen as rain many times since the world began. God can be trusted to know what he is doing.

The Lord uses vivid language to remind us that he is the one who keeps this water cycle going. He keeps the hail and the snow in his *storehouses*. He musters the lightning and the winds into *divisions*, preparing them for action like an army in its barracks.[4] He is like a *father* to the rain and dew, instructing them where to fall – not just where people need them, but also in uninhabited places, since this is an expression of his glorious character and not just a chore to keep the wheels of the world spinning around. The Lord takes delight in every aspect of his work that proclaims that we live in a well-ordered world.

In verses 29–30, the Lord turns our attention to how water turns to ice. Because H_2O is all around us, we tend to overlook what an extraordinary substance it is. Unlike other liquids, water expands rather than contracts when it gets cold. You don't have to know much about physics to spot that this is highly unusual. But if water didn't defy our expectations in this way, then ice would be denser than water and it would sink. The oceans and the lakes would therefore start to freeze from the

---

[4] God points out in 38:23 that rain and snow have been more decisive factors in the key battles of history than any general's cunning. The Lord has the last say on the battlefield (see Joshua 10:11).

bottom up. With no surface ice to hold in their heat, they would then become colder, resulting in more ice, which would also sink, making them even colder still. Eventually, the oceans and lakes would become nothing more than a massive hulk of ice, which would then cool down the land. Almost every living thing on earth would freeze to death, all because of a tiny variation in the properties of water.

But enough of the science lesson. God's main point in his speeches isn't about the wet stuff. It's about how little we understand about the world we live in and about how much the little that we do know cries out to us loud and clear: *Order, order!*

Water makes up two thirds of your body. It covers over two thirds of the earth's surface. And every molecule of H_2O responds to our questions about suffering. We don't know everything, but we do at least know something: God runs a very well-ordered world.

Stargazing (Job 38:31–33)

"Can you bring forth the constellations in their seasons or lead out the Bear with its cubs?"

(Job 38:32)

When Neil Armstrong and the other two astronauts who first landed on the moon came back to earth on 24th July 1969, they were met by an excited President Nixon. He told the TV reporters that *"This is the greatest week in the history of the world since Creation!"*

Now I don't want to take anything away from their achievement. People had been dreaming of travelling to the moon since the dawn of time, and it was the men and women of NASA who finally succeeded. But when we read what the Lord says to Job, we start to wonder whether President Nixon's excitement was a sign of humanity's greatness or an admission of just how puny we really are.

The moon is 238,900 miles away from earth. In the whole of human history, only twelve people have walked on it – all of them American men, and all of them within the space of three short years. After that, it was decided that getting people to the moon was far too difficult and costly for humanity to attempt such an endeavour again.

The Lord tells Job in these verses that the difficulties of space travel are meant to help us trust God to know what he is doing. Even when we find events on earth confusing, we are supposed to look up at the night sky and comfort ourselves that the Lord's plans are a lot higher than our own.[1] The Lord therefore invites Job to do a little stargazing with him. He asks him to look up at the Pleiades, one of the easiest constellations

---

[1] See Job 22:12, Psalms 8:3–4, 19:1–4 and 136:7–9, and Romans 1:18–20.

to see with the naked eye. You might know it better as the Seven Sisters, because it consists of seven bright stars, each of them a lot like our sun.[2] The Lord challenges Job to put a bridle on the Pleiades and to lead it across the night sky like a donkey. If he doesn't know how to do that, then perhaps he should stop questioning the wisdom of the God who can.

Next, the Lord turns Job's attention to Orion's Belt, another of the constellations we can see with our naked eye. It is also known as the Three Kings because it consists of three stars like our sun. The Lord gives Job a slightly easier challenge this time. Can he simply unbuckle Orion's Belt by a notch or two? If he can't even do this small thing to the stars, then perhaps he had better leave the running of planet Earth to the one who can.

The Lord gives Job a chance to pick any of the other constellations.[3] Are there any of them that he is able to move across the night sky? How about the Bear – better known to most of us as Ursa Major or the Big Dipper or the Plough? Can Job shift it a little? If that's too big, then how about Ursa Minor, one of its bear cubs? Job knows that the stars move across the sky, but he has probably given it very little consideration until this moment. He doesn't understand the laws of astronomy. He has no idea how they move and why. The Lord therefore points out that, if Job can trust him to rule the stars he sees above him, then he can also trust him with the things he struggles to understand on the earth below. Let's be honest. We all find this difficult. We find it easier to trust the Lord with the stars and constellations than we do with the detail of our own lives, because events on planet Earth feel a lot closer to home. But rather than dismiss the Lord's challenge to Job, let's take what

[2] There are actually more than seven stars in the Pleiades, but the rest can only be seen through a telescope. In the Hebrew text of 9:9, Job says literally that the whole constellation is like a mere *bedroom* to the Lord.

[3] The Hebrew word for *constellations* in 38:32 means literally *the zodiac*. People who consult their horoscope for guidance have confused God's creation with its Creator. They are as foolish as a person who studies their car engine in order to discover which route to take to work tomorrow.

he says seriously. Let's take a moment to ponder how the stars and planets teach us that we can always trust God to know what he is doing.

As mentioned before, the moon is 238,900 miles away from earth. That may seem a long way, but it's tiny in terms of astronomy. It isn't another planet; it is merely our own planet's moon. Mars is the nearest planet to earth, and it is 35 million miles away. Uranus and the dwarf planet Pluto are somewhat further – it's 1.6 billion miles to Uranus and 4.7 billion miles to Pluto. If those kind of distances make your mind boggle, they are meant to. God deliberately created a universe large enough to humble our hearts every time we look up into the night sky.

The Lord does not ask Job to look up at the planets in these verses. He asks him to look far beyond them. He invites him to stargaze by looking at constellations that represent solar systems that are so far away that it is hard to put the distances in words. We cannot measure the distances in miles. We have to use light years – that is, the amount of time that it would take us to go there if we ever invented a space rocket that could travel at the speed of light. That's 670 million miles per hour and, for now at least, the fastest rockets can only travel at a small fraction of that speed. The stars that form Orion's Belt are 1,262 light years away. The stars that form the Pleiades are nearer, a mere 444 light years away. The closest constellation that the Lord points out to Job is Ursa Major, which is 80 light years away. To put into perspective how far away that is, if Job had set off in a rocket travelling the same speed as Neil Armstrong's *Apollo 11* at the very moment that the Lord pointed out the constellation to him, and if he had travelled non-stop from then until now, he would not yet have completed even 2 per cent of his space odyssey!

That's why Isaiah 40:12–13 expects a bit of stargazing to silence our complaints against the Lord and to help us trust that God knows what he is doing. Isaiah says that the Lord is the one who *"with the breadth of his hand marked off the heavens"*. That's right, the many light years of the universe all fit snugly in the palm of the Lord's hand! Isaiah says this to encourage us. It is meant to help us trust the Lord to do his job without us. Isaiah asks us, *"Who can fathom the Spirit of the Lord or instruct the Lord as his counsellor?"*

On 24th December 1968, a few months before Neil Armstrong and his two friends landed on the moon, the crew of Apollo 8 became the first humans in history to lose sight of the earth, as they orbited the moon on an earlier mission. Moved by the vastness of space, the astronauts decided to read aloud the words of Genesis 1 in their Christmas Eve broadcast to the millions watching back on earth. Frank Borman ended the Bible reading with a prayer that echoed these verses in Job: *"Merry Christmas – and God bless all of you, all of you on the good Earth."*

---

[4] Genesis 1 offers similar encouragement by telling us in just two words in Hebrew that *"he also made the stars"* (Genesis 1:16). Astronomical distances are nothing to God. They are there to teach us his greatness.

Where the Wild Things are (Job 38:34–39:30)

"Who provides food for the raven when its young cry out to God...?"

(Job 38:41)

The Lord has blown Job's tiny mind. All this oceanography and meteorology and astronomy has left him reeling at the vastness of God's wisdom and of his power. The Lord therefore decides to take a different tack for the next chapter. If Job feels overwhelmed by looking up at celestial bodies, then he can look down at the tiny wonders of his own world. He can take a trip to where the wild things are.

In 38:34–38, the Lord tells Job to take a proper look at the birds.[1] The Ancient Egyptians depicted Thoth, their god of wisdom, with the head of an ibis because they believed that each ibis on the River Nile was an incarnation of the god. The Lord therefore asks Job if he knows who taught the ibis its wisdom, training it in how to read the river's ebb and flow so as to use its long, curved bill to find the best food hiding under the mud. It wasn't Job, any more than it is Job who calls down rainstorms and thunderbolts, so the Lord moves on to another bird.[2] Was it Job who taught the cockerel how to tell when it is time to wake up the world by crowing its early morning wake-up call?

In 38:39–41, the Lord asks similar rhetorical questions about the animals. Is it Job who helps the hungry lions to hunt

---

[1] This is not a one-off. Jesus also imparts wisdom to his disciples by telling them to *"Look at the birds!"* (Matthew 6:26 and 10:29–31, and Luke 12:24).

[2] The Lord depicts the rainclouds as his *water jars* and the lightning bolts as his *soldiers*, reporting to him as their commanding officer and trusting him to know the best battleplans. We need to trust him in this too.

for prey, ensuring that they catch enough to feed themselves, but not so much that they off-balance the food chain? Or is Job busy helping the ravens to fly from place to place in search of food to feed their young? Of course he isn't. Job wasn't able to protect his flocks and herds from foreign raiders, let alone protect the birds. The Lord, on the other hand, astonishes Job by revealing that the baby ravens cry out to *him* for their daily food. If even bird-brained creatures have the common sense to trust in God's goodness towards them, then surely Job and his friends ought to trust God's goodness in the midst of his suffering.[3]

In 39:1–18, the Lord points out that the day-to-day survival of every animal depends on whether or not he knows how to run a well-ordered world. Any zookeeper will tell you that one of the hardest aspects of their job is persuading animals to breed and bringing them safely to birth when they do, so the Lord tells Job that this is all a normal day's work for the Almighty. He isn't just the ruler of the oceans, the custodian of the rainclouds and the air-traffic controller for the planets and the stars. He is also the midwife for the mountain goats and deer. On top of this, he still has time to be the owner of the wild donkeys and wild oxen, which refuse to work for people yet recognize him as their Lord. The wild ostrich may be stupid, but even she would never dare to doubt the goodness of her Creator in the same way as Job and his friends.

In 39:19–30, the Lord finishes his nature documentary by pointing out to Job some of the mightiest creatures in the world. The warhorse is strong and fearless, but it derives all its strength and courage from the Lord. The hawk and eagle have the keenest eyesight and the largest wingspan, but they too receive their great attributes from the Lord.

The Lord could easily continue. He has only scratched the surface of the many wonderful animals that he has created to

---

[3] All of fallen creation has an awareness of God. That's why atheism is so foolish in humans (Psalm 53:1).

display his greatness.[4] But he knows that he has made his point. It isn't just the vastness of the oceans and of the rainclouds and of the universe which declare that God knows how to run a well-ordered world. It is also the smallest creatures. Wherever we look, the world is fearfully and wonderfully made.

That's why I find it so bizarre when people talk as if science and belief in God are incompatible. The message of these verses is that a study of our well-ordered universe will always point us towards its glorious Creator, unless we have determined in advance to close our eyes and our minds to that very possibility.

Our generation has more reason than any other to believe in God, as scientists discover miniature design of the highest order about which Job and his friends never knew. For example, they could not have known that every cell in our bodies is more complex than a large and well-run factory. They could never have known that, although most of those cells are barely two-hundredths of a millimetre wide, each contains several million molecules and many thousand mitochondria. They could never have imagined that 25 million of those cells die and are replaced by our bodies every single second. They had no idea how much each of us is a walking work of wonder, every detail of our bodies proclaiming the glory of God.

Job and his friends could not have known that the human brain has 100 billion neurons and over 500 trillion synaptic connections, allowing it to process 100 million new pieces of information every second. Science is not the enemy of faith in God. It ought to be its true companion. C.S. Lewis was right when he argued that *"In science we have been reading only the notes to a poem; in Christianity we find the poem itself."*[5]

Job, of course, is a believer. The Lord does not point out all these animals in order to convince him that God exists. He points them out to convince him *what kind of God* he is. He does so to reassure Job that he knows how to run a well-ordered world. If

---

[4] The Lord mentions the stork and the locust in passing (39:13 and 20), but he has made his point sufficiently.

[5] C.S. Lewis says this in his book *Miracles* (1947).

brute animals trust him to do his job and are not disappointed, then he can also be trusted to do his job by the likes of you and me. We can accuse God of injustice. We can accuse him of being cruel. But the whole created order will testify against us if we do.

Shortly before he died, I had the privilege of spending an afternoon with the great British philosopher Antony Flew. I was keen to ask the famous atheist and author of *Darwinian Evolution* why, in his final years, he had come to faith in God. He gave me the same simple explanation that he wrote in his final book before he died.

> *"I believe that this universe's intricate laws manifest what scientists have called the Mind of God... Why do I believe this, given that I expounded and defended atheism for more than a half century? The short answer is this: this is the world picture, as I see it, that has emerged from modern science... Nature obeys laws... intelligently organized and purpose-driven beings... When I finally came to recognize the existence of a God, it was not a paradigm shift, because my paradigm remains... 'We must follow the argument wherever it leads.'"[6]*

---

[6] Antony Flew in *There is a God: How the World's Most Notorious Atheist Changed His Mind* (2007).

The Thief of Joy
(Job 39:13–18)

"The wings of the ostrich flap joyfully, though they cannot compare with the wings and feathers of the stork."

(Job 39:13)

The Lord is a happy God. We saw in 38:7 that joy is an essential aspect of his character. We also saw that God wants to teach those who love him to be happy too. Yet far too many of us live our Christian lives down at the miserable end of the scale.

The book of Job talks a lot about misery and suffering. It tells us unequivocally that God has a bigger goal for our lives than ensuring that they are always problem-free. So it comes as a bit of a surprise that he pauses, part way through his nature documentary, to tell us the reason why so many of us are a lot less happy than he intends us to be.

The Lord devotes six whole verses to the ostrich. That's surprising, because it is such an ugly bird that we might have been tempted not to mention it at all. It has a small head and an even smaller brain. It has a long, scrawny neck and ungainly, featherless legs. It has wings, but they are far too small for it to take to the air. The ostrich is flightless, hardly worthy of being called a bird at all, and yet the Lord points out to Job that it flaps its wings *"joyfully"* and *"laughs"* as it runs. It clearly has something to teach us about how we can lay hold of the happiness that God wants to give to those who love him. So let's not rush on to the next animal until we have listened to what the ostrich has to say.

Theodore Roosevelt famously warned that *"Comparison is*

the thief of joy." That gets to the heart of what the ostrich has to teach us in these verses. The Lord points out that its wings are useless when compared to those of a stork, just as its nesting instinct and its parenting skills are useless when compared to those of almost any other bird. It is even more bird-brained than the raven and even more ungainly than the wild donkey, but the ostrich has one big thing going for it. It knows better than to compare itself with the birds that God has not created it to be.[1] Its wings are flightless but it flaps them joyfully because it knows what they are for. As the longest-legged bird in the world, it was given its wings to help it run even faster. The ostrich doesn't compare itself with storks or eagles – those are not what God created it to be – but with the horse and its rider. A horse struggles to sustain a gallop of thirty miles per hour for any real distance, but an ostrich can easily hit forty miles per hour and then keep on running.

The ostrich therefore teaches us that happiness is about keeping our eyes fixed on our Creator. Jesus says in John 10:10 that *"The thief comes only to steal and kill and destroy; I have come that they may have life, and have it to the full."* The Devil loves to steal away our happiness by making us wish we were other than God created us to be. The high school jock wishes he were an "A" student. The "A" student wishes he were sporty. The girl with blonde hair wishes it were curlier and her skin browner. The girl next to her wishes her hair were straighter and her skin whiter. The Bible teacher wishes he were an evangelist. The evangelist wishes that he led the team of pastors.[2] The Devil loves it most if he can make two people both covet what the other has. Two men thinking that the other's wife is prettier. Two friends thinking that the other's child is more gifted. The married person longing to be married while his married friend

---

[1] Note how 39:17 repeats one of the main recurring themes of the book of Job. Wisdom does not come through brainpower. It comes from the Lord (12:13, 17:10, 28:28, 32:8, 35:10–11 and 38:36).

[2] The Bible specifically warns us not to do this, in Romans 12:6–8 and 2 Corinthians 10:12.

wishes he were single. The detail doesn't matter, just so long as it makes us miserable. Can you hear the Devil laughing at you?

The American novelist Mark Twain jokes about a man who died and found himself at the Pearly Gates. He quickly asks:

> *"Saint Peter, I have been interested in military history for many years. Who was the greatest general of all time?" Peter points to a man who looks unimpressive. "You must be mistaken. I knew that man on earth, and he was just a common labourer." "That's right, my friend," Peter smiles back. "He would have been the greatest general of all time, if he had been a general."*[3]

We will never know in this life how much of our misery is self-inflicted, through comparing ourselves with the wrong people. The ostrich wants to teach us that happiness means discovering who God created us to be.

The ostrich also teaches us that happiness is about *being grateful for what we have*. It does not focus on its flightlessness or on its lack of parenting skills. Those are not its forte. Instead, it focuses on the fact that it is fleet of foot and that when it runs its feels God's pleasure. Whenever we focus our own eyes on the things God hasn't given us, it makes us miserable. Even if we get what we covet, we will still feel dissatisfied, since contentment is far more about our hearts than about our situations.[4] In our world of non-stop advertising and of photoshopped selfies and of carefully manicured social media feeds, our only real hope of happiness is to ask God to teach us the secret of contentment that the apostle Paul says God taught him in Philippians 4:11–12.

Finally, the ostrich teaches us that happiness is about *cultivating a simple trust in the Lord*. God tells us up front that the ostrich is stupid. It fails to protect its eggs and it has no idea

---

[3] John Maxwell retells Mark Twain's story in his book *Talent is Never Enough* (2007).

[4] Proverbs 27:20, Matthew 13:22 and 1 Timothy 6:6–11. Much of what we covet in others is not actually real. The stork migrates a long way south for winter, but it does so by riding on thermals, not just by flying.

how to bring up its chicks. But it has one thing going for it. It trusts in the Lord to offset its deficiencies. That's what Jesus says sets apart the happy believer from the stressed-out pagan, and it's what the apostle Paul says lies at the heart of his own contentment. *"And my God will meet all your needs according to the riches of his glory in Christ Jesus."*[5]

The Lord has much to say to us in these final speeches about why he allows suffering. He assures us that he runs a well-ordered world and that we can therefore trust him to work even our misery for our long-term good. But as he says all this, he uses the ostrich to challenge us that far too much of our misery is self-inflicted. Some of the suffering in the world is caused by adverse conditions, but far too much of it stems from our devilish habit of constantly comparing ourselves with others.

He warns us that, other than the Devil himself, comparison is the greatest thief of joy.

---

[5] Philippians 4:19. Also Luke 12:22–34 and 1 Timothy 6:17.

Mid-Course Correction
(Job 40:1–5)

"I spoke once, but I have no answer – twice, but I will say no more."

(Job 40:5)

In May 2019, Liverpool played away to Barcelona in the first leg semi-final of the Champions League. The result was a disaster. Swept away by the combined talent of Luis Suárez and Lionel Messi, they lost 3–0. Even their ever-optimistic manager, Jürgen Klopp, was pretty circumspect when a reporter asked him in the post-match interview whether he now believed there was any chance of their progressing through to the final in the second leg back home. He shot back, *"Before this game we had a bigger chance."*[1]

If you follow football, then you know what happened six days later in the second leg at Anfield. Against all odds and every prediction, Liverpool beat Barcelona 4–0. They made it through to the final and, three weeks later, they lifted the trophy as champions.

I wish I could have been a fly on the wall to listen to what Jürgen Klopp said to his players in between the two matches. I would love to know what he did to bring about such a massive mid-course correction to his team. But we've got another, even greater mid-course correction happening before our very eyes in these verses. We don't know what Jürgen Klopp said to Liverpool, but we do know what the Lord said to Job. We also know that Job took what God said on the chin and quickly changed his tune.

---

[1] Post-match interview with reporters, 1st May 2019.

In verse 1, the writer inserts a line of narrative into the text in order to separate the main body of the Lord's first speech from its closing challenge in verse 2. The Lord asks Job, *"Will the one who contends with the Almighty correct him? Let him who accuses God answer him!"* This is a direct reference to how Job ended his final speech in 31:35–37, so cocksure about defending his own righteousness before God in heaven's courtroom.[2] The Lord is giving Job an opportunity to retract his words. Does he still believe that God has wronged him, or would he like to make a mid-course correction?

In verses 3–5, Job grasps gladly at the opportunity. Note how different his words are here to those of his previous speeches. *"I am unworthy – how can I reply to you?"* he splutters. *"I put my hand over my mouth. I spoke once, but I have no answer – twice, but I will say no more."* So what has Job learned from the Lord's first speech that makes him perform such a sudden U-turn? What does he see now that he didn't see before?

First, Job recognizes how foolish he was ever to doubt that God knows what he is doing amidst our suffering. If we have learned anything together in this commentary from Stephen Fry and *Bruce Almighty* and David Attenborough and *Animal Farm* and Lucretius and *Changing Lanes* and Richard Dawkins and *Captain Corelli's Mandolin*, then it's that it is all too easy to jump to the conclusion that God is not up to his job. But looking at the oceans and the rainclouds and the stars and the animals has convinced Job that we live in a very well-ordered world. He doesn't know why his children died or why he lost his health and his possessions, but he recognizes that he was wrong to jump to the hasty conclusion that the problem must be at God's end.

Second, Job recognizes how foolish he was ever to think that he could ever fight the corner for his own righteousness in heaven's courtroom. While God remained a distant object of

---

[2] The Hebrew word *rîb* in 40:2 means *to contend a case*. The word *yākah* in 40:2 means *to rebuke* or *to correct*. Some translations render the second word *to accuse*, because the Lord is clearly speaking here in legal terms.

worship and a bullet point in debates with his friends, Job could fool himself that he had done little that needed forgiving. But now that he has heard the Lord speak, he has a far greater sense of the vast gulf that exists between feeling righteous compared to our neighbours and being truly righteous before the Lord.

The great twentieth-century preacher Martyn Lloyd-Jones argued that:

> *You are not a Christian unless you have been made speechless! How do you know whether you are a Christian or not? It is that you "stop talking". The trouble with the non-Christian is that he goes on talking... They are forever talking about God, and criticising God, and pontificating about what God should or should not do... You do not begin to be a Christian until your mouth is shut, is stopped, and you are speechless and have nothing to say.*[3]

That's what Job models for us here. He has made the mid-course correction that we are all told to make in Romans 3:19–20. His speech is only two verses long because he has found a new perspective on his soul.[4]

Third, Job recognizes that God knows what he is doing, even when we do not. The Lord has spoken to him out of a windstorm, knowing full well that his ten children were recently killed by one. The Lord has declared that the lightning bolts are his obedient foot-soldiers, knowing full well that Job's flocks were recently burned to a cinder by freak lightning bolts from heaven. Job reasons that, since the Lord knows all this yet makes no effort to conceal his sovereignty over those disasters, he must be pretty confident that they are leading to an outcome that will vindicate his wisdom in the end. Although it still looks like madness and cruelty from where

---

[3] Martyn Lloyd-Jones in *The Righteous Judgment of God* (1989).
[4] This is an importance lesson for Christian apologists and counsellors. Had the Lord merely answered Job's intellectual questions, they would still be arguing. We need to give people a bigger vision of God.

Job is standing, he trusts that God is able to see his life a lot more chess moves ahead than he can.

I find this very challenging personally. I can look back on many events in my life that I thought were complete disasters at the time – relationships that ended, hopes that were thwarted, house purchases that fell through, financial investments that went sour – and with the benefit of hindsight praise God for his wisdom in denying me what I wanted so that he could give me what I needed. Job pleads with us not to wait for hindsight, but to start praising God ahead of time. It is always a faulty premise, just because we cannot see a purpose in our suffering, to assume that there therefore isn't one.

Fourth, Job recognizes that God has led him on a spiritual journey through his suffering. Although the Lord has not told him about the conversations in his heavenly council in the first two chapters of the book of Job, he is grateful that the Lord has shown him what will happen in his heavenly courtroom at the end of time. Job would never have seen the light about heaven and hell, and about the great Redeemer of humankind, had God not led him through such dark places. None of his misery has been meaningless.

And so, as the Lord begins the second of his two speeches, he is addressing a very different man. Job has made a radical mid-course correction to his heart. He is now ready to receive the final jigsaw piece to our great puzzle: *Why does God allow suffering?*

Fantastic Beasts and Where to Find Them (Job 40:6–41:34)

"Look at Behemoth… Can you pull in Leviathan…?"
(Job 40:15 and 41:1)

The Lord's second speech feels a bit like watching *Jurassic Park* or *Fantastic Beasts and Where to Find Them*.[1] Two big words dominate this final speech and they are such vivid words that both of them have become part of the English language. We use the word *behemoth* to refer to any large and powerful organization. We use the word *leviathan* to refer to any political system that is too big and too powerful to challenge.[2]

In 40:6–14, the Lord explains what his second speech is going to be all about. It will answer Job's questions, but in ways that he might find challenging and scary. God speaks out of the same windstorm as before and he issues Job with the same warning: *"Brace yourself like a man"*. God is about to take him on a rollercoaster ride.[3]

The Lord does this because Job has been far too quick to assume that the suffering in the world proves that God is unjust, and far too slow to recognize his own sin. The key verse in this second speech is verse 8: *"Would you discredit my justice? Would*

---

[1] *Jurassic Park* (Amblin Entertainment, 1993) and *Fantastic Beasts and Where to Find Them* (Warner Bros Pictures, 2016).

[2] The English philosopher Thomas Hobbes published two famous reflections on the political lessons of the English Civil War entitled *Behemoth* (1668) and *Leviathan* (1651).

[3] We saw in 38:3 that this Hebrew phrase – literally, *"Gird up your loins!"* – was a call for Job to tuck the bottom of his robe into his belt to free up his legs to run fast with God. See 1 Kings 18:46 and 2 Kings 4:29.

you condemn me to justify yourself?"[4] We make two mistakes whenever we complain that God allows bad things to happen to good people. First, we assume that some people are good, when all of us are to some degree participatory in the sin that messes up our world. Second, we assume that we are qualified to spot the difference between good things and bad things. The Lord challenges Job, if he believes that he is qualified to do God's work for him, to prove it by unleashing his power on the wicked. After that, they can debate as equals.

In 40:15–24, the Lord suggests that Job start by unleashing his power on *Behemoth*, the first of the two fantastic beasts that he describes in this speech. Some readers have suggested that this colossally strong land animal is the hippopotamus, since it is a river-dwelling herbivore and a mighty mass of muscle, yet George Bernard Shaw rightly retorts that God needs to give us a better reply to our questions about suffering than *"I bet you couldn't make a hippo"*. Thank God that he does give us a better answer. We can tell that Behemoth is not a hippo from the fact that *"its tail swings like a cedar"* (verse 17). There are plenty of things to admire about a hippo, but its scraggly tail is not among them.

Other readers believe that Behemoth is a now-extinct dinosaur, such as a diplodocus or a brachiosaurus. But this poses unnecessary problems (does anybody actually believe that dinosaurs still roamed the earth less than 4,000 years ago?) and it fails to grasp the message of the book of Job so far. People have called into question God's ability to rule the world righteously. He has responded by pointing to the magnificent sense of order that permeates the whole of his creation. He has asked us to trust him, even in the face of suffering, because creation proves that he knows how to run a well-ordered world.

---

[4] The Hebrew word *mishpāt* in 40:8 means *justice* or *judgment* or *legal case*. The word *tsādaq* in 40:8 means *to vindicate* or *to justify* or *to declare righteous*.

Behemoth therefore represents the forces of chaos that only God can subdue.[5]

In 41:1–34, the Lord expresses this more clearly by suggesting that Job unleash his power on *Leviathan* instead. Many modern readers get confused about this second fantastic beast (some have suggested the crocodile, others a marine dinosaur known as the plesiosaurus), but what's at least clear is that Job *isn't* confused. He has already mentioned Leviathan five times in his own speeches, either as Leviathan or as Rahab or as *"the fleeing snake."*[6] He knows full well that the people of the ancient Middle East used the name Leviathan to describe the demon-monster that sought to keep the world in chaos before the Lord spoke his creation command over the primordial oceans: *"Let there be light!"* Many readers of the book of Job wonder why the Lord never tells Job about his conversations with Satan in his heavenly council, but the Lord does tell him. He tells him here, using the type of language that he knows Job will understand.[7]

Leviathan comes from two Hebrew words – *lāvāh* meaning *joined together*, and *tannīn*, which means *massive snake* or *dragon* or *sea monster*. It is more than just another name for Satan. It describes the Devil "joined together" with all the other demons that rebelled against God's rule.[8] It is a vivid description for all the evil forces that attempted to keep the world in chaos when God created it, and which still attempt to work their chaos throughout his well-ordered creation now.[9] Satan's hand

---

[5] The Lord emphasizes three times in 40:15 and 40:19 that he created mighty Behemoth. However much Satan and his demons pretend that they are rivals to God, he is their Creator and they are mere creatures.

[6] Job 3:8, 7:12, 9:13, 26:12 and 26:13. *Rahab* means *Proud* or *Insolent* or *Arrogant*. See also Psalms 74:12–17, 89:9–10 and 104:26, and Isaiah 27:1 and 51:9.

[7] Another clue that Leviathan is a not a flesh-and-blood animal is the fact that the Lord says in 41:18–21 that it breathes fire.

[8] John Milton likens Satan and his demons to Leviathan in his epic poem *Paradise Lost* (1667, 1.200–202).

[9] The word *tannīn* is used in 7:12 and 30:29. *Snakes* is a better translation than *jackals* in 30:29, since the same Hebrew word is used for the snakes that fight

has brought great misery to Job throughout this book, but the Lord declares that he has Satan on a leash. The Devil is more powerful than any earthly creature, but he is no match for his heavenly Creator.

When the apostle Paul ends his great vindication of God's justice, in Romans 9–11, he quotes from the Lord's speech to Job about Leviathan.[10] Paul has been grappling with similar questions to the book of Job. People have been asking him if God can be trusted to run a well-ordered world, given that the Jewish nation has largely rejected Jesus and the Church is filled with outcast Gentiles. Paul points the Romans back to what Job 41 tells us about Leviathan. The Lord has utterly subdued the evil forces that wish to work their chaos in the world. He has put Satan on a lead, like a household pet.[11] He has done what no mortal man could ever do, by making Satan beg for mercy and consent to serve out his doomed existence as God's skivvy. Paul quotes from 41:11 to exclaim in triumph:

Oh, the depth of the riches of the wisdom and knowledge of God! How unsearchable his judgments, and his paths beyond tracing out! "Who has known the mind of the Lord? Or who has been his counsellor?" "Who has ever given to God, that God should repay them?" For from him and through him and for him are all things. To him be the glory for ever! Amen.[12]

---

in front of Pharaoh in Exodus 7:9–12 and for the victory that God gives us over the great snake Satan in Psalm 91:13.

[10] Paul's quotation of 41:11 in Romans 11:35 is one of only two New Testament quotations from the book of Job. In 1 Corinthians 3:19, he also quotes the words of Eliphaz in 5:13.

[11] The Hebrew text uses *you* (*singular*) in 41:5. God is addressing Job personally, knowing full well that *"the young women in your house"* have been killed. He is unashamed, since it is all part of his perfect plan.

[12] Romans 11:33–36, quoting Isaiah 40:13 as well as Job 41:11.

Epilogue – Job 42:

Job's Comfort

What Job Discovered About God (Job 42:1–6)

"My ears had heard of you but now my eyes have seen you."

(Job 42:5)

People say all sorts of things online that they would never dare to say in person. When we cannot see the other person, they somehow seem less personal. We stop filtering what we say about them, and social media very quickly becomes antisocial media.

The epilogue to the book of Job begins by acknowledging this. Its first six verses record how Job replied to the Lord at the end of his speeches. Job confesses that he has said outrageous things about God from a distance that he would never dare repeat now that he has seen God up close and personal. *"My ears had heard of you but now my eyes have seen you. Therefore I despise myself and repent in dust and ashes"* (verses 5–6).

Job has discovered that God is *far greater* than he ever imagined. While God was the object of his dutiful worship and the subject of his theological discussions, it seemed a small thing to question God's justice. But now that he has seen God, he can hardly believe the recklessness of what he said.[1] The Hebrew phrase he uses in verse 5 (*shēma' shema'tīkā*) carries the sense of *"I heard a second-hand report about you"*. Job was already a believer at the start of the book, but now his second-hand faith has become first-hand.

---

[1] Job 7:20–21, 9:21–24, 12:4–9, 19:6 and 27:2. When the translators of the Greek Septuagint came to these passages, they toned down some of Job's language because they were so appalled at what he said.

Job has discovered that God is *far more glorious* than he ever imagined. What he said about God in his speeches was largely true (42:7), but now that he has seen God he realizes how much of it was truth dumbed-down. Even his greatest speculations about God's glory were at risk of insulting the Almighty by masking the true scale of his glory with faint praise. The Lord started his speeches by accusing Job of obscuring the true wisdom of his plans and purposes (38:2). Job responds at the end by freely confessing that this accusation is fair.[2] *"You asked, 'Who is this that obscures my plans without knowledge?' Surely I spoke of things I did not understand, things too wonderful for me to know"* (verse 3).

Job has discovered that God is *far more powerful* than he ever imagined. At the start of the book, he had some sense of God's sovereignty. He grasped that the good things and the bad things that befall us are equally acts of God. But he never reflected on the Lord's constant activity in creation until he heard him speak. He never considered what the oceans and the rainclouds and the ice and the constellations proclaim about God's well-ordered rule. He never stopped to recognize that the Lord is zookeeper to the ravens, midwife to the mountain goats, master to the wild donkey and commander of the eagles. Job never reflected on the power that the Lord asserted against the forces of chaos to create the world or on the power he continues to assert against those evil spirits now. At the start of the book, Job lived as though the Lord were the mightiest of creatures, but now he sees that this falls way short of the truth. God is the Almighty Creator. He confesses in verse 2, *"I know that you can do all things; no purpose of yours can be thwarted."*

Job has discovered that God is *far more righteous* than he ever imagined. The primary theme of the book of Job is the vindication of God's justice in the face of suffering, so we should see verses 4–6 as its great crescendo. Job ended his own

---

[2] The Hebrew word *hāshak* in 38:2 meant literally *to darken*. Job amplifies God's accusation in 42:3 by changing the word to *'ālam* meaning *to hide* or *to conceal*.

speeches by demanding a hearing from God in his heavenly courtroom, but now that Job has listened to the Lord's speeches any thought of defending his own righteousness has gone out of the window. He has been silenced by the Word of God, as the apostle Paul says in Romans 3:19–20 we all must be. Job admits that he is utterly out of answers. *"You said, 'Listen now, and I will speak; I will question you, and you shall answer me.' My eyes had heard of you but now my eyes have seen you. Therefore I despise myself and repent in dust and ashes."*[3]

Job has discovered that God is *far more merciful* than he ever imagined.[4] Conviction of sin alone is not enough to save us. Confession of sin must lead to faith in the Saviour. Job acknowledges this by declaring that he has seen the Lord, when on one level he hasn't. He has merely seen the windstorm out of which the Lord spoke to him. Exodus 33:20 warns us that nobody can ever see God and live to tell the tale, so Job must be referring to his fresh confidence that all the visions he saw earlier of a great Redeemer in heaven were genuinely visions of God. His sins will truly be atoned for. He takes what he saw of God in the windstorm as a down-payment on the promise he received in 19:25–27: *"I know that my redeemer lives, and that in the end he will stand on the earth. And after my skin has been destroyed, yet in my flesh I will see God; I myself will see him with my own eyes."*

Job has therefore discovered that God is *far more interested in friendship with us* than he ever imagined. The Lord refuses to play along with any of our slot-machine formulae because he does not want a human race of automatons. He wants friends who freely choose to worship him in spirit and in truth, not because they have to, but because they want to. If the Lord is willing to pay the ransom price for our sins as our Redeemer,

---

[3] 42:4–6. Job really means this. Most speeches in the book of Job are long. This one is only six verses.

[4] James 5:11 particularly emphasizes that Job's sufferings teach us that God is *"full of compassion and mercy"*.

then he must be serious about friendship with us. Discovering this was worth the pain!

Job therefore confesses that God is *far wiser* than he ever imagined. He knew what he was doing all along, even when Job started doubting him. What the narrator taught us in the interval was right. Wisdom is not to be found in man-made textbooks. It is only to be found in fearing the Lord and in learning to walk in friendship with him every day.[5]

The great Victorian preacher Charles Spurgeon taught his hearers that:

> *Any blessing that comes as the result of the Spirit's work in your soul is a true blessing; though it humbles you, though it strips you... Riches may not do it. There may be a golden wall between you and God. Health will not do it: even the strength and marrow of your bones may keep you at a distance from your God. But anything that draws you nearer to him is a true blessing.*[6]

Job believes it. He is no longer complaining about how much suffering the Lord has put him through. He is delighted with how much it has helped him to discover about God.

---

[5] We saw earlier that Job 28:28 is a summary of the book as a whole. Job's final words cry out that it is true.

[6] Taken from a sermon preached by Spurgeon at the Metropolitan Tabernacle in London on 11th June 1871.

What Job Discovered About Prayer (Job 42:7–9)

"My servant Job will pray for you, and I will accept his prayer…"

(Job 42:8)

God has a lot on his to-do list. If we didn't know that before we listened to his speeches, then we certainly know it now. He has planets to keep in orbit. He has the weather to oversee. He has battles to determine, animals to feed and the forces of evil to push back across the world. So we might have expected him to be in a hurry to tick forgiving Job's friends off his to-do list and to move on quickly to restoring Job's shattered fortunes. But he doesn't. He refuses to ride roughshod over the real choices made by humans. He wants to work with us, not instead of us. That's what Job discovers about prayer.[1]

In verse 7, Job discovers that God takes seriously the choices that we make. The Lord informs Eliphaz, Bildad and Zophar that he is angry with them for speaking half-truths regarding his character.[2] Elihu escapes God's censure, giving weight to his claim that the Holy Spirit inspired him to deliver his four speeches. Job also escapes censure, partly because his words were largely true and partly because he has already prayed a prayer of repentance in the first six verses of this chapter. His three friends have not, and the Lord makes it clear

---

[1] Job becomes such an expert on prayer that Ezekiel 14:14 and 14:20 list him in the top three intercessors of the Old Testament, alongside Noah and Daniel. That's quite a hall of fame!

[2] Some of what they said was so true that Paul quotes it in 1 Corinthians 3:19. It is important, then, that we note in 42:7 that the Lord places half-truths in the same category as lies.

that there is no forgiveness for them until they do so. The Lord longs to save all of us. He wants nobody to perish. But he refuses to act until we pray.

In verse 8, Job discovers that prayer is not virtuous in and of itself. The Lord won't forgive Job's three friends unless they ask him to, but nor will he forgive them simply because they ask him to. God never sweeps sin under the carpet, so he detests it when people think that they are doing him a favour by praying. The book of Proverbs tells us that *"The Lord detests the sacrifice of the wicked"* because *"Acquitting the guilty and condemning the innocent – the Lord detests them both."*[3] The Lord tells the three friends that he will only pay attention to their prayers if they are accompanied by the blood of an innocent sacrifice.[4] From our perspective, their burnt offering is a clear prophecy that forgiveness is only possible through faith in Jesus as the Lamb of God. Job and his friends cannot yet be expected to understand this fully. God simply calls them to obey.[5]

In verse 8, Job discovers that the state of a person's heart before the Lord makes a major difference to the power of their prayers. We don't like to talk much about this, because we rightly want to emphasize that nobody's heart is completely right before the Lord. The Gospel creates a level playing field. We have either been made wholly righteous through the blood of Jesus or we have not been made righteous at all. But what Job discovers in these verses is that *how much we put our faith in Jesus* does affect our prayers.

Why else would God tell Eliphaz, Bildad and Zophar to ask Job to pray for them? Why not cut out the middleman and simply pray themselves?[6] If your answer to that question is all

[3] Proverbs 15:8 and 17:15. See also 15:29, 21:13, 21:27 and 28:9. See also Psalm 66:18, Isaiah 1:15 and Zechariah 7:13.

[4] Isaiah 64:6, 1 Peter 2:5 and Revelation 8:3–5.

[5] This ought to answer our questions about whether or not the other religions of the world lead to salvation. Where is the crucified Jesus in Islam, in Buddhism, in Hinduism or in Judaism? Jesus alone can save.

[6] God does something very similar in Genesis 20, where he tells Abimelek to get Abraham to pray for him.

about the Old Testament priesthood, then note that the three friends do their own sacrificing. They only ask Job to pray. Note what the New Testament teaches us too. What does James mean when he tells us that *"the prayer of a **righteous person** is powerful and effective"*? What does Paul mean when he exhorts *"men everywhere to pray, lifting up **holy** hands"*? What does Peter mean when he warns husbands to be considerate towards their wives, *"so that nothing will hinder your prayers"*?[7] The Lord cannot be hoodwinked. He knows that Job's three friends have not yet surrendered to the Gospel as wholeheartedly as Job.[8] He asks Job to pray for them, because our prayers are only as powerful as our faith in God's Word.[9]

In verse 9, Job discovers that talking about prayer is no substitute for actually praying. Eliphaz, Bildad and Zophar do not receive forgiveness from the Lord in verse 7 by nodding their heads at the Lord's rebuke. They do not receive forgiveness in verse 8 by offering bulls and rams as instructed. They do not even receive forgiveness in verse 9 when they spill the blood of their innocent sacrifices on God's altar. They are only forgiven when Job opens his mouth to lay hold of the Lord's promises for them. Their nods and their actions were powerless to save them until *"the Lord accepted Job's prayer."*

The apostle Paul emphasizes this, after laying out the Gospel in Romans 1–8, and midway through his vindication of God's righteous rule in Romans 9–11. At the very heart of his New Testament equivalent of the book of Job lies this instruction:

> *But what does it say? "The word is near you; it is in your **mouth** and in your heart," that is, the message concerning*

---

[7] James 5:16, 1 Timothy 2:8 and 1 Peter 3:7.

[8] Job's repentance is proved by his willingness to forgive his friends. They have treated him so shamefully that Job might not have wanted to see them again for a long time – and yet he forgives. The fact that he goes on to have more children shows that he also forgives his wife! See Matthew 6:14–15 and James 2:13.

[9] Four times in 42:7–8, the Lord distinguishes Job from his friends by referring to him as *"my servant Job"*. While that's wonderful vindication for Job, it is also a damning spiritual assessment of his friends!

*faith that we proclaim: if you declare with your **mouth**, "Jesus is Lord," and believe in your heart that God raised him from the dead, you will be saved. For it is with your heart that you believe and are justified, and it is with your **mouth** that you profess your faith and are saved.*[10]

This insight is vital to us as we arrive at the end of the book of Job. We have learned so much together about God and about ourselves and about God's promises – yet none of it will benefit us unless we turn it to the Lord in prayer. Highlighting verses will not change you. Filling a notebook will not change you. Tweeting quotations from this commentary will not change you. The only thing that will change you is prayer, so take some time out to pray into all that you have learned.

In verse 9, Job discovers that God answers our prayers when we pray with faith and a sincere heart towards him. There is no delay to the Lord's answer. We are not told that God promised to get back to Job within five working days. Nor is there any probation period for his three friends. We are told that, instantly and totally, *"the Lord accepted Job's prayer"*. We discover in verse 10 that no sooner had Job said "Amen" to his prayers for his friends than the Lord started answering Job's prayers for his own fortunes too.

John Wesley told his followers that *"God does everything by prayer, and nothing without it."* Job has discovered that this is true. Take some time out as you come to the end of the book of Job to talk to God about what you have learned. Those new insights will only start transforming your life when you respond by taking them to the Lord in prayer.

---

[10] Romans 10:8–10. Paul also emphasizes in 10:13 that only those who *call* on the name of the Lord are saved.

What Job Discovered About the Devil (Job 42:10–11)

*"They comforted and consoled him over all the
trouble the Lord had brought on him..."*

(Job 42:11)

One of the biggest complaints from readers of the book of Job is that God never seems to tell Job about the Devil's role in all his sufferings. The Devil is mentioned by name fourteen times in the prologue – *Satan*, or strictly speaking **the** *Satan* meaning *the Accuser* – but he is not even mentioned in passing in the epilogue. The writer was so clear in the prologue that Satan's hand afflicted Job, rather than the Lord's, yet he talks in the epilogue about *"all the trouble the Lord had brought on him."* So how can this be fair? Why doesn't God reveal to Job the conversations that took place in his heavenly council?

We have probably learned too much through the book of Job to express our surprise to God in such strong terms. We are a bit more aware now that, whenever we feel confused by God's actions, the problem is unlikely to be at his end. And we are right. The truth is, the Lord *does* reveal plenty to Job about the Devil through his sufferings. Five times in his speeches, Job makes reference to Satan and his demons as *Leviathan* or as *Rahab* or as *"the fleeing snake"*.[1] During the good times Job probably never gave a second thought to the stories he had heard about the great sea monster that lurked in the darkness of the primordial oceans before the Lord created the world.

---

[1] Job 3:8, 7:12, 9:13, 26:12 and 26:13.

People rarely give spiritual warfare much thought when they are living in peace and prosperity. The disasters that befell Job changed all that. He became far more spiritually aware.

The Lord spoke to Job explicitly about the Devil and his demons in Job 41. Unlike many modern readers, who flounder around a bit with Leviathan, discussing crocodiles and plesiosaurs and krakens and Godzilla, Job was in no doubt as to the identity of Leviathan. We saw earlier that his name comes from two Hebrew words – *lāvāh* meaning *joined together*, and *tannīn* meaning *massive snake*. Job grasped that Leviathan was a collective name for Satan *"joined together"* with the other demons to oppose the rule of God. Leviathan had attempted to keep the world in chaos but had lost the fight when the Lord called out over the waters, *"Let there be light!"* Leviathan still tries to work its chaos throughout God's creation now. The Lord gave Job a whole chapter of teaching on this – it's just a chapter that many modern readers skim read and fail to understand.

So when the writer records in the epilogue that all of Job's brothers and sisters and friends came to offer him comfort as they feasted at his house, he isn't masking Satan's role in the drama by telling us that *"they comforted and consoled him over all the trouble the Lord had brought on him"*. He is zooming out so that we can see the full picture. He is inviting us to stop and take note of what Job discovered about the Devil.

Job discovered that the Devil was lurking in the darkness before God began his work of creating the world. The Bible gives us more detail about this elsewhere but, as in the book of Job, it keeps the focus much more on the glorious Creator God than on his fallen creature Satan. Isaiah 14:12–17 calls him a *"morning star"* (which ties in with the angels being described as *morning stars* in Job 38:7) but Satan was not content simply to serve God as an angel.[2] He wanted to be God, so he led some of the angels in rebellion. The Lord defeated them and cast them out of heaven.

---

[2] People tend to think of Satan as *the* morning star (the Latin word for morning star is *Lucifer*) but Job 38:7 suggests that he was merely one of many morning stars. He was a dazzling angel, but not uniquely dazzling.

We are told more about this in Ezekiel 28:11–19 and Luke 10:18 where Jesus recalls, *"I saw Satan fall like lightning from heaven."*

Job discovered that the Devil had real authority to work his evil in the world. He presided over the darkness and chaos until the Lord called the world to order in creation, then he found a way to infiltrate the perfect world that God had made. Job discovers in his suffering that the stories he has heard about Leviathan are true. Satan really is the Tempter who deceived Adam and Eve. He really is the great Fault Finder, who was only too happy to appear in God's heavenly courtroom when they did. Job doesn't grasp the detail of what we know from the prologue, but he discovers beyond all doubt that God is just. If Satan is at work in the world, then he has authority to do so.

Job discovered that the Lord had a plan to undo that authority once and for all. He grasps that God had drawn up a plan to save the world, not just by *might*, but by *right*. God never ignores genuine spiritual authority. That is what Satan does. The Lord calls everybody in his heavenly council to bear witness that he acts at all times with impeccable righteousness.[3] Job's vision of a Defence Lawyer in heaven showed him that the Lord was serious about launching legal action against Leviathan. His vision of a Redeemer in heaven's courtroom, getting ready to pay the ransom price for human sin convinced him that it involved far more than good intentions. When the Lord told Job's friends to shed the blood of innocent sacrifices to secure forgiveness for their sin, it was like the final jigsaw piece slotting into place in God's perfect plan to deal with Satan.[4]

So Job discovered that the Devil is a defeated foe. He may thrash around in the waters of our lives, causing chaos, but he knows his time is short. He may deceive himself at times that he can cling on a little longer, but deep down he knows the truth

---

[3] Ephesians 3:10–11 says that the Lord calls them all to examine the righteousness of his rule.

[4] Hebrews 2:14 tells us how much it cost Jesus to subdue Leviathan: "he too shared in their humanity so that by his death he might break the power of him who holds the power of death – that is, the devil".

of Job 41.[5] The Lord has him on a chain. In the words of Martin Luther, he is *"God's Satan"*. The writer emphasized this in the prologue by showing us that Satan has to ask permission to attack us and that each attack takes place within God's strict parameters. Job discovers this when the Lord informs him in Job 41 that he has caught the Devil and his demons on a fish-hook, that he has made them beg for mercy and that he has forced them to act as his servants. The Lord has domesticated them like household pets. He still allows them to work their mischief, but it is only to give them enough rope with which to hang themselves.

So don't imagine for a moment, when the epilogue of Job refers to *"all the trouble the Lord had brought on him"*, that not enough has been said about Satan. That statement is a victory-cry, declaring that God has been totally sovereign over Satan's actions all along. God is so full of wisdom that, even as the Devil and his demons celebrate their belief that their evil actions are winning, God is turning their attacks around for good.

If you are suffering right now, and if it feels to you as if the Devil is winning, then this is seriously good news. If God has allowed bad things to happen in your life, then it must be because he knows how to turn it around for good. So take heart. The battle between good and evil is not a battle of equals. Don't forget what Job discovered about the Devil.

---

[5] Matthew 8:29–31, Mark 5:6–13, Luke 8:28–33 and 22:31, and Revelation 12:1–12.

What Job Discovered About Prosperity (Job 42:10–17)

The Lord blessed the latter part of Job's life more than the former part.

(Job 42:12)

You can tell whether or not you have understood the message of the book of Job from how you react to the final eight verses of the story. Many readers finish the epilogue and conclude that God prospered Job because he was so patient in his sufferings. They don't seem to spot how much this sounds like the flawed formula of Eliphaz:

People who do evil + A loving, powerful God = People who are cursed
People who do good + A loving, powerful God = People who are blessed

So what *is* the message of these final eight verses? Why does God bless Job at the end, and what is he trying to teach us in doing so? What did Job discover about prosperity?

First, we should conclude from these verses that God wants those who love him to be happy. Yes, he wants us to be more than happy – we'll get to that in a moment – but more than happy does not mean less than happy! The Hebrew phrase the writer uses in verse 10 for God *restoring the fortunes* of Job is the same phrase that is used in several of the Psalms to encourage us to pray for restoration for ourselves.[1] We should

---

[1] Psalms 14:7, 53:6, 126:1 and 126:4.

never forget that the Lord always wants the best for us, and that this often means giving us a happy time.[2]

The Lord demonstrates this by making Job twice as prosperous by the end of the epilogue as he was at the start of the prologue. He lost 500 yoke of oxen and 500 donkeys to raiders, so the Lord restores to him 1,000 of each. He lost 7,000 sheep to a freak lightning storm, so the Lord restores to him 14,000. He lost 3,000 camels to raiders, so the Lord restores to him 6,000. Everything is doubled, which is a pretty good return on investment for all of Job's troubles. But God doesn't do everything that we might have expected here, in order to show us that there isn't a slot-machine recipe for happiness. Job lost seven sons and three daughters, so the Lord gives him seven sons and three daughters more. That's only doubling if you include the children who remain dead. This is meant to teach us that there is no formula for prosperity. The Lord gives us what he chooses to give us.[3]

Second, we should conclude from these verses that, in order to bless us, God withholds what we want so that he can give us what we need. He is the happy God and he wants to make us happy, but he is willing to thwart us in the short-term in order to bless us in the long-term. One of the reasons why suffering sends so many Christians into a tailspin is that they have failed to learn the lesson of Acts 14:22: *"We must go through many hardships to enter the kingdom of God".*[4] They think that happiness is the same thing as instant gratification, whereas God insists lovingly that it is not. That's why the so-called "prosperity gospel" is so dangerous, because it claims that God will give us whatever we think we need whenever we think we it. It is not the Gospel at all. It enlists greed as an ally for godliness, which never works for long. It spoils

---

[2] People coming to feast at Job's house is significant, since it reverses the rejection Job lamented in 19:13–21.

[3] Job only had one wife, so this may of course have been an act of God's mercy towards her!

[4] They are still thinking in terms of this world, not in terms of eternity (2 Corinthians 4:16–18).

us in the good times and disappoints us in the bad times. It keeps our eyes focused on this world instead of on eternity.[5] It is every bit as evil as the vilest speculations of Job's friends.

One of the ways in which the epilogue expresses this is by telling us a bit about Job's new daughters. The subtle hints that Job's first ten children may have been drunkards and blasphemers did not stop us from reeling with horror when they were killed in the prologue. We felt some of Job's pain. However, the writer clearly believes it is significant that Job's new children were of much better character. The beautiful looks of his daughters are matched by such beautiful character that Job entrusts them with an inheritance alongside their brothers, something very unusual for the ancient world. They are named Jemimah (meaning *Affectionate* or *Dove*), Keziah (meaning the *Cassia* spice) and Keren-Happuch (meaning *Hornful of Luxury Eyeshadow*).[6] Even their names are meant to teach us that God will often take things we love from us in order to clear the decks for something even better. Suffering is amplified when we only think short-term.

Third, we should conclude from these verses that both of these principles are equally true for our health as they are for our wealth. This is important, because people teach some strange things from the book of Job. I have heard cessationists (who do not believe in modern-day miracles of healing) use the book of Job to argue that sickness is part of God's perfect plan for us. They teach that God wants us to glorify him by the way we bear our sicknesses, despite the fact that God heals Job miraculously in these verses. No sooner has he repented and forgiven his friends than his skin disease starts fading and he remains fighting fit for well over a century![7] Seeing the old

---

[5] Jesus warns us that, unless we teach believers to expect suffering, trials and persecution, they will give up on their faith when things get hard (Matthew 13:20–21 and Mark 10:29–30).

[6] *Antimony* was a very expensive eyeshadow. It is mentioned in 2 Kings 9:30 and Jeremiah 4:30.

[7] Job 42:16 doesn't just say that Job lived to 140. It says that he lived for 140 years after this!

man Job, surrounded by his great-grandchildren, ought to stir our faith for similar miraculous healing ourselves.

At the other extreme, I have heard charismatics (who believe in modern-day healing) use these verses to argue that we can expect God to heal us every single time – despite the fact that Job has been ill for over forty chapters and the fact that he presumably dies from something in verse 17![8] I quite agree that the main thrust of Scripture is that God wants to heal us.[9] Jesus never turned anyone away on the basis that God wanted them to remain sick in order to glorify him.[10] It's true that the only time somebody questioned whether he was willing to heal them, Jesus shot back, *"I am willing!"*, before immediately healing them.[11] But we mustn't miss the way that the book of Job insists that God will sometimes put us on a bed of physical sickness in order to operate on our soul.[12]

Job dies prosperous, having discovered a lot about prosperity through his sufferings. He has learned that God wants us to be happy but often disappoints us in the short-term to bless us truly in the long-term. He has learned that God wants to make us healthy and wealthy, but he has also learned that God cares more about blessing us eternally than

263

---

[8] The Bible says that there is a time for each of us to die (Ecclesiastes 3:2–3 and 7:17, and Hebrews 9:27). It also insists that this is a good thing, enabling us to be raised again incorruptible (1 Corinthians 15:50).

[9] We could argue that the only reason Job was ill for over forty chapters is that the people around him were too busy theorising about why God might allow suffering to bother to pray for him to be healed!

[10] On the contrary, the gospel writers repeatedly tell us that people glorify God by being healed. See Matthew 15:31, Mark 2:12, Luke 5:26, 9:43, 18:43 and 19:37, and John 11:4 and 11:40.

[11] Matthew 8:2–3 and Mark 1:40–42. Believing for less than this is leprous theology.

[12] Paul, Epaphroditus and Trophimus all had to wait for their healing. Paul is grateful to God for it, because good came out of his delay. See Galatians 4:13–15, Philippians 2:25–27 and 2 Timothy 4:20.

blessing us instantly. Only when Job lost everything, did he discover lasting prosperity.[13]

---

[13] Job's prosperity in these verses was genuine earthly prosperity, but it also forms a prophetic picture of the glorious resurrection of the Suffering Servant. That's a blessing worth losing everything to obtain.

Conclusion: Why Does God Allow Suffering?

And so Job died, an old man and full of years.

(Job 42:17)

We have finally reached the end of the book of Job. Well done for making it all the way through. There have been plenty of highs and lows. A lot of speeches, a lot of truth, but it's also fair to say, a lot of blather and waffle too. So what have we learned from the book of Job? At the end of these forty-two chapters, *Why does God allow suffering?*

God allows suffering because we live in a fallen world. He pushed back the chaos when he created our well-ordered world, but he gave the human race real choice as to whether or not to allow the chaos back in. He did not want a race of robots, but of real worshippers who choose to love him willingly. This means that he allows us to choose to run the other way. More than any other book of the Old Testament, Job talks frankly about Satan. By choosing to side with the Devil and his demons in their rebellion against God, we have given them authority to unleash their chaos back into the world. Those who suffer most are rarely the ones who sin most, but we are all participators in the problem. The human race's suffering is self-inflicted.

God allows suffering because he rules the world in righteousness – that is to say, because he is committed to playing by his own just rules. Chaos started when Satan rebelled against the Lord's authority, so God knows better than to fight the chaos through more of the same. He recognizes that our sin gave the Devil real spiritual authority to work his chaos in our world. The more we play along with Satan, the more we give him a legal right to pursue his agenda to hurt and to destroy.

God allows suffering but he won't allow it forever. The book of Job says that he has been working a plan since the dawn of time to undo Satan's legitimate authority, one that will enable God to be both just and the one who justifies sinners. Job has caught glimpses of the plan in these forty-two chapters. He has seen our Defence Lawyer limbering up in heaven's courtroom. He has seen that this Man is our divine Redeemer too. God has stepped into our world as a human being to pay the ransom price that justice demands for our sin, and he has turned the evidence of that ransom – his own precious blood – into "Exhibit A" in the great and glorious courtroom drama of history.

That's right. The staggering message of the book of Job is that God is not a spectator when it comes to this world's suffering. The writer prophesies on almost every page about the coming of Jesus. Jesus is the true Righteous One. He is the true Suffering Servant. He is the true Blood Sacrifice, whose sufferings are foreshadowed by Job's own disfigured body and whose work is finally revealed when even Job's three false friends find forgiveness by shedding the blood of innocent sacrifices. Job lived almost as long before the coming of Jesus as we live after it, so what was prophecy to Job is now history to us. Let's not allow Job to be more excited about seeing this through a glass darkly, than we are about looking back to it as historical reality.

Somebody has put it this way, in the anonymous vision *The Long Silence*:

> *At the end of time, billions of people were seated on a great plain before God's throne. Most shrank back from the brilliant light before them. But some groups near the front talked heatedly, not cringing with shame – but with belligerence. "Can God judge us? How can He know about suffering?", snapped a pert young brunette. She ripped open a sleeve to reveal a tattooed number from a Nazi concentration camp. "We endured terror, beatings, torture, death!"*

In another group, a Negro boy lowered his collar. "What about this?" he demanded, showing an ugly rope burn. "Lynched, for no crime but being black!" In another crowd there was a pregnant schoolgirl with sullen eyes: "Why should I suffer?" she murmured. "It wasn't my fault." Far out across the plain were hundreds of such groups. Each had a complaint against God for the evil and suffering He had permitted in His world. How lucky God was to live in Heaven, where all was sweetness and light, where there was no weeping or fear, no hunger or hatred. What did God know of all that man had been forced to endure in this world? For God leads a pretty sheltered life, they said. So each of these groups sent forth their leader, chosen because he had suffered the most. A Jew, a negro, a person from Hiroshima, a horribly deformed arthritic, a thalidomide child. In the centre of the vast plain, they consulted with each other. At last they were ready to present their case. It was rather clever.

Before God could be qualified to be their judge, He must endure what they had endured. Their decision was that God should be sentenced to live on earth as a man. Let him be born a Jew. Let the legitimacy of his birth be doubted. Give him a work so difficult that even his family will think him out of his mind. Let him be betrayed by his closest friends. Let him face false charges, be tried by a prejudiced jury and convicted by a cowardly judge. Let him be tortured. At the last, let him see what it means to be terribly alone. Then let him die so there can be no doubt he died. Let there be a great host of witnesses to verify it. As each leader announced his portion of the sentence, loud murmurs of approval went up from the throng of people assembled. When the last had finished pronouncing sentence, there was a long silence. No one uttered a word. No one moved.

For suddenly, all knew that God had already served His sentence.

God allows suffering because he has suffered for us and because he knows that short-term suffering is the fastest way to make us to listen to him in order to be saved from far worse suffering throughout eternity. God wants to deliver us out of the chaos of our sin. He has paid the price to do so, but we each need to receive it. The book of Job has taught us that even the sacrifice of Jesus will not save anybody who refuses to pray.

God allows suffering, even after we have received his great gift of salvation, because he knows that it weans us away from the love of this fallen world and towards the love of our Creator and of his new world to come. The Christian writer A.W. Tozer claims that *"It is doubtful whether God can bless a man greatly until He has hurt him deeply."*[1] That's the message of the book of Job in a nutshell. It's the answer to our question: *Why does God allow suffering?* Job is dead. He has finished his life's race. He now sees his Redeemer face to face. And he isn't complaining about his suffering anymore.

So let's end the book of Job by worshipping God together for all he has taught us. Let's praise him for ruling righteously and with perfect wisdom over his well-ordered world.

That well-ordered world is still reeling in the face of chaos. People all around us are still asking: *Why does God allow suffering?* So let's go out and tell them about this Good News.

---

[1] He says this in his book *The Root of the Righteous* (1955).

Acknowledgments

Every effort has been made to trace copyright holders for the works reproduced in this book, and the publishers apologise for any inadvertent omissions.

Scripture quotations taken from the *Holy Bible, New International Version* Anglicised. Copyright © 1979, 1984, 2011 Biblica, formerly International Bible Society. Used by permission of Hodder & Stoughton Ltd, an Hachette UK company. All rights reserved. "NIV" is a registered trademark of Biblica. UK trademark number 1448790. Both 1984 and 2011 versions are quoted in this commentary.

Scripture quotations marked *English Standard Version* are taken from the Holy Bible, English Standard Version ® (ESV®) copyright © 2001 by Crossway, a publishing ministry of Good News Publishers. All rights reserved.

Scripture quotations marked *New English Translation* are used with permission, and taken from are from the NET Bible® copyright ©1996–2006 by Biblical Studies Press, L.L.C. http://bible.org All rights reserved.

Scripture quotations marked *The Message* are taken from *The Message* copyright © by Eugene H. Peterson 1993, 1994, 1995, 1996, 2000, 2001, 2002. Used by permission of NavPress Publishing Group.

Page 33, "Blessed Be Your Name" by Matt Redman & Beth Redman. Copyright © 2002 Thankyou Music (Adm. by CapitolCMGPublishing. com excl. UK & Europe, adm. by Integrity Music, part of the David C Cook family, songs@integritymusic.com)

Page 191, Sermon at Ebenezer Baptist Church by Dr Martin Luther King Jr. Reprinted by arrangement with The Heirs to the Estate of Martin Luther King Jr., c/o Writers House as agent for the proprietor New York, NY. Copyright © 1965 by Dr. Martin Luther King, Jr. Renewed © 1993 by Coretta Scott King.